through the tips, tricks, and techniques that will take your palate to new heights. Along with being one of my favorite people, I have never met someone so passionate and knowledgeable about spices, which is what makes his food so special. I can't wait until you dig into this book and watch your taste buds explode."

—MICHAEL SYMON,
James Beard Award–winning chef and
New York Times bestselling author

"Through history and storytelling, Lior takes the pantry out of the closet and puts it front and center exactly where it should be. Get ready to go on a transformative cultural journey that begins in your kitchen."

—CARLA HALL,
bestselling author of *Carla Hall's Soul Food*

"Lior is the only person I trust to spice up my life, and his Middle Eastern pantry is sure to liven up any kitchen. His knowledge of these ingredients is only matched by his mastery of how to use them in the most magical recipes!"

—JAKE COHEN, *New York Times*
bestselling author of *Jew-ish*

"Part cookbook, part history lesson, part beguiling travelogue, *A Middle Eastern Pantry* overdelivers on beauty, inspiration, and pure joy. Crisscrossing the region, ingredient by ingredient, Lior's book is a must-have for all who are intoxicated by the flavors of the Middle East. It's an instant classic that you'll return to again and again."

—NILOU MOTAMED, food and travel
expert and TV personality

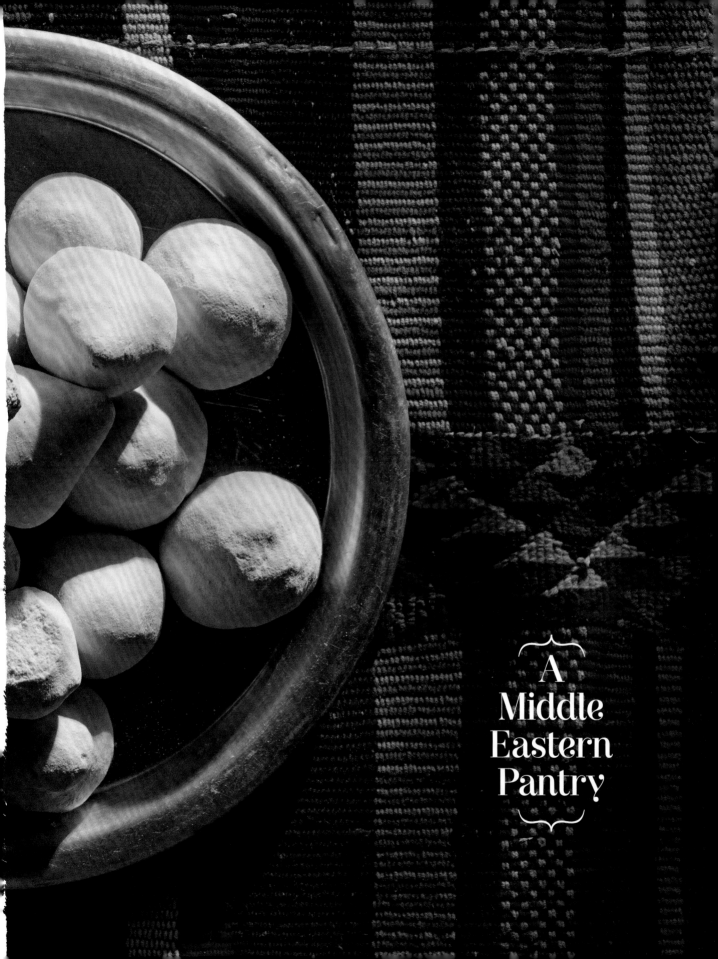

A
Middle
Eastern
Pantry

A
Middle
Eastern
Pantry

Essential Ingredients for
Classic and Contemporary Recipes

LIOR LEV SERCARZ
and Emily Stephenson

Photographs by DAN PEREZ

Clarkson Potter/Publishers
NEW YORK

To my parents,
Ayala and Moshe Lev Sercarz,
for letting me sail into the horizon

To
Lisa, Luca, and Lennon,
for the daily inspiration

CONTENTS

Introduction

Pantry cooking is not just for times when grocery shopping feels like too much of a chore. It's not about reaching into the dark corners of your cabinet to miraculously pull together dinner on a weeknight. For me, pantry cooking is the *best* kind of cooking. I love the ingredients that fill my shelves because I choose them with purpose—my pantry is a curated selection of items that add complexity, texture, richness, spice, acid, and more to whatever I'm making. Having a pantry that excites you can yield a more accommodating and flexible way of putting together a meal that allows for improvisation. Fresh produce or meat are essential, but you can't turn them into delicious meals day in and day out without these staples. (And, of course, there are some meals that are entirely based on pantry items.)

I was born in Israel and spent most of my childhood on a kibbutz in the north of the country. I roamed fields and orchards freely and foraged for pine nuts and berries with friends and for capers with my grandfather. While the food on the kibbutz was Ashkenazi Jewish–influenced, I was able to explore many of the various dishes of the Middle East when I went to friends' houses. Tasting extraordinarily flavorful dishes like gormeh sabzi made by a friend's mother was a formative experience for me. I soon learned about the food of my Iraqi, Turkish, and Egyptian neighbors.

When we traveled to the local market or visited family in other regions, street food was the main way I explored the food beyond our kibbutz. "Ethnic" restaurants didn't really exist in Israel in the 1980s, but there were plenty of stalls and carts at every market. Throughout the Middle East, a food market isn't just for shopping—there's also a sense of exploration. The market is where I first sampled Iraqi sabich sandwiches drizzled with amba (*page 59*), flaky Turkish bread called simit (*page 133*), and succulent shawarma seasoned with its namesake spice blend (*page 37*). The markets are one of the things I miss most now that I've moved away.

I finished school, and during my time in the

military, I realized how much I enjoyed cooking in the barracks and decided to become a professional chef. I worked in kitchens in Israel for several years, then moved to France to attend culinary school. I interned at the Michelin three-starred restaurant Les Maisons de Bricourt in Brittany—and it was there that I learned what extraordinary ingredients spices could be. The experience was remarkable.

After a few years cooking in France, I moved to New York City, where I continued my restaurant career working for Daniel Boulud. But after many years of the fast-paced, late-night, long-shift work, I needed a change. That's when I opened my spice business, La Boîte. And for the last decade-plus, I've focused my passion for cooking, culinary exploration, and working directly with farmers on spices (and other essential ingredients) on sourcing the best possible products for my customers. When I visit farms, I get to indulge my passion for learning about the origins of the foods we eat. Then I bring that knowledge and enthusiasm to my customers' tables through storytelling.

I really do believe that my loves of Middle Eastern pantry items and the region are deeply intertwined. Only now that I've been away for over twenty years do I see that I took it all for granted. Leaving the Middle East has given me a much better appreciation of the food I grew up with. I wish I had cherished it as much then as I do now. I was so lucky to grow up in a farm environment, to see the ways our communities were preserving agricultural products and the role the pantry and preservation play in the magnificent cuisines of the Middle East. Since the dawn of agrarian societies and because of the hot climate, cooks in the Middle East have had to preserve almost all of their harvests, from spices and grains to legumes and vegetables, to make long-lasting pantry staples.

As a chef who has worked on multiple continents and now calls New York City home, I still turn to these flavors and ingredients for inspiration—more so than ingredients from anywhere else. Most of them live in my pantry today. The ingredients I feature throughout this cookbook are an important part of my culture and history—and of so many others. This region's cuisine and its significance deserve to be celebrated. Plus, the ingredients are so versatile and translate very well to other cuisines you may cook, be it Moroccan, Indian, Italian, or Mexican, which makes them invaluable additions to your pantry.

I've divided this book into chapters based on pantry categories—for example, Nuts (*page 98*), Molasses (*page 156*), and Legumes (*page 226*). In addition to a basic description and recipes for using these ingredients, I offer more context about their history, agricultural origins, and how they've been traditionally made. I have a passion for sharing the origins and deepening our understanding of the food we eat. It's a huge part of the storytelling I do with my spice business, La Boîte, and in all the books I've written. I want readers of *A Middle Eastern Pantry* to think about where *all* of our food comes from—our capers and sesame seeds as well as our meat and fresh produce—which I think is a much bigger, culturally accepted conversation, especially when it comes to sustainability and quality. At their most basic, items in cans, jars, and bottles, like tomato paste, tahini, and rose water, are agricultural products captured at their peak by skilled and knowledgeable farmers who made them with care, using traditional preservation techniques. We take so many of our shelf-stable items for granted. It's time to celebrate them.

Perhaps you'll even be motivated to make some of these pantry staples yourself. There's nothing wrong with commercially produced ingredients, but I think it's exciting and important to take ownership of *almost* everything you make (you can skip making homemade tahini, which was never as good as store-bought in my experimentations!) so you know exactly what was used to make the torshi you're serving with dinner or the grape molasses in the salad dressing for Goat Cheese, Grape, and Walnut Salad (*page 165*). Preserving fresh produce will connect you to the whole cycle of seasonality, not just the harvest. We get so caught up in freshness and enjoying produce at its peak that we forget we can be eating these ingredients year-round in different, preserved forms: dried, pickled, fermented, and cured.

This is not meant to be the ultimate authority on the pantry items and recipes of the region, but a celebration of *my* Middle Eastern pantry. I've included dozens of my favorite ingredients that I use daily at home, and recipes to help you incorporate them into yours. Many of the recipes are my interpretation of traditional dishes, often made easier for the modern cook. I will always take the time to learn the history of a dish, but as a chef, I'm constantly reinterpreting what I experience. My versions of some of these dishes are not meant to be the definitive recipe or to disrespect the original (try telling any Middle Easterner that stews are easier made in an oven). I believe

that first we must understand where our culinary building blocks come from and why ingredients are used in certain ways—whether that's due to agricultural constraints or cultural significance. Then, by incorporating and interpreting them in our modern-day cooking, we can all help preserve—pun intended—these traditional ingredients and foods.

A fully stocked home pantry is what can make you a better, faster, more creative cook. It also can provide you peace of mind—I know that when I get home from work to make dinner for my family, having fantastic ingredients on hand to create an exceptionally tasty meal becomes many times easier. The addition of a new spice mix, fruit molasses in place of sugar, or a bit of cured meat can take a familiar dish to another level. These are flavorings and ingredients I get excited about using—and I want you to as well.

Yalla!
To the pantry . . .

How to use this book

This is a reference book and a cookbook, to be both read and cooked from. The chapters group similar ingredients— some are made from the same plant, as with olives and olive oil, some are categories, such as legumes, and some are similar preparations, like molasses. The introduction to each chapter gives some background on the category as a whole, then goes into detail for every pantry item. In each chapter you'll find the origin and history of the ingredient, production and/or agricultural details, a description of the appearance and flavor, guidance on sourcing and storing, info about traditional uses, and my own suggestions for how to incorporate the ingredients into your daily cooking.

After the in-depth explanation of the pantry ingredients, you'll find recipes that feature them. Of course, you'll often find the ingredients popping up in the recipes from other chapters, but the recipes that follow the backgrounds are meant to be either an introduction to these items or a whole new way to show them off.

What Makes a Pantry Item?

My brief definition of a pantry item is a shelf-stable, nonrefrigerated food. In order to last for several months at room temperature, fresh foods must be preserved in some way so they don't spoil. The preserving methods are very natural and simple—drying (like figs), adding acid or salt (such as torshi or salt cod), or using an uncomplicated cooking method like reducing fruit juice to make molasses. In this book, I chose not to include items that need to be refrigerated, even if they have a long shelf life, like yogurt. I want this book to be mainly about foods that cooks in the Middle East have been using for hundreds or thousands of years and are so integral to the cuisine, like lentils, pine nuts, and dates. There are also ingredients included that may be unfamiliar to some but are essential to Middle Eastern cooking, such as sujuk (*see page 267*), dried lime (*see page 33*), and mahlab (*see page 103*).

This is what pantry items are—from a technical point of view. Beyond the what (ingredient) and the how (to use it), I find the history and backstory of items we might never think twice about, like spice mixes or honey, to be fascinating. Where do these ingredients we see in grocery stores come from? How has our use of them changed over the course of history? There's so much more to food than just the physical aspect of nurturing the body. A better understanding of what you eat, where it's from, who's making it, and how it's made is just as important. We know that a jar of olives doesn't just materialize at a factory before being shipped to your grocery store—but we don't think about it much beyond that. Olives, like any fruit, are grown in an orchard by a farmer who must know when they are at peak ripeness for harvesting and curing. They need to know how to harvest the olives without damaging them (or the tree, many of which can live for hundreds of years), and exactly how long to cure them so they taste their best. That knowledge comes from the trial and error of generations of farmers, sometimes dating back thousands of years. It is important to be mindful of this when we shop.

Pantry items should be glorified. We should take the care to pick them out as many shoppers do fresh produce and meat. Just because they are in a bottle or jar does not mean that oils, spices, or honey are all the same or made without thought. Yes, there are many tomato pastes on our supermarket shelves, but I want to encourage you to seek out products that connect you to their agricultural roots and don't rely heavily on modern preservatives. When you use a thoughtfully made pantry item instead of a mass-produced option, your food will taste better and be better for you.

Nothing lasts forever

I've highlighted interesting, important, and delicious ingredients in this book that I hope you'll be inspired to incorporate into your cooking. But I'm not going to tell you exactly how to stock your pantry, because the list should be tailored to your taste and style of cooking. If baharat (*see page 27*) and jameen (*see page 246*) don't pique your interest, or you've tried them but never feel inspired to cook with them, then I'm not going to say you absolutely must have them at home. Try new ingredients you're intrigued by, and remember what you weren't enthusiastic about. If you buy bulgur (see Wheat, *page 209*) and find that you don't use it up within six months, don't buy it again.

Before going shopping, take an inventory. Check your cabinets to see what you have, how long it's been there, and what needs to be used. Smell and taste something that may be a few months old to see if it will be good for much longer.

When you come home from the store, make sure ingredients are transferred into proper containers (I give you guidance in the Sourcing and Storing section for each ingredient) and label them with the name and date. It's important to remember that these ingredients all have long shelf lives but not *eternal* shelf lives. I've given rough estimates of how long things will last, but always use your best judgment. A good rule of thumb is to buy only enough of an ingredient to use up in two or three months, and nothing should stay in your cabinets for more than a year. I've given examples of how to use every ingredient that I call out in this book. If you're still stuck for inspiration, you can never really go wrong with adding most of them to a pan of roasted vegetables or a pot of soup.

Preservation Methods

The modern concept of a fully stocked pantry would not exist without mostly ancient preservation techniques. Our ancestors filled their "pantries" because they needed to preserve their crops to feed themselves beyond the harvest season. They created and used numerous techniques so that fresh fruits, vegetables, foraged nuts and seeds, grains, legumes, meat, and dairy would keep for months.

When we talk in the US about seasonality, we always talk about freshness, but in the Middle East, each harvest is also the season to preserve and prepare for the upcoming months. With this foresight, peak-season produce needn't be fleeting. Also, some foods can't be enjoyed fresh, like olives, which are only edible after they are preserved. Preservation creates exciting flavors and textures that make food all the more delicious.

The following are the major preservation practices used in the Middle East, and each deserves to be highlighted. The main purpose of all of them is to stop, or dramatically slow down, the process of spoilage caused by naturally occurring enzymes in the food and their chemical reactions (think fruit ripening, then going too far); microorganisms such as bacteria, yeast, and molds; air exposure; too much light or moisture; and heat. Using one or a combination of these methods can extend the shelf life of fresh food by many months.

DRYING

One of the oldest methods of food preservation uses the sun, wind, or both to remove moisture from food (think fruit, legumes, and herbs that become spices, just to name a few). The lack of water incapacitates microorganisms and denatures the proteins in enzymes, which means they can no longer cause chemical reactions. Most drying does not completely stop all enzyme reactions, as evidenced by darkened (unsulfured) dried fruit, for example.

FERMENTING

This preservation technique encourages "good" types of bacteria, molds, and yeast and essentially constitutes "controlled" spoilage. Foods can be fermented by submerging them in a brine, as with pickles; by leaving them in open air, as with cheese and sausage; or by introducing microbes to liquids to create carbonation, alcohol, or both.

PICKLING

This is a loose term that can include a number of preparations, though here I mean submerging food (fruits, vegetables, meat, etc.) in a strong acidic solution, usually diluted vinegar. The low pH of the pickling liquid, plus no air exposure, inhibits both enzymes and bacterial growth.

SALT CURING

When salt is added to fresh food in high concentrations, it turns the water in the food into a salt solution through osmosis. This stops bacteria from growing and interferes with the chemical reactions of enzymes. Salt cod (*see page 269*) is, as you might guess, cured in salt, as are some capers and basturma (*see page 265*).

SUGARING

Jams, compotes, and foods suspended in sugar syrups (green walnuts or dried figs, for example) are popular forms of preservation. Sugar has the same effect on microorganisms as salt but does not denature enzymes, thus most foods preserved in sugar are also cooked first.

REDUCTION

A technique that is especially popular in the Middle East, reduction is used on a wide range of produce, from peppers to pomegranates. It essentially concentrates the food's natural sugars by long, slow cooking, which boils off much of the water, making pastes like pepper paste and syrups such as pomegranate molasses. The simmering or drying process kills bacteria and inhibits enzymes, and the remaining sugar content slows down bacterial growth (see Sugaring, above).

OIL PRESERVATION

Submerging foods in oil deprives bacteria of oxygen but has no effect on anaerobic bacteria or enzymes (and is why it's not advisable to preserve raw garlic, for example, in oil), so this needs to be combined with another technique such as fermentation, as with labne balls; pickling, as with some eggplant pickles; or drying, as with sun-dried tomatoes.

DISTILLATION

To distill a liquid or a solid suspended in water, the ingredient must be boiled in an alembic still, then the vapor collected and condensed back into liquid, which captures the original ingredient's scent for cooking and other uses. Flower waters (*see page 175*) are the most common example.

About the Region & Cuisine

The Middle East is both easily recognizable and blurry around the edges. For some, its western border ends at the continental divide before it extends into Africa; others include Egypt, Libya, and Sudan. Some definitions only go as far east as Iran; others also include its neighbor Afghanistan. To the north, Georgia is an obvious border, but Armenia and Azerbaijan could fall on either side of the border, as they have strong cultural ties to Turkey and Iran but are also former Soviet republics.

The reason for the confusion is that the concept of "the Middle East" is man-made. It's not a continent, though the majority of it is in Asia. The term "Middle East" is often used as shorthand for Arab or Muslim countries, but this fails to address the complexity of the region. The name, like quite a few of its current borders, comes from the British. It's in the "middle" of the rest of the world in relation to Europe, and lies between the antiquated "Near East" and "Far East" regions of the British Empire. Winston Churchill created a Middle Eastern Department when Britain took control of Iraq, Jordan, and Palestine from the Ottoman Empire, and the term began to be used outside of British bureaucracy during World War II. Much of the world has been defaulting to the term ever since, though not without controversy from its colonialist origins. "Western Asia" is a label that has been gaining popularity recently, albeit with slightly different borders.

Thus, because it's entirely man-made, not bound by geographic contents and strict borders, and more about culture, I, too, have a little flexibility in my definition of the Middle East and its food. The cuisines—and their ingredients—that I've included in this book are Armenian, Bahraini, Cypriot, Egyptian, Iranian, Iraqi, Israeli, Jordanian, Kuwaiti, Lebanese, Omani, Palestinian, Qatari, Saudi Arabian, Syrian, Turkish, Emirati, and Yemeni. For me, these cuisines are all connected; they are the cooking of *my* Middle East. To further acknowledge the diversity, I've added the chapter names in the major languages of the region: Arabic, Turkish, Hebrew, Farsi, Greek, and Armenian.

There are common flavors and attributes that make grouping these individual cuisines into one regional cuisine possible. All of them show an astonishing creativity when it comes to grains, legumes, and vegetables—meat and dairy are truly seasonings for their bounty of vegetarian building blocks. Within each, there is a contrast between the hyperseasonal, simple, fresh dishes and more intense, deep, slow-cooked stews. There is a love of sour flavors and proficient use of acidic ingredients. There is good use of—and there are lots of—spices, but there is little heat. Fat is used in abundance. The food is all wonderfully flavorful and incredibly well-seasoned. These similarities stem from common influences like religion, trade, and political history—but the most important is the climate that causes food to spoil astoundingly quickly and necessitates quick solutions for long-term storage.

Modern borders also explain why the cuisines of countries like Lebanon and Syria are similar—they used to be one country. Thus, there are some dishes that will have several names and multiple countries claim proprietorship. Grouping the countries into culinary subregions can be helpful—the countries of the Levant, a region along the Mediterranean that includes Jordan, Lebanon, Syria, and Israel, have a lot in common, such as falafel, baklava, and hummus. So do those of the Arabian Peninsula—Saudi Arabia, Kuwait, and the United Arab Emirates (to name just a few)—with rice dishes such as mushbuss, meat and grain stews known as harees, and balaleet, a sweet and savory vermicelli dish. Iran, with its elaborate stews, jewel-toned rice, and kebabs, could be considered a culinary region all its own, but it heavily influences its neighbors' cuisines, as does Turkey, with its own kebabs and many creative uses of peppers and grapes. When these subregions are combined, they show the full breadth of the exciting, bright, creative, and varied Middle Eastern cuisine.

A few notes for recipe success

You should follow the instructions, time, and measurements given in the recipes in this book—but don't give up on your senses. Taste as you go when possible, and if something needs more of one seasoning or another, or longer in the oven, trust yourself and your cooking ability. With so much variation in pans, burner strength, and ingredients, follow the visual cues and use the times more as a guideline. I guarantee this simple change will make you a better cook.

A few other things I think are important:

- An oven thermometer is an essential tool to have so your dishes cook through in roughly the amount of time given. (Also make sure you're using the right oven mode if your oven has convection.)

- Get a kitchen scale. I've included weights for all spices (including salt) and all the ingredients in baking recipes in this book because weights are consistent. I also think they're easier—you don't have to deal with cleaning measuring cups or the hassle of scooping and leveling flour. For spices, I recommend a precision, or spice, scale to get better accuracy for low weights. However, all amounts over 1 gram have been rounded to the nearest whole, so any digital scale should work. Any amount under 0.5 grams is marked as n/a (not applicable).

- Pull meat and fish out of the refrigerator before you cook with them; even 5 minutes will help take some of the chill off and cook your meat more evenly.

- The recipes are designed to work with many pans, but the one we use for nearly everything in our test kitchen is a deep, 12-inch, enamel-covered cast-iron skillet. I highly recommend buying one.

Right, near Umm al-Hiran, a Bedouin village in the Negev Desert, Israel

spices

{ SPICES }

بهارات

baharat

תַּבְלִינִים

ادویه‌ها

μπαχαρικά

համեմունքներ

The spices that I call out in this chapter include singular spices or herbs common to Middle Eastern cuisine, like sumac, as well as the most popular spice mixes used throughout the region (see Make Your Own Spice Blends, *page 35*, for recipes). They are the spices that make food taste "of a place" and that instantly bring back memories of home for me. I begin the chapter with an overall history of spices, offer instructions for storage and toasting, and then go into each spice in detail, followed by recipes for how to make your own blends and dishes to highlight them.

ORIGIN AND HISTORY

Spices have long been used in the Middle East for medicinal, spiritual, and gustatory purposes. There are spices native to specific parts of the Middle East, such as sumac, za'atar (the herb, which is essential for the blend of the same name), anise,

bay leaves, coriander, and cumin. But for much of history, abundant use of spices was limited to the wealthy, who could show off with extravagant meals full of spices imported from farther east like black pepper, nutmeg, and cloves.

The spice trade may have started as early as 3000 BC with Asian, Indian, and later Greco-Roman caravans traveling by land across the Middle East and by sea as they carried spices westward. Cities like Aden, Damascus, and Alexandria acted as waystations and became the spice emporiums for the world. By 900 BC the Arabs had their own caravans to connect themselves directly to the source of many spices, Southeast Asia. Their monopoly on the spice routes lasted until the Romans and Europeans started long, dangerous routes completely by sea (certain legs had always been by boat) to circumvent the geographic and commercial middlemen. Those routes led to the discovery of the New World and the introduction of new spices such as allspice and chiles.

The unique spice blends we associate with the Middle East were developed and refined over the long history of the spice trade, eventually combining ingredients native to the beginning, middle, and ends of the routes, thousands of miles apart. For example, hawayej (*see page 29*) from Yemen brings together cumin and coriander native to the Middle East, black pepper and turmeric from Southeast Asia, caraway from Europe, and cloves from Indonesia—and the blend flavors much of the food in the country to this day. The mixes in this chapter are used extensively in savory cooking, but many are also used in sweets and drinks, and though rare for spices, sometimes as a garnish. They're some of the defining flavors of Middle Eastern cooking.

SOURCING AND STORING

When shopping for spices, whether whole spices or ground, buy yours from a company or shop that pays attention to sourcing, has relationships with farmers, and values quality and freshness. If buying a blend, always read labels to make sure it doesn't contain fillers like salt and coloring agents. We sell many of the spice blends mentioned in this chapter at La Boîte, and if you'd like to make the blends yourself, we sell all of the individual spices called for.

I find people use ground spices more than whole, and what matters is that you actually *use* them. If you like to grind whole spices such as coriander seeds or cumin seeds before cooking, for the most powerful flavor, do that; if you prefer the convenience of ground spices, buy them. Do what works best for you and your cooking style, because this will encourage you to actually enjoy the spices and not let them linger on the shelf. Spices lose their flavor and potency over time, and there's no set rule about how long they're good for, but if the taste and smell is noticeably muted, it's time to part with those spices. Generally speaking, whole spices last a bit longer than preground.

For whole spices, the color should be uniform and vivid, which indicates everything was harvested ripe. A faded color probably indicates a faded taste—and that applies to ground spices, too. For both, a strong smell signals freshness.

Stored properly, your spices will be immune to spoilage, but the quality will fade over time. Keep spices out of the sun and away from the stove as both light and heat deteriorate their essential oils. Humidity also has a negative effect, so don't keep them in your freezer. Choose nonreactive containers such as metal or glass for storing, and make sure the containers won't conduct heat and that they're airtight. Then keep them in plain sight so you'll actually use them.

TOASTING SPICES

If you buy whole spices, you'll often need to toast them before grinding to bring the oils from the center to the surface, adding stronger, punchier flavor to your cooking. One of the questions I get most often from customers is how to properly toast spices. Here's my method:

For small quantities (up to 1 cup): In a small dry skillet over medium heat, toast the spices, swirling the pan often to make sure all sides are evenly heated, until they are fragrant, 3 to 4 minutes. Immediately transfer them to a bowl to stop any further toasting from the residual heat in the pan.

For 1 cup or more, I use the oven. With its heat from all directions (as opposed to just below), the oven is better for toasting, but it's not worth the effort to turn it on for a small amount of food. Preheat the oven to 350°F and do not use convection mode. Spread the spices onto a small sheet pan or ovenproof skillet and bake until the spices are fragrant, 8 to 10 minutes, checking often (that is a lot of spices to burn in one go). Transfer them to a bowl immediately to stop the cooking.

Toast spices on an as-needed basis so they're as fresh as possible. I don't recommend toasting a big batch to use for days or weeks on end because the fragrance will fade with long storage, defeating the purpose of toasting.

Sumac

I like to call sumac "Middle Eastern vinegar" because I use both the same way—as a wonderful condiment that imparts a sharp, tangy flavor to everything from kebabs to salads—but that is where their similarity ends. Sumac retains its acidity when heated, unlike vinegar and citrus, so it's a great addition to roasts, like the Palestinian chicken and bread dish musakhan.

ABOUT

The name *sumac* comes from the Aramaic word for "red." It's been used for thousands of years in the Middle East to add a sour note to dishes like rice pilafs outside of the citrus growing season, or in regions where citrus doesn't grow. The spice is made from the berries of a bush native to the Mediterranean and parts of Asia. It's currently cultivated and also grows wild in Turkey and Iran.

In the fall and after flowering, sumac bushes are covered in small, rust-colored, hair-covered berries that grow in dense clusters called bobs. When ripe, the sumac berries are dark red or even purple (*see the photo on page 22*)—however, they are actually harvested before fully ripe if used for culinary purposes. They are traditionally dried in the sun, then sold whole or ground. Some sumac is also cured in salt to preserve it, then ground and sold.

APPEARANCE AND FLAVOR

Ground sumac is most common. It's coarser and moister than most spices. If you do find the berries, they are quite small and hard. For both, the color can range from rust red to deep reddish purple. The berries' color isn't always consistent, so some producers add beet or hibiscus powder to get the deep burgundy color customers have come to expect. Because sumac berries aren't 100 percent dried; they contain some humidity and are prone to clumping, thus salt is often added, too. I only buy pure ground sumac so I can control the salt level in my food. Not all packaging will indicate if salt is added, so try to buy it from a source that you can talk to. If you're buying cured sumac, the salt level will obviously be higher.

The taste is famously astringent and sour with a floral touch and a dry, almost tannic finish.

TRADITIONAL USES

Garnish for hummus — *Levant*
Kebab topping — *Iran, Iraq, Turkey, and more*
Fattoush (fried bread salad) — *Levant*
Soaked sumac berry drink — *Turkey and more*

Recipe Ideas

1. Sprinkle over mild cheese as an appetizer.

2. Garnish fried eggs with a generous dusting before serving.

3. Use as a flavoring for grain or meat fillings for stuffed vegetables.

4. Mix into a salad for an additional acidic note, as in the Sumac Onion Salad (*page 39*).

Za'atar

Za'atar is an herb—and when the herb is combined with sumac and sesame seeds, it becomes the blend also known as za'atar—and it's one of the key flavors of the Levant.

ABOUT

Origanum syriacum, za'atar or Syrian oregano, is often confused with many similar herbs. A perennial plant in the mint family, it is native to the Middle East and grows wild in the mountains of Syria, Israel, and Lebanon and is now cultivated in Lebanon. The leaves are best when they're harvested before the plant flowers, then dried and crushed. The leaves can also be eaten fresh. Both the herb and blend are most popular in the Levant and in Egypt.

For me, the spice blend za'atar should always include the crushed herb, sumac, and sesame seeds. After that, cooks and vendors can add salt or other herbs as they please, and the proportions are up to interpretation.

APPEARANCE AND FLAVOR

Za'atar the herb has a warm, savory, herbaceous aroma and bitter, slightly salty-sweet flavor similar to hyssop, oregano, thyme, or savory. The leaves are grayish green when fresh.

The addition of tart sumac to the spice blend plays up the salinity of the herb, as does actual salt, which is sometimes added. Sesame brings a nutty warmth, and the result is a perfectly balanced blend. The mix should look moist, not dusty, and ranges from almost-brown to muted green. To make your own za'atar blend, *see page 36*.

TRADITIONAL USES

Mixed with oil and used as a dip — *Levant*
Manousheh (flatbread) — *Lebanon*
Coating for labne balls — *Levant*
Garnish for fried eggs — *Levant*

Recipe Ideas

1. Season a chicken with the dried leaves before roasting, as in Carob Molasses Roast Chicken (*page 168*).

2. Sprinkle vegetables with the blend before or after roasting—it can stand up to heat.

3. Mix the blend with olive oil to make a salad dressing.

4. Make Za'atar Laffa (*page 40*).

Baharat

Many sources will tell you that *baharat* translates to "spices" or "spice mix" from the Arabic word *biharat*, but albaharat and bahar are both Arabic for "allspice," and for me, baharat the blend is all about the allspice.

ABOUT

Baharat is an all-purpose mixture used heavily in the Persian Gulf region, Levant, Egypt, and North Africa. It's a direct product of the spice trading routes, as nearly all of the spices often used in the mix are not native to the Middle East, but cooks would have had exposure to new aromatics from countries farther east, like India and Indonesia, and to allspice from the Caribbean.

There are two main versions of baharat: one for meat or meatballs (such as Baharat Lamb Keftas) and one for fish. The first is the more common and usually includes allspice, nutmeg, cinnamon, black pepper, and bay leaves. The blend for fish contains cardamom, cumin, turmeric, and paprika. Beyond those versions, the ingredients and proportions vary greatly from person to person, by country, and also by culinary use.

APPEARANCE AND FLAVOR

Obviously, the exact flavor will depend on the mix of spices used, but generally speaking, baharat adds a highly aromatic, intense, slightly sweet note to food. The blend most often used for meatballs is very warm and a little floral from the nutmeg and allspice and has a reddish tinge. The fish blend is earthier and yellowish in color from the turmeric.

When shopping for preground spices, try a few to see what proportions of ingredients you prefer in your cooking. For example, my recipe for Baharat (*page 36*) leans heavily on allspice, cinnamon, and ginger for a sweeter, more floral mix. Try a few to see what you like.

TRADITIONAL USES

Mushbuss (chicken and rice dish) — *Qatar, UAE, Bahrain, and Kuwait*
Pilaf — *throughout the region*
Kibbeh — *throughout the region* (see Kibbeh with Pine Nuts, *page 106*)
Kofte and kefta — *throughout the region* (see Baharat Lamb Keftas, *page 45*)
Lamb marinade — *throughout the region*

Recipe Ideas

1. Use the fish baharat to flavor fish stews, legume dishes, or vegetable fritters.

2. Season roasted carrots or sweet potatoes with meat baharat.

3. Add meat baharat to apple, pear, stone fruit, or chocolate desserts as you would other sweet spice mixes.

Dukkah

This famous Egyptian spice blend has almost as much in common with granola as it does the other mixes in this chapter, as it's mainly made up of nuts and seeds. It's one spice mix that I think should always be made at home.

ABOUT

Dukkah is an Egyptian spice blend that is now eaten in other parts of the region. The name comes from the Arabic verb for "pound," because the nuts, seeds, and spices are traditionally pounded in a mortar and pestle—though now a food processor is used more often to make the blend. Dukkah was found in the Egyptian pyramids, where it was buried alongside the dead to help sustain them on their journey in the afterlife.

The "recipe" for dukkah varies from household to household and also from batch to batch, because unlike the other blends, it's a way to use up leftover ingredients like nuts. It will at the very least always contain toasted nuts and spices. Sometimes seeds, like sesame seeds, are added, as are toasted whole wheat berries or other grains, or ground and toasted legumes.

APPEARANCE AND FLAVOR

This is a coarsely ground mix, often a golden color. Along with the toasted nuts and seeds, whole spices like cumin and coriander are included, and occasionally fennel seeds or black pepper as well. Dukkah often contains salt to season the components. The flavor profile will vary between blends, but it is always toasty, very savory, and a little sweet.

I never buy dukkah because freshness is key, and I highly recommend you make it at home (see the recipe on *page 36*). If you do buy a premade mix, it's hard to know how long the nuts have been sitting on the shelf, and there's a chance they have already gone rancid.

TRADITIONAL USES

With oil, as a dip for bread at breakfast — *Egypt*
Alone as a snack — *Egypt*

Recipe Ideas

1. Sprinkle over cooked rice to add crunch.

2. Use to garnish fresh cheese before serving as an appetizer.

3. Toss into a salad for textural interest.

4. Add to roasted vegetables, such as the Dukkah Roasted Root Vegetables (*page 42*).

Hawayej

This Yemenite spice blend has two main types—a sweet version and a savory one. It can be spelled *hawayej* or *hawaij*.

ABOUT

The word *hawayej* translates from Arabic as "mixture" or sometimes "gathered stuff." The sweet kind (often called "hawayej for coffee" or "hawayej coffee") usually features cardamom, ginger, and allspice and may contain aniseed, fennel seeds, cloves, or cinnamon as well. The most common ingredients in the savory type ("hawayej for soup" or just "hawayej soup") are cumin, black pepper, and turmeric, and sometimes cardamom, coriander, and cinnamon.

APPEARANCE AND FLAVOR

Sweet hawayej is floral and bright with cardamom and has a duskier brown color. Some may have a licorice-like note from aniseed or fennel seeds. The soup blend is pungent and savory, with a golden hue from the turmeric.

TRADITIONAL USES

Yeminite Jewish lamb, beef, or chicken soup — *Yemen, Israel*
White coffee flavoring — *Yemen, Israel* (see Hawayej White Coffee, *page 47*)

Recipe Ideas

1. Use the soup blend for any bean soup or stew, especially Ful Medames (*page 236*).

2. Rub meat with the soup blend (as you would a dry rub) before grilling.

3. Flavor cookies with the coffee blend.

4. Mix the coffee blend into root vegetable purees.

Shawarma

This category of spice is as varied as the signature dish it's used for (are you sensing a pattern yet?). Shawarma, the dish, can be made from chicken, lamb, or even turkey, and the blends for each are curated as such, though I don't always stick with what's recommended by the name.

ABOUT

The shawarma technique, and thus the spice blends that go with it, is probably of Turkish origin and is very popular in many more countries now. The name comes from the Turkish word *cevirme*, which means "to turn."

There are two main approaches to the shawarma spice blend. The Turkish blend, similar to baharat (*see page 27*), has nutmeg, allspice, and clove, and is less common in stores. The other approach is used throughout the Levant and is a savory blend with cumin, turmeric, black pepper, and paprika. Other spice additions can include sumac, cayenne pepper, cinnamon, coriander, cloves, and cardamom.

APPEARANCE AND FLAVOR

Depending on what's in your blend, shawarma can be aromatic from allspice, tart from sumac, or can have some heat thanks to cayenne pepper. The Turkish take it in a subtly sweet direction with nutmeg and clove, and as such, it's brown in appearance. The Levantine mix is usually a reddish color from the paprika and is very savory, sometimes with a bit of heat.

TRADITIONAL USES

Shawarma — *Turkey and more*

Recipe Ideas

1. Use as a rub on any protein for any high-heat preparation, such as roasting and searing.

2. Season vegetables or fish generously with the spice before grilling.

3. Lamb is an especially good protein choice—season any cut before roasting, grilling, or sautéing.

Advieh

This wonderfully fragrant, floral spice blend is used mainly in Iran and Iraq, to my knowledge.

ABOUT

Advieh means "spices" in Farsi and comes from the Arabic word for "medicine." It's an old blend, and recipes date back several millennia. There are two basic varieties: *advieh polow,* or "rice spice" in Farsi, and *advieh khoresh*, which means "stew spice."

The classic blend contains cardamom, cinnamon, cumin, and rose petals. I put saffron in mine, because I think it sets it apart from the other blends of the region and makes it extra special. There is also a deep love of saffron in Iranian cuisine, which I emphasize with my blend. The rice blend usually contains the sweeter spices, and the one for stew has more savory additions like coriander or turmeric.

APPEARANCE AND FLAVOR

Sometimes the blend has a little texture with pieces of rose petal, or it can be uniformly ground. It's a light brown color, perhaps with a slight reddish tint. Both blends are sweet, with the rice blend being more noticeably so, while the stew version might have a bit of heat from black pepper or a savory hint from coriander.

TRADITIONAL USES

Multiple rice dishes — *Iran, Iraq*
Pickling spice — *Iran*
Stew seasoning — *Iran, Iraq*

Recipe Ideas

1. Both versions work as a dry rub for lamb or chicken.

2. Use either advieh in vegetable soups as a seasoning.

3. Flavor your favorite fried rice dish with either blend.

Seven Spice

If you assume that a name like "seven spice" is a set recipe, that assumption is unfortunately wrong. Seven spice always includes seven spices—but the exact spices that make it into the mix vary, as with the rest of the blends in this chapter.

ABOUT

While the exact formulation can change, usually the difference is just one or two ingredients. The most common components are coriander, cloves, allspice, cinnamon, cumin, and black pepper. Some blends contain white pepper, nutmeg, ground ginger, paprika, or fenugreek seeds. Like baharat, a spice blend that seven spice is often used interchangeably with, this is a multipurpose spice for almost all types of dishes. Seven spice is very popular in Lebanon and is often referred to as Lebanese Seven Spice (that's what I call my version of the blend on *page 37*).

APPEARANCE AND FLAVOR

The base of this blend is warm and slightly sweet, with heat from pepper or ginger and a little bitterness from fenugreek. It's finely ground and usually a darkish brown color, though if paprika is added it might have a warmer tone.

TRADITIONAL USES

All-purpose seasoning — *Lebanon, Syria, and Iraq*

Recipe Ideas

1. Use as a dry rub on meats for grilling or high-heat roasting.

2. Season roasted or pureed sweet root vegetables with it.

3. Add to tomato sauce in the early stages of cooking.

Dried Lime

This is an exceptional ingredient used to add earthy, citrusy flavors to dishes in Iran, Iraq, and cuisines from the Gulf Peninsula. I think it's one of the essential, unique spices of the Middle East. Dried limes are most often added to long-simmering stews to rehydrate and impart their flavor—and can even be eaten after cooking—but they can also be ground or grated dry for a zesty burst of flavor.

ABOUT

Dried lime is probably native to Oman, and is also called Omani lime, Persian lime, black lime, limon omani, or, sometimes confusingly, dried lemon. In Iraq, it's known as noomi basara, after Basra, the port in the country where the limes probably first arrived.

The small fruits used to make dried limes are about the size of Key limes. They are not made from the types of limes available in grocery stores—those would be unbearably bitter when dried. The fruit is sometimes cured with salt and traditionally dried in the sun, though increased demand means many are now (quickly) dried in ovens.

APPEARANCE AND FLAVOR

Dried lime has all the sour flavor of fresh limes with less bitterness and a slightly fermented funk. It's sold whole, and the size can vary quite a bit; look for ones that are about the size of unshelled walnuts or golf balls. Seek out limes that are still a little moist inside, if you can test them (they should have some give and not sound hollow when tapped). The color ranges from a very light brown to almost black, depending on how long they've been dried. The lighter limes are slightly more bitter than the black, muskier-tasting ones.

TRADITIONAL USES

Gormeh sabzi (herb stew) — *Iran*
Mushbuss (chicken and rice dish) — *Qatar, UAE, Bahrain, and Kuwait*
Digestive tea — *Iran, Iraq, and more*

Recipe Ideas

1. Grate over raw and cooked dishes—like lime zest but more interesting.

2. Add to a pot of green lentils to make a deeply flavored soup, then either discard the limes or serve them alongside the lentils.

3. Make Verjus and Lamb Stew with Eggplant (*page 65*), which is flavored with dried limes.

DUKKAH

ZA'ATAR

LEBANESE
SEVEN
SPICE

HAWAYEJ
SOUP

ADVIEH

BAHARAT

SHAWARMA

Make Your Own Spice Blends

As you've probably gathered, spice blends in the Middle East are a very personal matter. These are my versions, and while they are certainly not definitive, I think they're perfectly balanced. Try them once as is, then customize however you see fit. For information on how to pick quality spices and properly store them, see Sourcing and Storing (*page 23*).

Meet some of the defining flavors of the Middle East.

Za'atar

Makes about 1½ cups (178 grams)

½ **cup** sesame seeds, preferably unhulled (70 grams)

1½ **cups** (packed) dried za'atar leaves (42 grams), or use a combination of 1 **cup** dried marjoram (16 grams), ⅓ **cup** dried oregano (10 grams), and 3 **tablespoons** dried thyme (9 grams)

½ **cup** crushed or ground sumac (56 grams)

2 **teaspoons** fine sea salt (10 grams)

Optional additions: pinch of nigella seeds, dried ground savory, dried ground rosemary, to taste

In a small skillet, toast the sesame seeds over low heat until fragrant, about 5 minutes. Remove from the pan and set aside to cool. Using a coffee grinder or mortar and pestle, grind the za'atar leaves with the sumac and salt until coarsely ground. Pour into a small bowl and mix in the toasted sesame seeds.

Baharat

Makes about ½ cup (46 grams)

⅓ **cup** loosely packed dried rose petals (5 grams), ground

2 **tablespoons plus** 1½ **teaspoons** allspice berries (15 grams), toasted (see page 24) and ground

2 **tablespoons** ground cinnamon (10 grams)

1 **tablespoon plus** 2 **teaspoons** ground ginger (10 grams)

1 **teaspoon** black peppercorns (3 grams), ground

1 **teaspoon** caraway seeds (3 grams), toasted and ground

In a small bowl, mix the rose petals, allspice, cinnamon, ginger, pepper, and caraway until evenly combined.

Dukkah

Makes about 1 cup (83 grams)

¼ **cup** hazelnuts (30 grams), toasted (see page 99) and finely chopped

3 **tablespoons** coriander seeds (15 grams), toasted and coarsely ground

2 **tablespoons** crushed dried mint leaves (5 grams)

2 **tablespoons** cumin seeds (15 grams), toasted and coarsely ground

1 **tablespoon plus** 2 **teaspoons** sesame seeds (15 grams), toasted

1 **tablespoon** dried thyme (3 grams)

In a small bowl, mix the hazelnuts, coriander, mint, cumin, sesame seeds, and thyme until evenly combined.

Hawayej Soup

**Makes about ½ cup
(56 grams)**

This is for the savory spice blend. For the sweet version of hawayej, make the spice blend included in the Hawayej White Coffee (*page 47*), but omit the white coffee.

2 tablespoons cumin seeds (15 grams), ground

**1 tablespoon plus
1½ teaspoons** black peppercorns (14 grams), ground

**1 tablespoon plus
1½ teaspoons** ground turmeric (13 grams)

1 tablespoon caraway seeds (8 grams), ground

1 tablespoon coriander seeds (5 grams), ground

¼ teaspoon ground cloves (0.5 grams)

In a small bowl, mix the cumin, pepper, turmeric, caraway, coriander, and cloves until evenly combined.

Advieh

**Makes about ¼ cup
(20 grams)**

1 tablespoon ground cinnamon (5 grams)

1 tablespoon coriander seeds (5 grams), ground

2 teaspoons ground turmeric (5 grams)

1 teaspoon black peppercorns (3 grams), ground

1 teaspoon ground nutmeg (2 grams)

Pinch of saffron threads, ground (n/a)

In a small bowl, mix the cinnamon, coriander, turmeric, pepper, nutmeg, and saffron until evenly combined.

Shawarma

**Makes about ½ cup
(48 grams)**

2 tablespoons cumin seeds (15 grams), ground

1 tablespoon coriander seeds (5 grams), ground

1 tablespoon dried garlic slices (5 grams), ground

1 tablespoon sweet paprika (8 grams)

2 teaspoons black peppercorns (6 grams), ground

2 teaspoons ground turmeric (5 grams)

1 teaspoon ground cardamom (2 grams)

1 teaspoon ground cloves (2 grams)

In a small bowl, mix the cumin, coriander, garlic, paprika, pepper, turmeric, cardamom, and cloves until evenly combined.

Lebanese Seven Spice

**Makes about ¼ cup
(29 grams)**

**1 tablespoon plus
1 teaspoon** ground cinnamon (7 grams)

2¼ teaspoons black peppercorns (7 grams), ground

1½ teaspoons ground ginger (3 grams)

1½ teaspoons allspice berries (3 grams), ground

1½ teaspoons ground cloves (3 grams)

1½ teaspoons ground nutmeg (3 grams)

½ teaspoon fenugreek seeds (3 grams), ground

In a small bowl, mix the cinnamon, pepper, ginger, allspice, clove, nutmeg, and fenugreek until evenly combined.

Sumac Onion Salad

In the upper eastern Galilee region of Israel, where you can actually see into neighboring Lebanon and Syria with the naked eye, there is a large Druze community whose cuisine is heavily inspired by its neighbors. One of the many small salads you get before every Druze meal consists of soaked red onions seasoned with tangy sumac. I didn't think much of it for years but eventually learned to appreciate its simplicity along with the intriguing layers of sweet and sour. A mandoline is helpful for slicing the onions paper thin, but a sharp knife works (almost) as well.

Serves 6

1	large red onion, halved and very thinly sliced lengthwise
2 tablespoons	extra-virgin olive oil
1 tablespoon	freshly squeezed lemon juice
1 tablespoon	pomegranate molasses
1 tablespoon	ground sumac (9 grams)
½ teaspoon	fine sea salt (3 grams)
½ teaspoon	freshly ground black pepper (1 gram)
¼ cup	roughly chopped fresh flat parsley leaves
¼ cup	fresh pomegranate arils

Fill a large bowl with ice water. Soak the onion slices for 1 hour to crisp them up. Drain well and blot dry with paper towels, being careful not to damage the delicate slices.

Meanwhile, in a small bowl, whisk together the oil, lemon juice, pomegranate molasses, sumac, salt, and pepper to combine well. Set aside to allow the spices to bloom while the onion soaks.

Transfer the drained onion slices to a clean bowl. Add the dressing, parsley, and pomegranate arils, toss, and serve.

Za'atar Laffa

Any type of bread topped with or dipped into za'atar is a no-brainer: The two are truly a perfect match. Laffa is a large, soft, and bubbly flatbread from Iraq, also popular in Israel, traditionally baked in a clay oven, or, in this version, it's in a skillet. I rub the dough with olive oil and then season it with salt and a generous amount of za'atar so the spice blend adheres and completely covers the bread and even toasts a little in the pan. You can also get creative and knead some into the dough once you master this recipe.

Makes 8 large flatbreads

Dough

1 tablespoon	sugar (13 grams)
1 tablespoon	instant yeast (10 grams)
2¾ cups	water (650 grams)
7 cups plus 2 tablespoons	all-purpose flour (1 kilogram)
¼ cup	extra-virgin olive oil (50 grams), plus more as needed
1 tablespoon	fine sea salt (16 grams)

Toppings

Extra-virgin olive oil

Salt

Za'atar (*page 36*)

Variation

Replace up to 25 percent of the flour with whole wheat or barley flour.

Storage Directions

Cooked laffa can be cooled completely and stored in a sealed bag in the freezer for a few weeks.

Make the dough: In a stand mixer fitted with the dough hook, combine the sugar, yeast, and water and whisk to combine and break up the yeast. Set aside for 1 minute to activate the yeast.

Add the flour, oil, and salt and mix on low speed until a rough dough forms, about 1 minute. Increase the speed to medium and knead, stopping to pull the dough off the hook, if needed, until the dough is smooth, elastic, and slightly sticky, 6 to 7 minutes.

Lightly oil a large bowl, add the dough, and cover with plastic wrap. Let rise until doubled in size, about 1 hour, or in the refrigerator for up to 24 hours.

Lightly oil a sheet pan. Divide the dough into 8 equal pieces (about 215 grams each). Shape them into balls and place them on the oiled pan. Flip them once so they are coated on both sides with oil. Cover the dough with a clean kitchen towel and let rest for 30 minutes.

Heat a 12-inch nonstick skillet over medium-high heat. Lightly oil a second sheet pan. Working with one at a time, flatten a ball on the second oiled pan until it's about 8 inches across and ½ inch thick, using a bit more oil if necessary. Do not overstretch the dough on the work surface or it will be hard to lift.

Top the dough: Using your fingers, generously rub the top of a dough with oil, then sprinkle with salt and a good amount of za'atar. Gently press the za'atar into the dough.

Carefully lift the dough and very slightly stretch it by hand so it's about 10 inches across, then place it in the hot skillet, za'atar-side up. Cook until golden brown in spots, 2 to 3 minutes, then flip and cook the other side until the bread is cooked through, making sure the za'atar doesn't burn, another 1 to 2 minutes. Remove the laffa to a plate and cover it with a towel. Brush any za'atar out of the pan and repeat with the remaining dough balls (start prepping the next laffa while the previous is cooking so it's ready to add to the pan immediately). Serve hot or warm.

Dukkah Roasted Root Vegetables

I roast seasonal vegetables every week for my family and serve them as a side dish, a salad, or even a main course. Roasting is a simple preparation for any vegetable (in any combination) and only requires they be cut in roughly the same size. This root vegetable dish works fall through spring, and mixing up the spices keeps the vegetables interesting week after week. Here, dukkah adds a nutty flavor and lightly crunchy texture, and this is one of the few times I will actually *cook* this spice blend rather than use it only as a garnish or dip.

Serves 6

2	medium beets, peeled and cut into ¾-inch wedges
2	medium turnips, peeled and cut into ¾-inch wedges
2	medium carrots, sliced on the diagonal
1	medium red onion, cut into ¾-inch wedges
2 tablespoons	extra-virgin olive oil
1 tablespoon	honey
1 tablespoon	verjus, homemade (*page 56*) or store-bought, plus more for serving
2 teaspoons	fine sea salt (10 grams)
3 tablespoons	Dukkah (*page 36*; 21 grams)

Preheat the oven to 375°F. Line a sheet pan with parchment paper or use an unlined roasting pan.

In a large bowl, toss the beets, turnips, carrots, and onion with the oil, honey, verjus, salt, and 2 tablespoons (14 grams) of the dukkah. Spread the mixture in an even layer in the prepared pan.

Bake, gently stirring every 15 minutes, until the vegetables are tender and lightly caramelized, about 50 minutes. Sprinkle the remaining 1 tablespoon (7 grams) dukkah on top and drizzle with verjus before serving warm.

Baharat Lamb Keftas

Ground meat, especially lamb and baharat, are a perfect match, as the sweet spices in the blend tone down the lightly gamy notes of the meat. I like to cook these meatballs with salted butter for added flavor, but there's no need to run out and buy it if you only have unsalted at home—the feta and olives in the mix season the kefta very well.

Serves 4

1 pound	ground lamb
⅓ cup	finely crumbled feta cheese
⅓ cup	pitted black olives, preferably oil-cured, finely chopped
¼ cup	finely chopped almonds
1	large egg
1	garlic clove, finely chopped
3 teaspoons	Baharat (*page 36*; 5 grams)
½ teaspoon	Urfa chile (1 gram)
⅛ teaspoon	fine sea salt (1 gram)
	Extra-virgin olive oil, for pan-frying
1 tablespoon	salted butter

In a large bowl, combine the lamb, feta, olives, almonds, egg, garlic, 2 teaspoons (4 grams) of the baharat, the Urfa chile, and salt. Mix well so the ingredients are evenly distributed.

Divide the kefta mix into 12 equal portions (about 53 grams each) and roll each until round and smooth, taking care to not overwork the mixture. Gently press each ball so the top and bottom flatten and the kefta is 1 inch thick or slightly thinner.

In a large skillet, heat a thin layer of oil over medium-low heat. When the oil is hot, add the kefta and cook until nicely browned but still pink in the middle, 4 to 5 minutes per side. Add the butter and remaining 1 teaspoon (1 gram) baharat and baste the kefta while cooking for another 2 minutes, or until well-browned all over. Serve hot.

Hawayej White Coffee

A few years ago, a Yemenite friend introduced me to white coffee, and I was blown away by the floral, elegant beverage prepared with it. White coffee beans are only partially roasted and at a lower temperature than the dark coffee beans we're used to. They're a hard-to-get item as they are very traditional and made by only a few producers, but with a little searching (on foot or on-screen) you can find them. I'm so excited for you to try this unique spiced drink.

Makes enough spice blend for about 20 servings

Coffee Hawayej

3 tablespoons	ground ginger (18 grams)
1 tablespoon	ground cinnamon (5 grams)
2 teaspoons	ground cardamom (4 grams)
2 teaspoons	ground cloves (4 grams)
1 cup	ground white coffee (124 grams)

For Serving

1 cup	boiling water per person

Make the coffee hawayej: In a small bowl, stir together the ginger, cinnamon, cardamom, and cloves until evenly combined. Mix in the ground coffee.

Serve: Pour the boiling water into a mug and stir in 1 tablespoon (8 grams) of the coffee hawayej. Steep for 4 minutes, after which the solids should have settled to the bottom (no need to strain). Serve right away.

Storage Directions
The coffee spice blend will keep in an airtight container in a cool, dark place for several weeks.

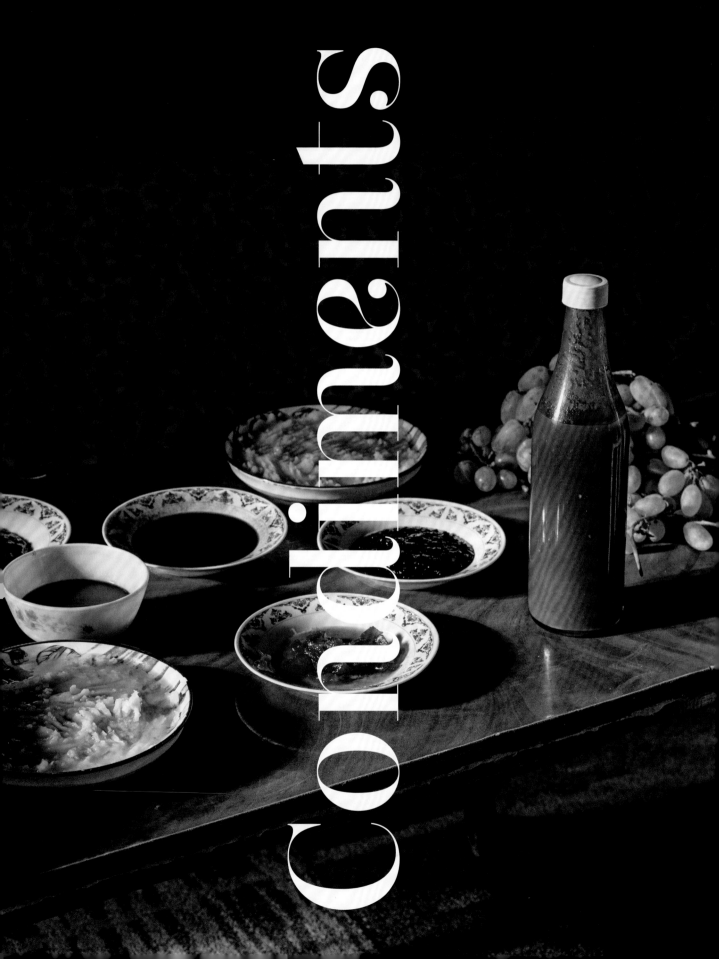

Condiments

صلصات

çeşniler

רְטָבִים וּ מִמְרַחִים

چاشنی‌ها

καρυκεύματα

սամունրեր

Pepper Paste

Biber salçası, which is Turkish for "pepper paste," is made from sweet and hot red peppers. It is a uniquely Middle Eastern source of umami: Just a spoonful gives body and depth of flavor to stews, soups, stuffed vegetables, rice dishes, legume dishes, and nearly every other kind of fare you can think of.

ORIGIN AND HISTORY

Biber salçası is a marriage of a New World crop and an Old World technique. Peppers and chiles, *Capsicum annuum*, were brought back by Europeans from the Americas at the end of the fifteenth century. At the time, they were believed to be related to black pepper, which is probably the origin of the chile vs pepper naming confusion—and also why they were more quickly integrated into local cuisines than other New World foods.

Turkey was one of the earliest enthusiasts of this new fruit. Sailors in the Ottoman navy had been introduced to peppers in the early 1500s, and the high vitamin C content was later discovered to cure their scurvy. The exact moment pepper paste was "invented" isn't known, but clearly when the novel fruit was introduced to Turkish cooks and deemed delicious, they applied their traditional preservation techniques (*see page 16*) to it as they would any other produce.

PRODUCTION

Large, sweet red peppers such as salçalık or kapya biberi are used to make the paste. For hot pepper paste, spicy peppers are added to the mix. A hot version of the kapya pepper called acı kapya

Pepper paste, amba, and verjus are three of my favorite flavorful condiments. I use them to add deep, nuanced flavor to my food with just a spoonful of their concentrated fruit taste. Tomato paste isn't a traditional condiment in that it does benefit from cooking to temper its flavor—but I included it here anyway since it's such an important ingredient in cuisines of the Middle East. It deserves a spot in this book and your kitchen.

biberi is often used. When the peppers are red and ripe, usually in the fall, they are harvested and then turned into a paste.

The paste can be made several ways. The trimmed peppers are pureed raw (or sometimes roasted first) and then spread into thin layers and dried in the sun, which, depending on the conditions, can take up to a week to get the right consistency. The puree can also be baked or reduced on the stovetop, or the whole peppers can be partially dried, then pureed. The paste is seasoned with salt and oil before being sealed in an airtight container and stored.

APPEARANCE AND FLAVOR

Pepper paste is very savory, a little sweet, and has a slight acidity. It's jammy without being cloying. The spicy version isn't intense—think mild jalapeño. The paste is thick and smooth like tomato paste, and a brick- to dark-red color. Note that some brands can be fairly salty.

SOURCING AND STORING

The ingredients on the label should be limited to peppers, salt, and oil. Some preservatives may be added to commercial versions to preserve the color, but you should try to avoid them. You can choose between mild acı biber salçası and hot tatı biber salçası, though they both may just be labeled "pepper paste."

The paste is often sold in large jars at Turkish, Armenian, or Middle Eastern grocers. After opening, add a thin layer of olive or neutral vegetable oil to the top of the paste, cover, and refrigerate. It will last for months this way. (The paste has a tendency to dry out and develop mold on the surface after the jar has been opened, so the oil prevents air exposure. Every time you use it, top up the oil layer.)

TRADITIONAL USES

Grilled cheese sandwich filling — *Turkey*
Pide (flatbread) — *Turkey*
Menemen (egg and vegetable dish) — *Turkey*
Kisir (bulgur salad) — *Turkey*
Cevizli biber (pepper and walnut spread) — *Turkey* (see recipe, *page 60*)

Recipe Ideas

1. Incorporate into meatball mix or a meat or grain stuffing.

2. Fry in oil to develop the flavor before adding it to tomato sauce.

3. Spread onto toast with other toppings such as cheese for a snack or appetizer.

Tomato Paste

Rich, concentrated tomato paste is one of the products that best embodies the evolution of so many pantry ingredients for me. We imagine it being made in huge batches and in industrial facilities, destined to fill tubes and cans that line a supermarket shelf, without even the vaguest notion of a farm or field. But, though it rarely is now, it used to be made by anyone with access to ripe tomatoes and strong sunlight.

ORIGIN AND HISTORY

The origin of tomato paste closely follows that of pepper paste (*see page 49*) with one notable exception: Tomatoes seem to have taken much longer to catch on. While chiles and peppers were already being used in the early sixteenth century in Turkey, by contrast, some of the earliest evidence of tomatoes in the Ottoman Empire doesn't come until nearly the end of the eighteenth century. Tomatoes were virtually absent from cooking on the Arabian Peninsula until the second half of the twentieth century.

But slowly, over the course of a few hundred years, tomatoes were adopted by cooks. They were most commonly used as a preserved paste to thicken stews and add color, replacing more expensive ingredients that accomplished the same, like ground nuts and saffron. The paste also adds a subtle tart note to cooked dishes the same way more familiar native ingredients like fruit juice or molasses do, making it easy to incorporate into all of the cuisines.

PRODUCTION

So-called paste tomatoes—a variety that has a firm texture and less moisture and seeds—are harvested in the summer. To make the paste, the tomatoes will either be run through a food mill first to remove any skin and seeds, then boiled for several hours until most of the moisture is cooked off. Or, the tomatoes can be cooked down until they've nearly disintegrated, strained, and then either returned to the pot to further reduce or spread into a thin layer on a tray to dry in the sun. For either method, when the paste is thick enough, in many parts of the Middle East it's salted, flavored with sugar and/or olive oil, then jarred and stored.

APPEARANCE AND FLAVOR

Tomato paste is sweet, tangy, a little acidic, and fruity. It's savory due to the umami qualities of tomatoes. It can have a raw edge to it before cooking, but it mellows and deepens with the application of just a little heat. The color is a rich red, and the texture is dense and smooth. Some jarred brands of paste from the Middle East can be saltier than Italian or American brands, which have no seasonings.

SOURCING AND STORING

The ingredients on a label should be just tomato, salt, perhaps oil, and maybe a sulfur additive to preserve the color. If you can see the color, it should be a nice deep red, almost brick-like. Buy organic if that's important to you, but it's not an indicator of better taste.

European and American tomato pastes are sold in small tubes or cans. Middle Eastern brands are often a looser texture and sold in large jars, which are certainly more economical. Like pepper paste, tomato paste is prone to spoiling on the surface, so store opened containers in the refrigerator topped with a thin layer of olive or neutral vegetable oil to prevent mold. Kept this way, it should last for several months (or just buy the paste in a resealable tube—a good solution if you don't use it very often).

TRADITIONAL USES

Thareed (meat and vegetable stew) — *Gulf countries*
Madhruba (meat porridge) — *Qatar*
Lahm bi ajeen (meat-topped flatbread) — *Turkey*
Duggus (tomato relish) — *Saudi Arabia*

Recipe Ideas

1. Make a sweet and sour sauce by mixing with sugar or pomegranate molasses.

2. Coat vegetables with the paste before roasting for flavor and texture.

3. Flavor meat, grain, and vegetable stuffings with a spoonful.

Verjus

In the family of products made from grapes, verjus is a tart liquid made from the juice of underripe white and red grapes. It is known for its gentle acidity, and some chefs prefer it to vinegar and grape juice because it doesn't clash with any wine drunk with the meal and isn't too sweet. For much of the Muslim Middle East, its lack of alcohol is also a bonus. I was surprised to learn there is a long history of using it in the region—and think it's a great addition to pantries due to its complex grape flavor that complements other flavors without overpowering them.

ORIGIN AND HISTORY

In Farsi, verjus is known as abghooreh and it is a common ingredient in Iranian cuisine. In Arabic it is called hosrum, and is used often in Syrian and Lebanese cooking.

Verjus is made from unripe grapes that have been trimmed off of vines destined to become wine, molasses, or table grapes (see Production, below). It was referenced in Roman recipes as far back as the first century AD; by the thirteenth century, the tart juice pressed from the grapes was used in Arabic recipes as a substitute for lemon juice, or sometimes in conjunction with it, and for pickling instead of vinegar. In medieval texts, it was often listed as interchangeable with sumac juice, pomegranate juice, lemon juice, and vinegar.

PRODUCTION

Verjus can be made both midway through the grape-growing season and at harvest. Grape clusters are pruned from the vines midseason to encourage better flavor on the fruit that is left. These trimmed, partially ripe, and semisoft grapes become verjus. When grapes for making wine or table grapes are harvested, there are often some grapes that aren't yet ripe enough to be used. These grapes also become verjus. Similarly, grapes are used from young vines that aren't producing quality fruit for wine yet, or from vines that produce fruit that isn't good enough for any other purposes. These underripe grapes have started to change color from opaque green, are high-acid and low-sugar, and are soft enough to press. Red verjus is made from red grapes or a mix of red and white grapes, and white verjus is made from only white grapes.

Once the grapes are pressed, the juice may be allowed to settle and is then filtered for a clearer final product. It *can* be bottled at this stage, but it will likely ferment. To prevent fermentation, a few traditional methods may be used: The juice can be salted, boiled (and often salted, too) to sterilize it, or it can be bottled and topped with a thin layer of olive oil to prevent air exposure. Adding a small amount of citric acid will help stave off fermentation for a few months. Commercial producers will use more high-tech methods of sterilization for the bottles or add preservatives such as sulfates, which are hard to avoid in products available here in the US.

APPEARANCE AND FLAVOR

The flavor of white verjus is fresh and crisp with a slight acidity and no prominent sweetness. Red verjus is earthier and a little less crisp. Both are lighter in color than the wines made from the same grapes.

SOURCING AND STORING

Strength varies from brand to brand, and if you're lucky enough to try a homemade batch of verjus, it is usually a lot tarter than store-bought. Look for a short, clean ingredient list, ideally with no preservatives beyond citric acid (this might not always be possible). Any indication of the country or region of origin and the grape varietal is nice to know. As with wine, you can begin to develop preferences. A lot of wineries actually make verjus, so your favorite producer may also sell it. It's not a very common product, but it is becoming easier to find at specialty food shops and online.

Unopened verjus will keep in a cool dark spot for a year, though some may ferment slightly. Once opened, store it in the refrigerator for up to 3 months, or freeze it in small portions for up to 6 months.

TRADITIONAL USES

Lemon juice substitute — *Lebanon, Syria, and more*
Sweet and sour sauce, with grape molasses — *Turkey*

Recipe Ideas

1. Use in salad dressing for a less harsh acid than vinegar.

2. Deglaze the pan with verjus after searing vegetables or proteins.

3. Add to poaching liquids for a subtle tartness.

4. Make Verjus and Lamb Stew with Eggplant (*page 65*).

5. Make your own Simplified Verjus (*page 56*) from ripe grapes.

Amba

This fluorescent yellow-orange sharp and sweet sauce, made from mango and flavored with fenugreek, is a staple of every falafel and shawarma stand in Israel and a household staple in Iraq.

ORIGIN AND HISTORY

Amba is popular in Iraqi, Israeli, and Saudi cuisines and has roots in India. The name probably comes from India, where *amba* means "mango" in the language Marathi spoken in Maharashtra. Amba was most likely invented at the end of the nineteenth century by the Iraqi Jewish Sassoon family of exporters in Bombay. When they arrived in India and discovered new-to-them mangoes, they decided to export them to Iraq. But the fruit would not survive the long journey, so it was pickled with vinegar and spices for preservation, and the original "chunky" form of amba was born. It's similar to Indian achar and Caribbean mango chutney, but it really does have a unique flavor profile because of the fenugreek. Unlike these other pickles, it is also pureed and used as a sauce.

The pickled mango was quickly popularized in Iraq, where it is sometimes called simply torshi anbeh, or "mango pickle." From Iraq, it spread to neighboring Saudi Arabia. It was brought to Israel in the mid-twentieth century by emigrating Iraqi Jews, who ate it with their traditional Shabbat breakfast of eggs cooked with eggplant. In the next few decades, the sauce became a common sandwich topping there (sabich without amba is like falafel without tahini sauce).

PRODUCTION

The key ingredients in amba are green (unripe) mango, turmeric, fenugreek, and perhaps fresh or dried chiles. Traditionally it's made by peeling and chopping the green mango, mixing it with salt, and letting it ferment for a few days, enough time for the sauce to develop a tart flavor (this step can also be skipped—in which case vinegar or citric acid might be added instead). The mango slices may be left out to dry in the sun for a few hours as well. (Many home cooks now skip the sun-drying stage, too.) Once the mango has been fermented, it's cooked with sugar and turmeric, fenugreek, and other spices such as mustard seeds or paprika. After the amba is prepared, it can be left chunky or pureed. If green mangoes are hard to find, amba can be made with ripe mangoes or even other fruit with less sugar added. It's a flexible preparation.

APPEARANCE AND FLAVOR

The sauce is a heady mixture of fruity and earthy flavors, with some sharp notes and a slightly funky tang. The distinctive scent comes from the fenugreek, which smells like maple syrup but has a savory, bitter flavor. Fenugreek also acts as a thickener and gives amba a viscous texture.

SOURCING AND STORING

You can buy either jarred prepared amba or amba spice blend to add to green mango—or you can make it yourself (*see page 59*). If buying amba from a market, be sure the label has a short ingredient list of just the key items and citric acid, which should be the only preservative. Prepared amba can be pureed and smooth or with chunks of mango. I love both. You may also find amba made with other fruit, such as papaya. They all have the unique vivid color and flavor that comes from the spices.

Store the spice blend as you would any other spice (*see page 23*). Once opened, keep jarred amba in the fridge and use it up within a few months.

Tomato salad — *Iraq*
Sabich sandwich — *Iraq and Israel*
Falafel condiment — *Israel*
Rice accompaniment — *Saudi Arabia*

Recipe Ideas

1. Mix a spoonful into a marinade for chicken or lamb.

2. Stir it into a salad dressing.

3. Top fried eggs with a spoonful.

4. Make the Mushbuss Rubyan (*page 62*), seasoned with Amba Spice Blend (*page 59*).

Simplified Verjus

I'm delighted to see more and more wineries producing verjus nowadays, making it much easier to find. But I also wanted to share a homemade version that is based on fully ripe green grapes plus a dose of citric acid (the acid found in citrus fruit). Unless you know of someone who owns a vineyard to get unripe grapes from, this is a great stand-in that you can make all year round. It has the same balance of sweetness and sour, minus the harshness of vinegar. As a bonus, the citric acid slows down fermentation.

Makes about 2 cups

2 pounds	seedless green grapes, stemmed
2 teaspoons	citric acid (7 grams), plus more as needed
½ teaspoon	fine sea salt (3 grams)

Put the medium disk into a food mill and fit the mill over a large bowl. Process the grapes in small batches until all of them have been juiced and no fruit is left on the skin. Discard the solids.

Pour the juice through a fine-mesh sieve into a bowl (discard any solids). Add the citric acid and salt and stir until dissolved. Taste the mixture. Depending on how ripe the grapes are, you may need to add more citric acid to get the signature tart flavor of verjus (the mixture should be as tart as fresh lemon juice, if not slightly more so). To make it tarter, add ¼ teaspoon (1 gram) more citric acid at a time until it makes your mouth pucker, but stop before all you can taste is the citric acid. The mixture will be cloudy.

Transfer to a glass container that holds at least 3 cups. Leave the verjus out overnight at room temperature. The next day, the fine sediment will have settled to the bottom and the clearer verjus can be decanted into another container, if you like.

Storage Directions
The verjus will keep in an airtight glass container in the refrigerator for up to 2 weeks.

More ways to use verjus

FROM JIM MEEHAN

One trendy use of verjus is in cocktails—both with alcohol and without. Jim Meehan is a world-renowned mixologist—author of *The PDT Cocktail Book* and *Meehan's Bartender Manual*—and a longtime friend. I knew he would have some smart insight on this modern appetite for an ancient ingredient and a recipe for how to use it.

"High-acid, subtly flavored verjus typically turns up in sauces and salad dressings, but it can also be incorporated into mixed drinks, which typically rely on citrus juice for acidity to balance sweetness. For me, verjus is less sharp than citrus and weightier on the palate.

"Apple and grape brandies distilled from fruits with prominent malic acid (such as cherries, apricot, plums, and grapes) are natural partners for verjus. On the nonalcoholic side, I'd stick with it as the sole acidic component with berries and stone fruit. Naturally fruity oolong tea has a pleasant affinity with verjus, as do flavorful sweeteners like honey and agave syrup. I tend to observe the maxim that, "if it grows with it, it goes with it," and procure ingredients either produced where the verjus is pressed or when the grapes are harvested. Freshly squeezed citrus produces a cloudy drink, so anytime I can use verjus to balance sweetness while preserving clarity and harmonious flavors, I'll also reach for it."

Secret Agent

A combination of botanicals and verjus stands in for Lillet Blanc in this alcohol-free riff on the Vesper Martini.

Makes 1 drink

1¾ ounces	Wilderton Lustre Botanical Distillate
1½ ounces	Seedlip Garden
1 ounce	Fusion Napa Valley Verjus Blanc
	Ice
3	pitted green olives

In a glass, combine the Lustre, Seedlip, and verjus with ice. Stir until chilled and strain into a chilled martini glass. Garnish with 3 olives on a pick and serve.

Amba

This Iraqi sauce is a signature condiment found in every sabich and falafel stand in Israel. It's a combination of sour green (unripe) mango and savory fenugreek that pairs so well with rich fried food and meats. It's beginning to be embraced beyond Israel and Iraq and get more recognition around the world as a versatile condiment—it's even available at some national American supermarket chains. Many store-bought brands can be over-the-top salty and tart, so for a homemade version, I've found that ripe mango works just as well when combined with amchoor, an Indian dried green mango powder. I've also dialed back the salt in the spice blend to let all the other spices shine.

Makes about 1 cup

Amba Spice Blend

1 tablespoon	ground amchoor (8 grams)
1 tablespoon	ground turmeric (8 grams)
2 teaspoons	citric acid (7 grams)
2 teaspoons	fine sea salt (10 grams)
1 teaspoon	fenugreek seeds (3 grams), ground
¼ teaspoon	cayenne pepper (0.5 grams)

Amba Sauce

1	ripe, medium mango, peeled, pitted, and chopped
1 tablespoon	honey

Make the Amba Spice Blend: In a small bowl, mix the amchoor, turmeric, citric acid, salt, fenugreek, and cayenne until well combined. This recipe makes more than you need for one batch of amba (about ¼ cup / 37 grams). Use the extra spice blend to season vegetable, fish, and meat dishes.

Make the Amba Sauce: In a blender, combine the mango, honey, 2 teaspoons (5 grams) of spice blend, and ¼ cup water and blend until smooth.

Variation
Replace the mango with 1 cup chopped peeled ripe papaya.

Amba Spice Blend Storage Directions
The spice blend will keep in an airtight container in a cool, dark place for several months.

Amba Sauce Storage Directions
Store the amba in an airtight container in the refrigerator for up to 5 days.

Cevizli Biber
(Turkish Pepper and Walnut Spread)

I had the chance to visit Turkey a few years ago and was blown away by the cuisine and all its flavor combinations. This pepper and walnut spread was one of my favorites, particularly because it highlights umami-rich Turkish pepper paste. It's a versatile condiment to have handy for sandwiches or a mezze spread.

Makes about 1½ cups

3	slices white bread (crusts discarded), coarsely chopped
1 cup	walnuts
½ cup	chopped yellow onion
¼ cup	extra-virgin olive oil
3 tablespoons	sweet Turkish pepper paste
1 tablespoon	distilled white vinegar
1 teaspoon	ground cumin (2 grams)
1 teaspoon	Urfa chile (2 grams)
	Salt

For Serving

Extra-virgin olive oil, for drizzling

Toasted baguette slices, crackers, or flatbread

In a food processor, pulse the bread, walnuts, onion, oil, pepper paste, vinegar, cumin, Urfa chile, and 2 tablespoons water until you have a spreadable paste, but stopping before the mix is completely smooth. Transfer to a bowl. Taste and season with salt, then cover. Refrigerate until chilled and the flavors have time to combine, at least 2 hours.

Serve: Spread the paste on a serving platter with a well in the center. Drizzle with plenty of oil and serve with crackers or toasts on the side.

Storage Directions
The spread will keep covered in the refrigerator for up to 1 week.

Mushbuss Rubyan
(Shrimp and Rice with Amba)

Think of this seafood and rice dish as Middle Eastern paella. In my take, it gets a flavor-packed kick from sweet-sour amba spice mix. The classic version from the Gulf region is made with many spice blends, but I love the flavor of mango with the shrimp. It's so simple to make and uses only one pan, which is always a bonus.

Serves 4

1 cup	basmati rice
1 pound	jumbo shrimp (12/16 count), peeled, deveined, and tail left on
3 teaspoons	amba spice blend (8 grams), homemade (*page 59*) or store-bought
2 tablespoons	unsalted butter
2 tablespoons	extra-virgin olive oil, plus more for serving
1	medium onion, diced
	Salt
3	garlic cloves, finely chopped
1	medium plum tomato, diced
1 tablespoon	tomato paste
10 sprigs	fresh cilantro leaves, half roughly chopped and half left whole for garnish

Wash the rice in a large bowl of cold water by swirling it with your hand, then pour off the water while keeping the rice in the bowl. Repeat until the water runs clear. Cover with room-temperature water and soak for 30 minutes, then drain.

In a medium bowl, gently coat the shrimp with 1½ teaspoons (4 grams) of the amba spice blend and marinate for 10 minutes.

Heat a 10-inch skillet over medium-high heat. Add the butter and cook until the butter is foamy and smells nutty, about 1 minute. Remove the shrimp from the bowl and add to the pan in a single layer. Cook for 30 seconds on each side before removing the shrimp to a plate and setting aside.

Reduce the heat to medium. Add the oil and onion and season with salt. Cook, stirring occasionally, until translucent, making sure the onion does not burn, about 5 minutes. Stir in the garlic and cook for 1 minute, until fragrant.

Add the diced tomato, tomato paste, chopped cilantro, and remaining 1½ teaspoons (4 grams) amba spice blend and stir. Add the drained rice and 1 cup water. Bring the mixture to a simmer, cover, and reduce the heat to low so the mixture simmers gently. Cook for 10 minutes.

Remove the lid and place the shrimp on top in a single layer. Cover and cook for another 10 minutes. Remove from the heat and wait 2 minutes before lifting the lid.

Serve hot, garnished with the cilantro and a drizzle of oil.

Verjus and Lamb Stew with Eggplant

This slow-roasted lamb dish is inspired by the classic Iranian stew khoresh bademjan. The verjus adds a fresh citrus note that cuts through the fat of the lamb. The eggplant and tomato add savory depth and stretch out the relatively small amount of meat to make it almost a complete dish—all it needs is rice to accompany it (try the tahdig on *page 218*). Seek out long, thin purple Chinese eggplants, which are easier to fry and less seedy than rounder, Italian eggplants.

Serves 6

3	large Chinese eggplants (about 1½ pounds), cut on a slight diagonal into 1-inch-thick pieces
1 teaspoon	fine sea salt (5 grams), plus more as needed
	Extra-virgin olive oil
1 pound	lamb stew meat, cubed
1	medium yellow onion, cut into ½-inch cubes
4	garlic cloves, thinly sliced
¼ cup	tomato paste
¼ cup	verjus, homemade (*page 56*) or store-bought, or freshly squeezed lime juice
2	dried limes (limon omani), broken in half (8 grams)
1 teaspoon	freshly ground black pepper (2 grams)
1 teaspoon	ground turmeric (3 grams)
¼ teaspoon	ground cinnamon (0.5 grams)
¼ teaspoon	saffron threads (n/a)
5	medium plum tomatoes, cored and halved lengthwise
	Yogurt, for serving

Preheat the oven to 350°F.

Season the eggplant with salt. In a large, deep, heavy-bottomed ovenproof skillet, heat a thin layer of the oil over high heat until hot. Working in batches if necessary, add the eggplant in a single layer and brown on both sides, 3 to 6 minutes per side, adding a little oil if the pan is dry when you flip it or add a new batch. Remove the eggplant to a plate as it browns, then repeat with the remaining eggplant.

Season the lamb lightly with salt. Make sure there is a thin layer of oil in the pan (add more if necessary) and add the lamb. Cook until browned on all sides, turning the cubes as they brown, 2 to 5 minutes per side. Transfer to the plate with the eggplant.

Reduce the heat to medium and add the onion, garlic, and 1 teaspoon (5 grams) salt. Cook, stirring occasionally, to soften the onion and deglaze the pan, 3 to 5 minutes. Add the tomato paste, verjus, dried limes, pepper, turmeric, cinnamon, saffron, and ½ cup water. Stir with a wooden spoon to incorporate any caramelization from the bottom of the pan.

Arrange the cooked eggplant, lamb, and the tomatoes together in the pan in one layer, or with as little overlap as possible, and add enough water to just barely cover the ingredients. Increase the heat to bring the mixture to a boil.

Transfer the pan to the oven and bake, making sure the liquid maintains a simmer, until the lamb is tender and the liquid has a thick, saucy consistency, about 2 hours.

Serve warm with a spoonful of yogurt on top.

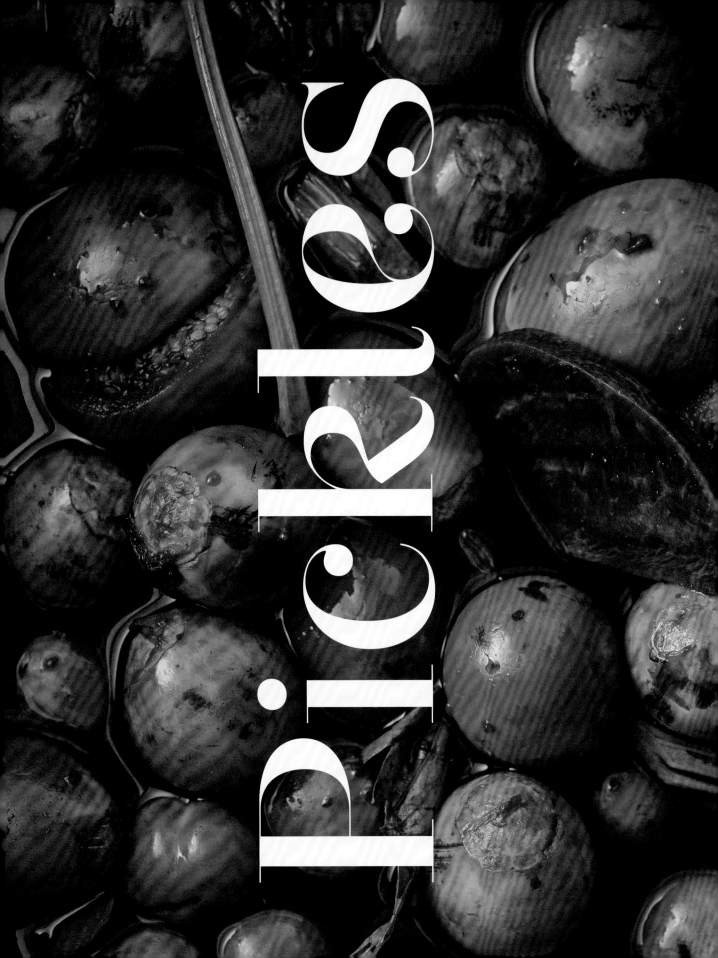

Pickles

{ PICKLES }

مخللات

turşu

חֲמוּצִים

ترشيجات

τουρσιά

թթու

I find that when many Americans hear the word "pickle," they think of just cucumber pickles. In actuality, there is a truly astounding variety of produce (and more!) that can be pickled, especially in the Middle East. There is never a shortage of tangy, salty accompaniments at every meal. I highly encourage you to branch out from the usual suspects. To start, try my all-time favorite, Eggplant Pickles (pictured on *page 66* and recipe on *page 76*).

ORIGIN AND HISTORY

It's thought that as early as 2400 BC, the Mesopotamians were pickling food by fully submerging it in an acidic liquid to greatly slow down spoilage. Many Middle Eastern pickles are made with vinegar and salt like traditional American cucumber pickles—though fermented pickles are popular as well, often submerged in a salt brine. (I may be biased in my view of what is more common, as I prefer vinegar pickles.)

We don't know exactly when and why it was discovered that storing foods in an acidic, salty solution kept them edible for many months. But once it was, the process was used on many agricultural products. The pickles provided sustenance outside of the growing season and variety (and vitamins) available to Middle Eastern diets. Before the invention of now-ubiquitous glass jars, pickles were stored in earthenware jars and sealed with clay that was dried by the sun. The vinegar used was commonly made from dates, grapes, or apples.

SOURCING AND STORING

When shopping for pickles, it's most important that you keep trying new varieties and taking advantage of the huge selection available. All pickles should look like they've retained some texture, even if they're chopped up into a relish. Any pickles, grape leaves, or capers that seem to be disintegrating or mushy should be avoided, as they're probably old or overbrined.

If you're buying jarred pickles, look for the shortest possible ingredient list: water, vinegar, salt, a few seasonings. Sometimes preservatives can't be avoided, especially with grape leaves or eggplant, which often have additives to preserve their color. If made without preservatives, some pickles will have a darker brine, and the color of the produce will be more faded, which I don't mind. Unopened shelf-stable pickles will keep for up to a year, stored in a cool, dry place out of direct sunlight, which can fade their color. Once opened, they should be kept in the refrigerator and will be good for several months.

Torshi

When I first tried them, I thought *torshi* was a word for the delicious pickled green tomatoes that were shared with me by an Armenian co-worker, but torshi, I soon discovered, is simply the Farsi word for "pickle."

ABOUT

From the Farsi word *torsh*, meaning "sour," torshi are also known as tursu in Turkey, toursi in Greece, and tourchi in Armenia. The Arabic word for "pickles," *kabees*, comes from the word *kabassa*, which means "compressed" (as they are when fermented). They're also known as mukhalal or mukhalat in Arabic.

I'd say the majority of Middle Eastern pickles are made with diluted vinegar and salt, but there are plenty of fermented pickles—those made in a salt brine. Growing up in Israel, you pick a side—fermented or vinegar pickles—and I am firmly in the latter group. Vinegar tends to keep vegetables crisper than a brine, but fermented pickles have both taste and health benefits. It really is a matter of personal preference.

Torshi are an essential part of the Middle Eastern diet. Some of the most popular are cucumber, cauliflower, garlic, onions, peppers, eggplant, and chiles. The vegetables can be whole or finely chopped and are often mixed. Immature fruits and vegetables, such as green almonds, green tomatoes, or green walnuts, are also popular.

PRODUCTION

Some vegetables can be pickled raw, such as cucumber or any unripe fruits or vegetables like green plums. Many vegetables are parcooked, salted, or both (especially eggplant), and even left in the sun to dry for a few days before moving on to the next step. Vinegar pickling won't soften the vegetables much further, so they need to be a pleasant crisp-tender texture before preserving.

Once the vegetables are ready, they are packed into a jar and covered in liquid. The liquid can be vinegar-based or a brine to encourage lacto-fermentation. Distilled white vinegar, apple vinegar, verjus, and grape vinegar (made from grape must as opposed to wine) are all popular choices. To flavor the pickles, herbs, spices, and aromatics are added. Sometimes a slice of beet is added to the jar to color the vegetables, as with pink pickled turnips and cabbage.

The pickles need to cure or ferment for at least a few days, depending on the type and personal preference. Jars of refrigerator pickles are not boiled or sterilized—they're called "quick pickles" because you can skip the boiling water–bath step. For long-term storage, vinegar pickle jars may be boiled to sterilize them. Once packed and sealed, the jars can sit on a shelf for up to 1 year.

APPEARANCE AND FLAVOR

Often the pickling process will mute the color of vegetables, and any especially bright colors may indicate preservatives beyond salt and vinegar. The texture should be crisp and firm, though lacto-fermented pickles are often a bit softer due to the slightly different way fermentation preserves food.

Pickles in the Middle East are often flavored with aromatics like garlic, herbs like dill, and spices like coriander and peppercorns, though often the main flavor is the vinegar and brine they're packed in. They can be spicy, herbaceous, or peppery but are rarely sweet.

TRADITIONAL USES

Meal accompaniment — *throughout the region*
Sandwich filling — *throughout the region*

Recipe Ideas

1. Chop them up and use them as a condiment for grilled meat or fish—anything grilled, really.

2. Thinly slice and use as a garnish for a hamburger.

3. You really don't need to do much more than remove them from the jar and eat them as a snack. Try Cucumber Pickles (*page 74*), Eggplant Pickles (*page 76*), and Torshi (*page 73*).

Grape Leaves

I've probably made thousands of stuffed grape leaves in my lifetime. Whether long and thin or a little fatter, warm or cold, stuffed with meat or grains, I love to eat them even more. I appreciate how unique grape leaves are as an ingredient, that another part of the grapevine isn't wasted, and that through pickling, a formerly inedible part of the plant becomes delicious.

ABOUT

Grapes are native to the region between the Black Sea and Caspian Sea that now makes up parts of Turkey, Armenia, and Iran. They've been cultivated by humans for thousands of years, with some of the earliest mentions appearing in ancient Egyptian texts.

Grapes were grown not only for wine making but also for making molasses (*see page 159*), drying (raisins), and eating fresh. The leaves are most commonly associated with dolma, which is both the name of the stuffed grape leaf as well as a broader category of stuffed vegetables that is probably of Persian origin. Some of the earliest references to stuffed grape leaves are from Egypt in the third century BC, but any other history is murky. What we do know is that grape leaf dolma were so popular, they spread to almost every country in the Middle East and even farther west into the Mediterranean.

PRODUCTION

Grape leaves are harvested by hand in the spring, when they are large enough to stuff but still fairly tender. Traditionally, the leaves are packed tightly into a jar, covered in a brine—sometimes with lemon juice, vinegar, or nowadays citric acid to give them an even more tart flavor—or packed only in salt. (Some commercially jarred varieties include additives to preserve the color of the leaves.) The jars are left to cure or ferment for a few days or up to a few weeks, depending on personal preference. Many people in the Middle East now preserve their own grape leaves by blanching and freezing them, but they lack the salty, sour taste I love.

APPEARANCE AND FLAVOR

Grape leaves have a tart, briny taste. Depending on the brand, the brine can be quite strong, so I like to rinse them before using. Even after rinsing, they will retain a lemony flavor, which adds a nice acidic note that doesn't fade with cooking. The leaves are dark green with a texture similar to collard greens. The smaller leaves are more tender, but all leaves require cooking before consuming.

TRADITIONAL USES

Dolmas (stuffed grape leaves) — *throughout the region* (see recipe, *page 79*)

Recipe Ideas

1. Wrap small fish like sardines, or any fish fillet, in grape leaves before grilling to impart flavor and preserve moisture.

2. Slice them up and add them to soup for a tart, briny flavor.

3. Chop the leaves, pan-fry in olive oil with your favorite spice blend, and serve as a side dish.

Capers

To some, caper bushes are something you pass without thinking twice about—or perhaps without even noticing. But not my grandfather. He foraged for wild caper buds in the Galilee, where we lived, and brined them to last the whole year.

ABOUT

Capers are the preserved, unopened flower bud of the short, hardy shrub *Capparis spinosa* that is native to the Mediterranean and Middle East. It grows in hot, dry climates in sandy soil and can notoriously be found in cracks in the pavement and by the side of the road. In the Middle East, capers grow wild in Cyprus, Egypt, Israel, and Lebanon, and in the salty, arid areas around the Caspian Sea in Iran and Black Sea in Armenia. If the flowers do bloom, they are stunning white blossoms with long purple stamens, and if pollinated, the fruits that form are known as caper berries, which can also be picked and pickled.

Capers are mentioned in the epic poem *Gilgamesh* dating from 2000 BC. Despite their long history, there aren't many traditional recipes that include them, but there have always been enthusiasts, like my grandfather, who will use them in cooking or simply snack on them like any other pickle.

PRODUCTION

The buds must be picked by hand in the early morning before they open. From spring through summer, the caper bush produces buds every ten to twelve days and can be continually picked. Once harvested, the buds are preserved in one of two ways. If stored in liquid, they're often soaked in salt water first, then packed in a brine or vinegar. If packed in salt, they are mixed with salt and left to sit for several days to draw out the moisture and cure, then the process is repeated with fresh salt, at which point they are ready. Some producers cure them for up to two months.

Caper berries, the fruit of the bush, are soaked in salt water, rinsed, and packed in vinegar.

APPEARANCE AND FLAVOR

Capers are ¼ to ½ inch wide. The smallest, called nonpareils, are the most expensive because hand-picking takes so long. The buds are dark green and sometimes speckled white on the outside with rutin, a crystallized flavonoid compound found in the flower. They have a meaty texture if properly preserved, and the very soft ones should be avoided. You can also buy caper berries, which are about the size of a large olive and are crunchy and seedy with a briny flavor.

The main flavor of capers is the brine or salt they're packed in. They do have herbaceous notes, similar to olives. The salt-packed variety need to be rinsed and soaked in water before use so they are not overwhelmingly salty.

TRADITIONAL USES

Seasoning for fish — *Cyprus, Lebanon, and more*
Salads — *Cyprus, Lebanon, and more*

Recipe Ideas

1. While searing meat or fish, add them to the pan with a splash of brine near the end of cooking.

2. Chop up and mix with yogurt for an easy sauce.

3. Blend with olive oil and cilantro for a quick dressing.

Storage Directions
The torshi will keep
in a sealed container
in the refrigerator for
several weeks.

Torshi

Torshi is endlessly adaptable—you can make it with whatever produce your local market has to offer. You can, of course, also start with the recommended vegetable mix here. Serve torshi with nearly every meal as a briny, lightly spiced complement.

Makes 2 quarts

Pickling Liquid

1 cup	cider vinegar
2 tablespoons	sugar
1 tablespoon	fine sea salt (16 grams)

Vegetable Mix

½	small head cauliflower, cut into bite-size florets
2	small carrots, peeled and cut on the diagonal into slices ¼ inch thick
2	celery stalks, cut into ½-inch pieces
2	medium Persian (mini) cucumbers, cut into slices ¼ inch thick
2	small turnips, peeled and cut into slices ¼ inch thick and then into strips
1	jalapeño, cut into ¼-inch rings
5	garlic cloves, smashed
1 tablespoon	coriander seeds (5 grams)
1 tablespoon	dried dill (3 grams)
1 tablespoon	fennel seeds (6 grams)

Make the pickling liquid: In a large measuring cup or bowl, combine 4 cups water, the vinegar, sugar, and salt and stir until the sugar and salt are completely dissolved.

Prepare the vegetable mix: In a lidded container that can hold at least 3 quarts (12 cups), combine the cauliflower, carrots, celery, cucumbers, turnips, jalapeño, garlic, coriander seeds, dried dill, and fennel seeds. Pour the pickling liquid over to submerge the vegetables (you may have extra liquid). Seal the jar.

Leave at room temperature until the vegetables taste pickled to your liking, 5 to 7 days. Serve immediately or transfer to the refrigerator.

Cucumber Pickles

The question among pickle fans is: Are you a vinegar person or a salt brine person? I am firmly in the vinegar camp, not to mention that I'm a huge fan of dill (there are two kinds in these pickles—fresh sprigs and dried seeds). I hope this recipe offers a good compromise for all pickle lovers with its numerous spices and slightly sweet vinegar brine.

Makes 1 quart

¼ cup	cider vinegar or sherry vinegar
2 tablespoons	fine sea salt (33 grams)
1 tablespoon	sugar
5	medium Persian (mini) cucumbers
5	sprigs fresh dill
1 tablespoon	white peppercorns (11 grams)
2 teaspoons	dill seeds (5 grams)
2 teaspoons	black peppercorns (6 grams)
2 teaspoons	green peppercorns (2 grams)
1 teaspoon	ajwain seeds (2 grams)

In a small saucepan, combine the vinegar, salt, sugar, and 3 cups water and bring to a simmer, stirring occasionally to dissolve the salt and sugar.

Meanwhile, in a sterilized tall 1-quart glass jar, fit the cucumbers and dill, then add the white peppercorns, dill seeds, black peppercorns, green peppercorns, and ajwain seeds.

Pour the hot brine over the cucumbers until it reaches the top of the jar (you may have extra brine). Seal the jar immediately and leave at room temperature for 48 hours. Serve the pickles right away or transfer to the refrigerator.

Variations
Using the same brine, you can pickle thinly sliced carrots, small cauliflower florets, sliced bell peppers, chiles, and trimmed green beans.

Storage Directions
The pickles will keep in a sealed container in the refrigerator for several weeks.

Eggplant Pickles

Tart pickled eggplants can be found at many falafel and shawarma stands throughout the Middle East. They're not as popular as other pickles and I've never understood why, especially considering eggplant's famous ability to soak up liquid and seasonings. Small round eggplants are always used—they can be eaten in just a few bites—because they maintain a meaty texture even after they're pickled. The smaller eggplants can be difficult to source and pickle successfully, so I've adapted the method to be used with much more readily available long, thin Chinese eggplants, which are ready in a fraction of the time it takes the round eggplant to pickle. The curious can find canned or jarred small pickled eggplant at Middle Eastern grocery stores, or try round eggplants (as in the photo), but be aware they will take weeks to pickle.

Makes 1 quart

Pickling Liquid
½ cup cider vinegar
1 tablespoon sugar
1½ teaspoons fine sea salt (8 grams)

Eggplant
3 thin Chinese eggplants (about 1 pound), quartered lengthwise and cut into 1-inch pieces
2 small red beets, peeled and cut into 12 wedges each

Make the pickling liquid: In a large measuring cup or bowl, combine 2 cups water, the vinegar, sugar, and salt and stir until the sugar and salt are completely dissolved.

Prepare the eggplant: In a sterilized 1-quart jar, pack alternating layers of eggplant pieces and beets, until you've added all the vegetables.

Pour the pickling liquid over the vegetables until it reaches the top of the jar (you may have extra liquid).

To keep the eggplant submerged, cut a plastic disk (for example, from an old plastic container) that will fit just below the lip inside the jar. It should be a tight enough fit that it holds the vegetables down, but not so tight you can't remove it easily to test the pickles. Put it into the jar, making sure it keeps the vegetables below the liquid. Put an object on top of the plastic to hold it—and the vegetables—under the liquid when the jar is closed. Something nonreactive like a smaller jar lid or a ball of plastic wrap is great.

Leave at room temperature until the eggplant tastes pickled and the texture retains some bite, about 7 days. Serve immediately or transfer to the refrigerator.

Storage Directions
The pickles will keep in a sealed container in the refrigerator for several weeks.

Dolmas

Aside from eating dolmas, one of my favorite things to do in the kitchen is stuff and roll them, making sure they are all uniform—it's very relaxing! You'll need to do the same to ensure they fit into a single layer in the pan.

Makes 39 pieces

1 cup	basmati rice
2½ teaspoons	fine sea salt (13 grams), plus more as needed
2 tablespoons	extra-virgin olive oil
1	small yellow onion, diced
2	garlic cloves, finely chopped
¼ cup	finely diced (about ⅛-inch) dried apricot
3 tablespoons	roughly chopped fresh cilantro
3 tablespoons	roughly chopped fresh dill
1 tablespoon	apricot jam
½ teaspoon	freshly ground black pepper (1 gram)
¼ teaspoon	celery seeds (0.5 grams)
¼ teaspoon	ground ginger (0.5 grams)
⅛ teaspoon	ground cinnamon (0.5 grams)
⅛ teaspoon	ground nutmeg (0.5 grams)
1	(8-ounce) jar pickled grape leaves (or about 45 leaves), drained and stems removed with scissors
1	lemon, thinly sliced
5	sprigs fresh dill

Wash the rice in a large bowl of cold water by swirling it with your hand, then pour off the water while keeping the rice in the bowl. Repeat until the water runs clear. Cover with room-temperature water and soak for 20 minutes, then drain.

In a medium pot, bring 8 cups water to a boil and add 1½ teaspoons (8 grams) of the salt. Add the rice and cook for 6 minutes, then drain in a fine-mesh sieve. Run the rice under cold water to stop the cooking, then drain and let cool.

In a small skillet, heat the oil over medium heat until hot. Add the onion and a pinch of salt and cook until translucent, about 5 minutes. Add the garlic and cook until softened, about 2 minutes.

Put the cooled rice in a large bowl and fold in the onion mixture, dried apricot, cilantro, dill, jam, remaining 1 teaspoon (5 grams) salt, the pepper, celery seeds, ginger, cinnamon, and nutmeg. Make sure the seasonings are evenly distributed.

Preheat the oven to 375°F.

Lay 1 pickled grape leaf flat on your work surface with the stem end facing you. Put 1 tablespoon of the rice filling in the center of the bottom part of the leaf, near the stem. Starting with the bottom edge, roll the leaf snugly around the rice filling at least one-third of the way up the leaf. Fold the sides of the leaf in to make a 2½-inch-wide log and seal in the filling (if they are any wider, they won't all fit in the pan). Continue rolling the leaf until the tip is wrapped around the roll. It should look like a nice cylinder, with the stuffing evenly rolled inside.

Put the stuffed leaf into a 9 × 13-inch baking dish. Repeat with the remaining leaves, discarding any that are torn, fitting them into a single layer of 3 rows of 13 dolmas. Pour 3 cups water into the pan of stuffed leaves and top the rolls with the lemon slices and dill sprigs. Cover the pan with parchment paper, then foil.

Bake until the rice is cooked, the leaves are tender, and there is almost no liquid left in the pan, 1 hour to 1 hour 20 minutes. Serve hot, warm, or chilled.

Storage Directions

The dolmas will keep covered in the refrigerator for up to 3 days.

OLIVES

{ OLIVES }

زيتون

zeytin

זֵיתִים

زيتونها

ελιές

ձիթապտուղ

The olive tree is culturally very significant in the Middle East. Every part of the tree is used, from the wood, to the leaves, to the small, hard, bitter fruits that our ancestors miraculously discovered could be made edible. It also has a lot of personal significance for me. One of the most important products from the tree is, of course, olive oil. My father, Moshe, has owned an olive orchard for the last three decades. It's become a family affair, with me being the distributor for his oil in the United States, and I've even managed to make it back for the harvest a few times.

ORIGIN AND HISTORY

Wild olive trees are native to the eastern Mediterranean, and the fruit was gathered by Neolithic peoples as many as ten thousand years ago. The trees were most likely first cultivated in the Levant, probably between 4000 and 3000 BC, then gradually spread west to Greece, and north and east to what are now parts of Turkey and Armenia. As the trees were cultivated, people selected those that produced fleshier fruits. As a result, wild olives today have a much lower flesh-to-pit ratio than the cultivated fruit.

When olives were first eaten on their own is unknown, but olive oil has a long history that goes back at least eight thousand years. The oil pressed from the fruit was used to light lamps in mosques and temples, for anointing during religious ceremonies, as temple offerings, and for soapmaking and cooking. The Romans planted olive trees across their holdings to produce lamp fuel and cooking oil. Outside of the Levant and the Roman Empire, olive oil was also used in Persia, but it didn't catch on as a cooking oil in Turkey until the late seventeenth century.

AGRICULTURAL DETAILS

The olive tree, *Olea europaea*, is an evergreen with silvery green leaves and small white flowers. The flowers produce the olive fruit, which is green when unripe and purple to black when ripe. Olives usually ripen in mid to late autumn and are between 12 and 35 percent fat by weight. They are a drupe, meaning a fleshy fruit surrounding a hard pit that contains the seed. The trees have deep root systems that allow them to thrive in poor-quality soil and on steep hillsides. Olive trees can live for over one hundred years, fruiting for many of them. They tend to have a production cycle with smaller yields every two or three years, so the tree can focus on growth.

The olives can be harvested at any ripeness and are usually harvested by hand. Sometimes a tractor may be employed to help shake the tree, but that's about as high-tech as it gets. Turkey is the biggest producer of both olives and olive oil in the region, followed by Egypt for olive production and Syria for olive oil. Of the olives harvested worldwide, 90 percent will be pressed for oil.

Olive Oil

If you've ever traveled to the Middle East and wondered why the food tastes so good, I can guarantee it was the olive oil used to make it.

PRODUCTION

The olive harvest is usually October through December. Olives can be harvested black or green to make oil. Some producers wait until their olives are completely black, but there is a risk that the olives could start dropping off the tree, or that rain might knock them off, which damages them. Green olives make a more peppery oil, whereas black, ripe fruits produce fruity, mellow oils. Some producers state that oil made from green olives has more antioxidants and may have a longer shelf life. Thus, when to pick is a matter of risk tolerance and personal taste.

Olives are harvested by hand or by machine, the former less likely to bruise the olives and cause oxidation, the latter obviously much more efficient. Once harvested, the olives must be processed very quickly—within hours or a day or two if refrigerated—before they start to turn.

To make the best-quality olive oil (without the use of heat or chemicals; see more in Sourcing and Storing, at right), the olives are first crushed in a press without breaking the pits. Traditional stone mills have mostly been replaced by metal grinders. The resulting paste is further pressed to extrude the liquid. Traditionally, the paste was spread onto fibrous mats that were stacked so gravity pressed out the liquid, but now many producers use a centrifuge. The liquid will separate into oil and any remaining liquid. The oil may be filtered or bottled right after separation.

APPEARANCE AND FLAVOR

Olive oil is herbaceous, peppery, bitter, and nutty. There can be notes of almond or even a hint of vanilla in some varieties. Some may have a slight acidic taste and some are delicate, while others can be quite bitter. I like oil that's on the more pungent, botanic side and has a fresh-cut grass flavor.

Olive oils can range from a clear, light golden color to dark, green, and cloudy. Again, it's all a matter of personal preference—a cloudy oil doesn't signify poor quality.

SOURCING AND STORING

I like my oil green and dark—meaning it was pressed quickly after harvesting while there was still some chlorophyll, which starts to fade as soon as the olive is picked. But you may prefer a lighter or more golden oil. On the packaging, I want to know the varietal and where it was produced, as this helps me know what I like so I can buy it again. The date of pressing or harvesting on the tin is helpful and shows that the producer is mindful of details (or not trying to hide anything). The date should be less than a year from purchase, preferably just a few weeks or months before.

These days, "extra-virgin" is not a sign of quality. It simply means that the oil was extracted only by mechanical means and has an acidity level of less than 0.8 percent. Similarly, "first pressed" and "cold pressed" don't mean much from huge producers, who use such large, efficient presses that all oil is only processed once, and cold pressed is implied by the word "virgin" on the label. "Pure" is sometimes helpful; otherwise you might end up with a blended oil. (Real, pure olive oil solidifies in the refrigerator.)

Middle Eastern olive oil varieties are less common than European ones (such as Arbequina or Koroneiki) in the United States, but you can find a few, such as Barnea, Maalot, Nabali, Tzouri, Gemlik, Domat, and Memecik.

My best advice is to keep trying lots of different oils to get a sense of what you like. When you do find one that you really like, it's more economical to buy in bulk. Keep a smaller bottle on the counter and the big canister in a dark cupboard. Try to limit how much you open and close the big container. Quality oil can keep for up to a year, but you shouldn't hold on to any oil that long. Buy only what you'll use up in two or three months.

TRADITIONAL USES

Imam bayildi (braised eggplant) — *Turkey*
Labne balls — *Levant* (see recipe, *page 248*)
Poached vegetables — *Levant and Turkey*

Recipe Ideas

1. Use olive oil to replace some of the butter in cookie recipes.

2. For desserts, pair olive oil with fruit and honey (in cakes or composed dishes).

3. Drizzle it over raw or cooked vegetables as a garnish.

4. Make Olive Oil Confit Vegetables (*page 97*).

5. Consider starting your day, as I sometimes do, with a shot of olive oil!

Moshe oil

My father, Moshe, has about seven hundred Tzouri olive trees that he has been caring for since 1993. Tzouri is a varietal from Tzor, Lebanon; it's known for its oil-producing olives and quality wood. My father waits every fall until about 70 percent of the olives in a plot are black and ripe before harvesting.

Once he deems the olives ready, he sets up nets below the trees because he only uses olives that he shakes off—never any from the ground. He harvests the olives by hand and doesn't use rakes or tractors because he believes if you hurt the tree, you hurt the oil. This reduces the chances of bruising, which causes oxidation and lower quality oil.

He then separates the olives from the leaves and branches by hand and sprints to the olive oil press. Most small and medium-size olive oil producers do not have their own press, so they must go to a communal facility. The one my father goes to is first come, first served. Slightly complicating the procedure is the fact that he will not stand in line behind anyone whose oil he doesn't like, despite the fact that the machines are cleaned after each use. He could also store his olives for a day or two in a refrigerator to wait for a better spot, but he refuses. The longer the olives sit, the more chance of oxidation and an acidic taste.

The press my father brings his olives to uses a large mixer to separate out the liquid from the solids. The resulting liquid will naturally settle and separate into oil and water. Once separated, the oil is ready, as there's no need to filter it. All of this takes just a few hours at the press.

Bruised fruit, too much exposure to air, and improper storage can all affect quality. But because my father pays such attention to detail, I have some bottles of his oil from several years ago that are still good today. And my customers know to ask for the oil by name—Moshe oil.

Olives

Second only to my love of olive oil is my love of olives. Try to buy yours from a store with an expansive selection so you can move beyond the most common varieties.

PRODUCTION

Green olives are unripe; black olives are fully ripe; and other colors fall somewhere in between. Olives don't ripen off the tree, so they must be picked at the exact stage of ripeness in which they are to be sold and must be processed very quickly—ideally the same day but within three days at the very most if they're refrigerated. Otherwise they oxidize and turn unpleasantly sour.

Olives are extremely bitter when harvested, due to a glucoside compound called oleuropein. They must be cured to be edible, and there are four main ways to cure them.

Water-curing: Olives are soaked in repeated changes of fresh water to draw out the oleuropein. This can take a few days if another curing process is going to be used after or happen over the course of many months if this is the only method. Fully water-cured olives are rare and taste less salty than other olives.

Lye-curing: This is the fastest way to remove the bitterness, but it also removes flavor. Olives are soaked in a strong alkaline lye solution (made with wood ash or sodium hydroxide) until the solution penetrates to the pit, which can take a few hours or up to a day. The lye must then be leached out by another long soaking, this time in fresh water, before the olives are ready. This process is mainly used on green olives. (Introducing air during the process will turn green olives black, which is how American canned black olives are made.)

Brine-curing: Any olives can be fermented in a brine, but it can take quite a long time for the olives to be ready, sometimes up to a year if fresh green olives are used. Water-curing green olives for a few days first, or using less bitter black olives, takes much less time.

Dry-curing: Commonly used for black olives, this method consists of packing olives in salt for a few days, which draws out the bitterness and removes some of the moisture from the flesh. Once they are cured, they are usually rubbed with oil or stored in oil to preserve the remaining moisture, which is why they are also called oil-cured olives.

Any curing process can be sped up by cutting the flesh or cracking the olives so the curing solution penetrates faster. Flavorings like herbs, spices, lemons, and other aromatics can be added during brine-curing or after any olives are fully cured and ready to be stored.

APPEARANCE AND FLAVOR

The range of flavor is quite large in the world of olives, but most are rich and fatty. They are often slightly bitter and possibly a little peppery. They are salty and may be tart if brine-cured. Black olives will have a milder, more fruity taste than grassy green olives.

Green olives are firmer and cling to the pit

while black olives are softer and separate more easily. In between, there are pink olives and purple olives, which are only semiripe and will fall somewhere between the texture of green and black. Some green olives are nearly brown in color, but they, too, are unripe. All olives have a meaty, chewy texture. Olives vary greatly in size, from around ½ inch to well over 1 inch long.

SOURCING AND STORING

I like to buy olives in bulk as it's usually more cost-effective, sampling is often encouraged, and I'm not limited to what is in small, sometimes tiny jars on the shelves. Regardless of how they're sold, the olives should be whole and firm. A soft, mushy olive may be old or low quality. Cracked olives will be split but should still have very firm, intact flesh. Pitted olives should not be overly soft.

The varieties you're probably familiar with—picholine, Castelvetrano, kalamata—are not native to the Middle East. Olive varieties from the region aren't really commercially available elsewhere. But no matter where you live, there is a large selection to choose from, and I can only encourage you to explore them all. To me, they're all good. I have several varieties that I like, for different purposes: black salt-cured for cooking, and cracked olives or any type marinated with herbs and chiles for snacking.

Olives don't need to be stored in the refrigerator if kept covered in brine in an airtight container in a cool, dark place. If you are keeping them in the refrigerator, they should be submerged in brine and well sealed.

TRADITIONAL USES

Mezze spread component — *throughout the region*
Zeytoon parvardeh (appetizer) — *Iran*
Yesil zeytin salatsi (olive salad) — *Turkey*

Recipe Ideas

1. Add olives to roasted vegetables or meat dishes so they develop a nice char and texture in the oven.

2. Include olives in a stew so they will soften as they cook, hydrate a little, and infuse everything with a briny flavor.

3. Rinse the brine off store-bought olives and marinate them in a mix of lemon juice and oil, with or without other herbs and aromatics, and serve as an appetizer.

4. Make Stewed Olives (*page 95*) or Olive Spread (*page 92*).

DIY Cured Cracked Olives

If there is something I always have at home, it's olives. Green, black, oil-cured—I eat them all. I snack on them but also add them to all sorts of dishes for an extra-briny note. And it turns out, it's not so difficult to make them yourself. The two hard parts are securing fresh olives (surprisingly, Etsy and eBay are great sources in the summer and fall, when olives are harvested) and waiting the two to three weeks for them to be ready to eat. So I can eat them sooner, I crack the olives, which greatly speeds up the curing process. This is my preferred seasoning mix, but you can really add any herbs or aromatics: woody herbs like rosemary, thyme, and bay leaves; whole dried or fresh chiles; fresh garlic. Or keep the brine very simple and marinate the olives in a flavored oil after curing.

Makes about 3 quarts

3 pounds	fresh olives, any variety
	Filtered water
	Salt
1	lemon, cut into 6 wedges
2 tablespoons	dried garlic slices (10 grams)
2½ teaspoons	Aleppo pepper (5 grams)

Put the olives in a very large bowl and cover with plenty of water. Leave the olives out at room temperature for 1 week, changing the water every 12 hours, to draw out the bitterness.

Put a 1-gallon container on a kitchen scale and tare it (so it reads zero with the container on top). Fill the container about halfway with filtered water and record the weight in grams (half a gallon is 8 cups, which should be about 1.9 kilograms). Multiply that weight by 0.05 to determine how much salt you'll need to make a 5% solution—in this case that comes to 95 grams of salt. Stir the measured salt into the water until it is completely dissolved.

Drain the olives. Using a rolling pin or mallet, "crack" the olives by hitting them with enough force to split the flesh but not so much to completely smash them (it may take a few tries to get the amount of force right). Put each olive into the brine immediately after cracking or it will start to oxidize. When you've finished cracking the olives and adding them to the container, add the lemon, dried garlic, and Aleppo pepper to the container and stir.

Loosely cover the jar with the lid or with cheesecloth. Leave the olives out at room temperature, skimming any white yeast that may appear on the surface daily.

After 5 days, taste an olive. You're looking for a pleasantly salty, only slightly bitter taste. Small olives should be ready in about 1 week; larger olives need up to 3 weeks of fermenting. Serve right away or transfer to the refrigerator.

Storage Directions
The olives will keep in a sealed jar in the refrigerator for several months.

Olive and Citrus Salad

Make this classic pairing when citrus is at its best. This winter salad is salty, sweet, and bright, with thinly sliced fennel bringing crunch and a fresh anise taste, and the olives adding salinity and meaty texture.

Serves 4

1	large orange
1	medium grapefruit
1	lemon
	Freshly squeezed orange or lemon juice, as needed
¼ cup	extra-virgin olive oil
	Salt
1	medium bulb fennel, halved and thinly sliced lengthwise
½	medium red onion, halved and thinly sliced lengthwise
1 cup	oil-cured black olives, pitted
¼ cup	fresh dill, torn into small pieces
¼ cup	fresh mint

Using a Microplane, zest the orange into a small bowl. Trim the top and bottom of the orange so that it sits flat on your cutting board. Peel the skin by following the round shape of the orange with a knife, cutting from top to bottom, and discarding strips of peel. Remove the segments by cutting along the inside of the membranes on either side so the flesh separates easily, in one piece. Repeat until all of the segments have been removed. Squeeze any remaining juice from the segmented orange into another small bowl or measuring cup.

Repeat the zesting, peeling, segmenting, and juicing of the grapefruit, adding the grapefruit zest to the bowl with the orange zest and the grapefruit juice to the bowl with the orange juice. Finally, zest, peel, segment, and juice the lemon, collecting the zest and juice the same way. Measure out ¼ cup of citrus juice (a little more than ¼ cup is fine, but if you don't have enough, supplement with additional orange or lemon juice). Pour the juice into the bowl with the zest and whisk in the oil and a pinch of salt. Taste and adjust the seasoning.

On a serving platter, layer the fennel, onion, olives, citrus segments, dill, and mint. Just before serving, drizzle on the dressing.

Olive Spread

This condiment-meets-appetizer is best made with strongly flavored green olives like picholine, Manzanilla, or Cerignola, not buttery, mild olives like Castelvetrano. Try spreading it over slices of fresh bread, serving it on top of grilled fish such as branzino, or using it as a seasoning paste on a rack of lamb before cooking.

Makes about 1 cup

1 to 1½ cups	pitted green olives, such as picholine, as needed
¼ cup	pistachios
¼ cup	extra-virgin olive oil
2 tablespoons	pomegranate molasses
1	small garlic clove, peeled
1 tablespoon	loosely packed dried rose petals (1 gram), crumbled or roughly chopped, plus more for serving
1 tablespoon	finely diced shallot
1 tablespoon	rose water
1 tablespoon	pistachio oil, plus more for serving
	Salt
	Fresh pomegranate arils, for serving

In a food processor, pulse 1 cup of the olives, the pistachios, olive oil, pomegranate molasses, and garlic until finely chopped but not yet pureed. Transfer the mixture to a bowl and gently stir in the rose petals, shallot, rose water, and pistachio oil. The mixture should be the texture of a coarse tapenade. Depending on the type of olives used, it may be too runny. If so, add the remaining ½ cup olives to the food processor to chop, then stir into the spread.

Taste and add salt if necessary. Serve right away, or cover and refrigerate, then bring back to room temperature before serving.

To serve, spread the mixture in a serving dish and garnish with a drizzle of pistachio oil, crumbled rose petals, and pomegranate arils.

Storage Directions
The mixture will keep in the refrigerator, covered, for up to 1 week.

Stewed Olives

Despite the fact you don't find them very often in Middle Eastern cuisines, I'm a big fan of cooked olives. Stewing them with ample spices and Turkish pepper paste really showcases how their meaty texture and toothsome flavor can be the star of a dish. I use these olives as a condiment for grilled meats or roasted vegetables, include them as part of a mezze spread, or garnish a bowl of Hummus Tahina (*page 235*) with them.

Makes about 2 cups

¼ cup	extra-virgin olive oil
1 cup	pitted kalamata olives
1 cup	diced yellow onion (cut the same size as the olives)
1	garlic clove, sliced
1 tablespoon	sweet Turkish pepper paste
1 tablespoon	tomato paste
2 teaspoons	ground allspice (4 grams)
2 teaspoons	ground coriander (4 grams)
2 teaspoons	ground cumin (4 grams)
½ teaspoon	Aleppo pepper (1 gram)
½ teaspoon	fine sea salt (3 grams)
¼ cup	honey
¼ cup	distilled white vinegar

In a heavy-bottomed saucepan, combine the oil, olives, onion, and garlic. Cook over medium heat, stirring occasionally, until the onion and garlic are softened but have not yet started to color, 8 to 10 minutes.

Add the pepper paste, tomato paste, allspice, coriander, cumin, Aleppo pepper, and salt and cook until everything is well incorporated, stirring occasionally, about 5 minutes.

Add the honey and 1 cup water and bring to a boil. Reduce the heat so the mixture simmers, and cook until the onion is tender and the liquid has thickened and looks glossy, 10 to 15 minutes. (If you'd like to further reduce the liquid, continue cooking for another 5 to 10 minutes.)

Remove from the heat and stir in the vinegar. Serve warm.

Storage Directions
Cool the mixture completely, then store, covered, in the refrigerator for up to 1 week.

Storage Directions
The vegetables will keep in the
oil for 10 days in the refrigerator.
Strain the oil before serving,
discarding the spices, or use the
oil for salads or any recipes that
call for olive oil. (The strained
oil keeps for about 10 days.)

Olive Oil Confit Vegetables

The term *confit* originally meant stewing meat or fish in its own fat until tender, but now it just means slowly cooking anything in fat. Vegetables turn out wonderfully using the same technique. Submerging vegetables and olives in olive oil allows them to leisurely simmer so the vegetables retain some texture while still being fully cooked. The ample cooking time means they absorb all the flavors of the olive oil, spices, and aromatics like chiles, garlic, and lemon.

Serves 6

4⅓ cups	extra-virgin olive oil, or more as needed
3	medium jalapeños, sliced
2	bay leaves
1 tablespoon	coriander seeds (5 grams)
2 teaspoons	cumin seeds (5 grams)
2 teaspoons	fennel seeds (4 grams)
2 teaspoons	fine sea salt (10 grams)
1 teaspoon	dried rosemary (2 grams)
1 teaspoon	dried thyme (1 gram)
1	medium bulb fennel, cut into ¾-inch wedges
1	medium Yukon Gold potato, unpeeled and cut into ¾-inch wedges
1	medium red onion, root end left intact and cut into ¾-inch wedges
1	medium turnip, unpeeled and cut into ¾-inch wedges
1	medium carrot, cut into ¼-inch-thick pieces
5	garlic cloves, peeled
½ cup	pitted green olives
½	lemon, cut into ¾-inch wedges

Clip a thermometer to the side of a large heavy-bottomed pot, then add the oil, jalapeños, bay leaves, coriander seeds, cumin seeds, fennel seeds, salt, rosemary, and thyme. Bring the oil to about 250°F.

Add the fennel, potato, onion, turnip, carrot, garlic, olives, and lemon and make sure they are completely submerged in the oil, adding more oil if necessary. Reduce the heat to low, cover, and bring the oil to 180°F. Adjust the heat as necessary to keep the temperature consistent and cook until the vegetables are tender, starting to check after 45 minutes. It may take up to 2 hours.

Serve the vegetables hot or warm. If refrigerating before serving, let the vegetables come to room temperature for about 30 minutes, or lightly warm them in a pan so the solidified oil melts.

NUTS

المكسرات

kabuklu kuruyemiş

אֱגוֹזִים

آجيل

ξηροι καρποι

ընդեղեն

Along with bakeries, fishmongers, butchers, and greengrocers, there's another type of shop in a Middle Eastern market: the nut (and dried fruit) vendor. In Hebrew, they're known as pitzuchia, which comes from the verb "to crack." While they're all over the Middle East, I rarely see them outside of the region. It's part of Middle Eastern culture to go to these stores and shop for the freshest nuts and seeds, often in preparation for weekend guests and family gatherings. The kinds featured in this chapter are the most versatile and popular ones consumed, plus one with no substitute: mahlab.

SOURCING AND STORING

Always purchase nuts from a store that does brisk business, as they have a high oil content and go rancid quickly when exposed to air, heat, and/or humidity for too long. If you can't sample them or buy them in bulk, seek out whole, firm ones that haven't crumbled or become dusty (especially walnuts). Look for the variety and source on the packaging—"Turkish Antep Pistachios" indicates more attention to detail than "Pistachios" does—and details are always a good thing because to me they mean exacting sourcing and a better product. A "best by" date is helpful, too. There should be no preservatives (aside from salt if you like salted nuts and seeds). Buying them in the shell isn't necessarily a sign of better quality, and with shelled nuts, at least you can see what they look like. Really the best advice is to find a source you trust and that has high turnover. And then keep shopping there.

At home, keep nuts in an airtight container, for the shortest amount of time possible. I recommend buying them in quantities you'll use in a month or less. If you buy more than you'll get through in a few weeks, keep the extras in the freezer. Properly stored, in an airtight container to protect the nuts from humidity and freezer burn, nuts will keep for several months (note I didn't say "forever"). To thaw, simply leave them out at room temperature for a few minutes.

TOASTING

Toasting nuts extends their shelf life by removing moisture and adds flavor. Buy pretoasted nuts or toast them right after purchase and before storing. The stovetop is the fastest way to toast nuts and seeds, but you have to watch the pan closely to prevent burning, and the nuts must be stirred often for even browning. The better option is on a sheet pan in a 350°F oven. Put the nuts into the oven for 6 minutes, then test often (convection ovens will toast faster than regular, and a nut with a lot of fat, such as pine nuts, will be ready sooner than almonds, for example). Once you get a feel for your oven, you can adjust the time and temperature to suit your needs. You can also add oil and spices to the nuts to flavor them. Cool completely before storing.

Pistachios

This is one of my favorite nuts, whether they're in the shell or not. I love the bright green peeled Sicilian varieties or the Middle Eastern kind, roasted or raw.

ORIGIN AND HISTORY

Pistachios are thought to be native to Iran, where they have long been an important crop. The name comes from the Farsi word for the nut, *pesteh*. The hardy tree grows throughout the Middle East from Turkey as far east as Afghanistan. Archaeological evidence suggests humans have been eating them since at least 7000 BC, and by the first century BC they were grown in the Hanging Gardens of Babylon.

The pistachio has quite a rich history and lore. They were thought to be brought by Adam from the Garden of Eden. It is one of only two nuts (along with almonds) mentioned in the Old Testament. And according to legend, the Queen of Sheba claimed all pistachio production for herself.

AGRICULTURAL DETAILS

The pistachio tree, *Pistacia vera*, is well suited to arid areas because its deep root system reaches groundwater many other plants cannot. The product we eat is not a nut in the botanical sense but the seed of a drupe, a tree fruit consisting of an outer skin, a fleshy middle, and a hard pit. The small fruits of the pistachio tree resemble olives in shape and size. The fruit surrounds the pit, which is the shell and seed you purchase and what we call a "nut."

Pistachios are harvested in the fall, when the fruit is ripe and loosens around the pit, and the shell that surrounds the seed splits. To process the pistachios, the fruit is removed by smashing, splitting by hand, or by machine. If the shells have not split, the pits were traditionally spread out to dry in indirect sunlight until they did. They were then usually dried in direct sun for a few days; nowadays, commercial ovens remove the humidity for longer storage. Iran produces the most pistachios in the region by far.

APPEARANCE AND FLAVOR

These nuts are small, less than ½ inch, and green, with red skin and a light tan, very hard shell. The green color is due to chlorophyll and compounds called carotenes (and the purple and yellow hues come from additional compounds within the nuts) and the bright green pistachios are the most sought-after. All pistachios are sweet with a little earthiness and a rich, oily fattiness. Pistachios are fairly crunchy, and if they still have the papery skin (and most of the Middle Eastern ones do), they also have a coarse texture.

TRADITIONAL USES

Roasted with lemon — *Iran*
Pilaf — *Iran and elsewhere*
Saweeyah bil haleeb (sweet vermicelli pudding) — *Oman*
Ashoura (wheat berry pudding) — *Egypt*
Ice cream — *throughout the region*

Recipe Ideas

1. Use as a garnish for nearly any savory dish, adding just before serving.

2. Sprinkle whole or chopped on salads.

3. Make Pistachio Marzipan (*page 114*).

Almonds

When I was growing up, seeing the plentiful almond trees blossom in winter was a sign that spring was on the way.

ORIGIN AND HISTORY

Native to the Middle East, most likely Iran, the almonds we eat are probably a mutation of the bitter almond. Around 3000 BC—or some believe up to one thousand years earlier—humans began to cultivate the sweet, nontoxic almonds and differentiate them from the bitter variety.

Almonds were an important part of the diet of early Persian civilizations. It was most likely the Persians who introduced Arabs to almonds, and eventually they traveled far enough that almond trees grew all along the Silk Road trading routes from China to the Mediterranean. By the fourteenth century BC, they were found in King Tut's tomb in Egypt.

AGRICULTURAL DETAILS

Prunus amygdalus, the small almond tree, produces several varieties of almonds. The sweet almond (*Prunus amygdalus* var. *dulcis*) is the almond we consume. Almonds are not a botanical nut but a drupe, like pistachios (*see page 100*).

Almond trees grow in the temperate areas of the Middle East and all around the Mediterranean. The trees grow to be anywhere from thirteen to thirty feet tall and produce white flowers. Once the flowers are pollinated by bees, the resulting unripe and fuzzy green fruit can be eaten whole, when the pit is tender and edible. Green almonds are harvested and consumed in the late spring. As the remaining fruit ripens, the outer flesh dries out and the shell containing the seed—the nut we eat—hardens. Once the fruit dries and pulls away from the hardened pit, the almond inside the pit is mature and ready to be harvested. This happens in the late summer or fall. Iran and Turkey produce the most almonds in the Middle East.

APPEARANCE AND FLAVOR

The flavor of almond is a perfect combination of sweet and bitter. They are quite crunchy, even more so when toasted. Almonds are teardrop shaped, less than ½ inch long, and covered in a papery brown skin. Blanched almonds are a pale tan color, as the skin has been removed.

TRADITIONAL USES

Fried in oil as a garnish — *Lebanon, Syria, and more*
Khoshaf (dried fruit compote) — *throughout the region*
Ghoraiybah (cookie) — *throughout the region*
H'riri (almond milk drink) — *Iraq*
Keşkül (pudding) — *Turkey*
Soumádha (syrup) — *Cyprus*
Served on ice as a snack — *Turkey*

Recipe Ideas

1. Add texture to meat stuffings, rice stuffings for dolmas, and meatballs (such as Baharat Lamb Keftas, *page 45*).

2. Substitute the pistachios in Pistachio Marzipan (*page 114*) with 8 ounces blanched almonds to make traditional marzipan.

3. Replace a portion of all-purpose flour in doughs with almond flour to add texture and a sweet flavor.

Walnuts

Rich, oily, and pleasantly complex, walnuts are delicious in all kinds of dishes, especially savory ones.

ORIGIN AND HISTORY

While there are types of walnuts native to North and South America, Europe, and parts of Asia, the variety we most often consume, *Juglans regia*, is most likely native to an area in western Asia that includes Iran. They are thought to have been consumed by humans up to eight thousand years ago and dispersed along the Silk Road trading routes by the first millennium BC, and over the next many centuries they were carried as far as China and England.

The walnut has many royal associations. The botanical name features the Latin word for "royal." And it is said that the nuts were so revered by ancient Persians that they could only be eaten by the king. The walnut is still often referred to as the "king of nuts."

AGRICULTURAL DETAILS

The best-known and highest-quality variety of walnut is called the Persian walnut—or, for some reason in the United States, the English walnut. The trees can grow to over one hundred feet tall and are fairly drought-resistant. They are cultivated in Turkey, Egypt, and Iran. As with many of the other nuts, Iran and Turkey are the biggest producers in the region.

The walnut is also a drupe, though to create some confusion, tree nuts like walnuts and pecans are known as drupaceous nuts. What we eat is the seed of the walnut tree. It's surrounded by a hard shell and fruit that dries out and splits as it ripens and the pit grows. The sour green fruit can be harvested in the spring and preserved in brine or sugar syrup. Fully ripe, hardened walnuts are harvested in the fall.

APPEARANCE AND FLAVOR

These nuts are very oily (which is part of their appeal), a little sweet, and slightly astringent, not in an unpleasant way. Good-quality walnuts will have less astringency.

TRADITIONAL USES

Cevizli biber (pepper and walnut spread) — *Turkey* (see recipe, *page 60*)
Fesenjan (pomegranate stew) — *Iran* (see recipe, *page 113*)
Circassian chicken — *Turkey, Egypt, and more*

Recipe Ideas

1. Add chopped walnuts to marinades for an extra-oily component.

2. Mix walnuts with a simple sugar or honey syrup to make a quick topping for sweets.

3. Lightly toast them (watch them closely, as they burn quickly) for a garnish.

4. Fill pastries with walnuts mixed with spices (see Baklava, *page 117*).

Mahlab

These tiny nuts are the wild card of the chapter and an ingredient rarely seen outside of the Middle East or Middle Eastern preparations (namely, baked goods). Also unique for nuts, mahlab is used as a spice, usually ground and in relatively small amounts to flavor other foods.

ORIGIN AND HISTORY

Mahlab are the kernels of a cherry tree native to the Middle East and southern Europe. They have been used ground for centuries in the Middle East and are rare to see in recipes from outside of the region. The Arabic word for the tree, *halub*, is referenced in the ancient poem *The Epic of Gilgamesh*, though there is no mention of the spice.

Mahlab's original use may have been for perfumes and in soaps, as that's where many of the medieval references to mahlab are found. Indeed, the sweet, nutty scent is what makes this ingredient so enchanting. I suppose it's only natural that innovative cooks at some point wanted to have that sensory experience when eating as well.

AGRICULTURAL DETAILS

Prunus mahaleb, the St. Lucie cherry tree, is a small tree or shrub in the rose family. It's fairly hardy, with white flowers that yield small cherries that are purplish black when fully ripe, toward the end of summer. While the cherries are edible, they are unpleasantly sour to eat. They are harvested specifically for the kernel, which is extracted from the pit and then dried. As with almonds, the kernels can be blanched to remove the skin. The trees are cultivated in Syria, Iran, and Turkey.

APPEARANCE AND FLAVOR

Mahlab has a pleasant, light bitterness when used sparingly, with a hint of sweetness and an almond- or vanilla-like scent. The kernels are about the size of peppercorns, teardrop-shaped, and cream colored. They lose their potency when ground, so buying them whole is preferable.

TRADITIONAL USES

Ma'amoul (cookie) — *throughout the region*
Ka'ak (cracker) — *throughout the region* (see recipe, *page 108*)
Kandil simidi (pastry) — *Turkey*
Flaounes (pastry) — *Cyprus*
Chorek (sweet rolls) — *Armenia*
Nabulsi cheese — *Levant*

Recipe Ideas

1. Add with a light hand to spice blends for the pleasant bitterness and nutty aroma.

2. Incorporate a small amount into cookie and cracker recipes.

3. Lightly fry in olive oil, season with salt, and sprinkle sparingly on salads.

Pine Nuts

As kids in northern Israel, we could spend a whole afternoon foraging for pine nuts, which took a surprising amount of skill we often didn't have. Thinking back on those forays, I understand why pine nuts are so expensive.

ORIGIN AND HISTORY

There are about thirty varieties of pine nuts that are considered edible, even fewer of which are large enough to be worth the effort of harvesting. The nuts consumed in the Middle East come from the stone pine, a species native to regions surrounding the Mediterranean with a distinctive umbrella-like shape.

Humans have been foraging for pine nuts in the Middle East, North America, Asia, and Europe since prehistoric times. The trees have been cultivated for their nuts for at least six thousand years. They were a popular snack in both ancient Greece and Rome and appear in medieval Arab cookbooks dating back to the fourteenth century AD.

AGRICULTURAL DETAILS

The stone pine, *Pinus pinea*, grows in coastal areas with sandy soil and a temperate climate. Pine nuts, really the seeds of the tree, are found in pine cones. The scales of the cones open and separate when they ripen, making the seeds much easier to collect.

Pine cones can be collected for much of the year. They grow until the end of summer, then become dormant for the fall and winter, and reach maturity and ripen the following summer. If gathered in the fall and winter, the cones are often stored until the following summer, then spread out in the hot sun to help them open. Or, in the summer, the tree can be shaken and the nuts from ripened cones will drop down. Once the seeds are removed, each must be cracked to break the shell but not the kernel inside. In the Middle East, Turkey is a big producer of pine nuts, and the trees also grow in Lebanon, Cyprus, and Israel.

APPEARANCE AND FLAVOR

Most of the pine nuts you'll see are small, ½ inch or smaller, and have a long pointed shape and ivory color. Some varieties are longer, others are more squat.

Pine nuts are absolutely delicious. They're tender, creamy, and so rich they sometimes can seem like eating butter. As you toast them, they release a beautiful nutty scent. However, some pine nuts can cause everything you eat to taste bitter for up to a few weeks after consuming. The exact reason is unknown. If you do end up eating some of the offending nuts, know that the side effects are not harmful and will eventually subside.

TRADITIONAL USES

Stuffing for whole fish — *Lebanon*
Tarator (sauce) — *Lebanon, Syria, Egypt*
Cookie and pastry garnish — *throughout the region*
Drink garnish — *throughout the region*

Recipe Ideas

1. Toast the nuts (in oil, if you like) and sprinkle liberally on cheese or hummus as an appetizer.

2. Mix them into meat, rice, or vegetable stuffings, such as the meat mixture inside Kibbeh with Pine Nuts (*page 106*).

3. Stir into Halva (*page 139*) before setting.

---

recipe Kibbeh with Pine Nuts ◆▸ *page 106*

Kibbeh with Pine Nuts

These golden, crispy famously torpedo-shaped fritters are filled with a tender and fragrant meat mixture studded with pine nuts. Kibbeh do require some time to prepare and are notoriously finicky to make, but have some patience and after the first few, you'll get the hang of filling and shaping them. The trick with this version is to have just enough water left on the soaked bulgur to bind the dough but not so much that the dough is sopping wet—which would cause the kibbeh to come apart in the fryer. As you form them, the thinner the dough, the better they'll fry up, so work carefully and test a few if you need to, as described in the recipe. Every second spent on assembly will be worth the end result. To make a vegetarian version, use 1 pound of finely chopped mushrooms in place of the meat, browned as directed.

Makes about 6 dozen

Filling

8 ounces	ground beef
8 ounces	ground lamb
1½ teaspoons	Baharat (*page 36*; 3 grams)
¼ teaspoon	fine sea salt (8 grams), plus more as needed
⅛ teaspoon	Aleppo pepper (0.5 grams)
½	medium yellow onion, finely diced
1	garlic clove, finely chopped
¼ cup	pine nuts
2 tablespoons	roughly chopped fresh cilantro
2 tablespoons	roughly chopped fresh flat-leaf parsley

Make the filling: In a large heavy-bottomed skillet over medium heat, cook the beef, lamb, Baharat, salt, and Aleppo pepper until the meats are browned and broken up into small pieces, 8 to 10 minutes. Add the onion and garlic and stir to combine well.

Set a fine-mesh sieve over a small bowl and drain the mixture, reserving the fat in the bowl for the dough. Transfer the meat mixture to a large bowl and stir in the pine nuts, cilantro, and parsley. Taste and adjust the seasoning.

Meanwhile, make the dough: Put the bulgur in a large bowl and cover with the warm water, making sure the grains are submerged. Soak the bulgur until it is tender with a nut-like texture but not mushy, about 20 minutes. Strain through a fine-mesh sieve and set aside to drain.

In a 10-inch nonstick skillet, heat the oil over medium heat until hot. Add the onion, garlic, and salt and cook until the onion is soft and translucent, about 5 minutes.

Add the drained bulgur to the skillet and cook until the mixture is warm and no water pools in the pan, 3 to 4 minutes. Transfer the mixture to a large bowl and add the semolina and 3 tablespoons of the reserved fat from cooking the meat (supplement with olive oil if you don't have enough, or use all olive oil, if you like). Using your hands or a spatula, mix everything together to form a soft, slightly sticky, and not completely smooth dough.

To stuff the kibbeh, it helps to have damp hands. Place a small bowl of water next to your work surface. Line two sheet pans with parchment paper.

Dough

2 cups	fine bulgur wheat
6 cups	warm water
2 tablespoons	extra-virgin olive oil, plus more as needed
1	medium yellow onion, finely diced
2	garlic cloves, finely chopped
2 teaspoons	fine sea salt (10 grams), plus more as needed
½ cup	fine semolina flour
	Neutral vegetable oil, for frying

Dampen your hands and gently shape 1 tablespoon of the dough into a flat, oval-shaped disk in the palm of your hand. Make a dent in the middle of the disk to start to form a long cupped shape so that the kibbeh is almost entirely formed and can be easily closed. Place 1 teaspoon of the meat filling in the hollow and seal by closing the dough lengthwise around the filling. Shape to close the seam, patching any holes or cracks, and form an elongated sphere that is pointed at the ends (a bit like a football). The dough should be about ¼ inch thick around the filling when closed, and the kibbeh should be 2½ to 3 inches long.

(If you've never made kibbeh before, it's helpful to test at this point to make sure the dough holds together in the oil. Pour 1 inch of oil into a small saucepan and heat to 350°F. Fry 1 or 2 kibbeh and if they hold, proceed. If not, try adding just a little bit of water to the dough and testing another.)

As you form the kibbeh, set them on the prepared pans. Continue shaping and filling the remaining dough and filling. Chill the kibbeh for at least 1 hour to set, or up to overnight. (The kibbeh can also be frozen at this point. Place the sheet pans in the freezer, in batches if necessary, with space between the kibbeh to prevent sticking. Once frozen, transfer them to a container until ready to fry; no need to thaw.)

Line a plate or sheet pan with paper towels. Pour 3 inches of oil into a large heavy-bottomed pot (or half the depth of the pot if it is less than 6 inches deep). Bring the oil to 350°F.

When the oil is ready, fry the kibbeh in batches, taking care not to crowd the pan and adjusting the heat as necessary to keep the temperature consistent. Carefully put the kibbeh in the oil and do not disturb until the shell has set. Fry until the kibbeh is browned and really crispy—almost crunchy—3 to 5 minutes. Use a slotted spoon or spider to transfer the kibbeh to the paper towels to drain. Season with salt. Repeat with as many kibbeh as you like. Serve warm.

Ka'ak

This deceptively simple-looking cracker gets its addictive quality from a very special ingredient—mahlab. The uniquely Middle Eastern spice adds nutty and slightly bitter undertones to the dough. The recipe makes quite a few crackers, but I find they still go too quickly, so you might consider making even bigger batches. *Ka'ak* is Arabic for "biscuit," and the word can be used to refer to any number of baked goods, but this crispy, savory cracker is my favorite.

Makes 40 crackers

2 cups plus 2 tablespoons	all-purpose flour (300 grams)
½ cup	sesame seeds (70 grams)
1 tablespoon	ground mahlab (5 grams)
1¼ teaspoons	baking powder (5 grams)
1 teaspoon	fine sea salt (5 grams)
½ cup	extra-virgin olive oil (100 grams)

Preheat the oven to 350°F. Line two sheet pans with parchment paper.

In a large bowl, whisk together the flour, sesame seeds, mahlab, baking powder, and salt. Make a well in the middle. Pour the oil and ½ cup (120 grams) water into the well and stir with a fork, starting from the center, to combine. Turn the dough out onto a work surface and knead until it is soft and malleable and the sesame seeds are fully incorporated, 2 to 3 minutes.

Divide the dough into 8 equal portions (about 78 grams each). Roll each portion into a log about as thick as your finger. Cut each log into 5 equal pieces.

Working with one piece at a time, roll each piece into a rope 3 inches long and ½ inch thick, then shape it into a ring and press the ends together. Seal the cracker by putting your finger inside the ring and rolling the closure on your work surface a few times. Transfer to the prepared pan. Repeat with the remaining dough.

Evenly space the crackers on the sheet pans so they are not touching. Bake one pan until lightly golden, 30 to 35 minutes. Let the crackers cool completely on the sheet pan. Repeat with the other pan.

Storage Directions

The crackers can be stored in an airtight glass container for up to 3 weeks. They must be cooled completely for storage, otherwise they will not stay crunchy.

Muhammara

Roasted red peppers and toasted walnuts are the main components of this classic Levantine dish that's one of my go-to condiments. While most recipes call for blending and for adding bread to thicken it, I prefer to chop the ingredients by hand for a more rustic texture. I do include crusty bread, but served alongside, to soak up the sweet and sour seasoning.

Makes about 3 cups

3	medium red bell peppers
2	medium green bell peppers
3	medium jalapeños
5 tablespoons	extra-virgin olive oil, plus more for serving
4 teaspoons	fine sea salt (20 grams)
1 cup	walnuts, toasted (*see page 99*) and roughly chopped
3 tablespoons	pomegranate molasses
1 tablespoon	sherry vinegar
2 teaspoons	sweet paprika (4 grams)
¼ teaspoon	Aleppo pepper (0.5 grams)

Position an oven rack about 4 inches from the heating element and heat the broiler. Line a sheet pan with foil.

Cut each of the bell peppers along the grooves to separate the sections, and remove the core, seeds, and stem. Halve the jalapeños lengthwise and remove the seeds and ribs.

In a large bowl, toss the vegetables with 4 tablespoons of the oil and 2 teaspoons (10 grams) of the salt, making sure the skins are well coated with oil.

Arrange the peppers skin-side up on the prepared pan. Broil them, checking often and rotating the pan front to back for even cooking, until the skin is fully charred and the peppers are tender but not yet mushy, about 20 minutes.

Transfer the cooked peppers to a large bowl and immediately cover the bowl with plastic wrap to steam. Let sit, undisturbed, until the peppers are at room temperature. Peel the skin from the peppers and discard. Finely chop the pepper flesh.

In a medium bowl, mix the chopped peppers with the walnuts, pomegranate molasses, vinegar, remaining 2 teaspoons (10 grams) salt, the paprika, Aleppo pepper, and remaining 1 tablespoon oil. Taste and adjust seasoning as needed.

Refrigerate for at least 2 hours to allow the spices to hydrate and the flavors to come together. Serve with a drizzle of rich, flavorful olive oil.

Storage Directions
The muhammara will keep in an airtight container in the refrigerator for up to 1 week.

Fesenjan

This Persian dish traditionally consists of a pomegranate and walnut sauce that's assembled over the course of a few different steps and that is then used for poaching chicken (or duck or meatballs) right in the pot. When I was working on my own version, I wanted to simplify the cooking process while still honoring the recipe. I also wanted crispy chicken skin. I think this end result is a perfect blend of new and old techniques. The walnuts and chicken release oils during cooking, so I like to whisk the sauce to emulsify and make it glossy before serving, but you can skip this step and take the pan right from the oven to the table.

Serves 4 or 5

½ cup	extra-virgin olive oil
3 pounds	bone-in, skin-on chicken thighs
2	medium onions, halved and thinly sliced lengthwise
2½ teaspoons	fine sea salt (13 grams)
8 ounces	walnuts
2 cups	pomegranate juice
½ cup	pomegranate molasses
2 teaspoons	freshly ground black pepper (4 grams)
	Fresh pomegranate arils, for garnish
	Roughly chopped fresh cilantro, for garnish

In a large, deep, heavy-bottomed ovenproof skillet, heat the oil over medium heat until hot. Working in batches if necessary, add the chicken in a single layer skin-side down and cook until the fat is completely rendered and the skin is nicely browned and crispy, 10 to 15 minutes. Flip the pieces over to quickly sear the other side, 1 to 2 minutes, then remove from the pan to a plate. Repeat with the remaining chicken.

Pour off all but ¼ cup of the fat in the pan. Add the onions and ½ teaspoon (3 grams) of the salt and cook over medium heat, stirring occasionally, until the onions are very soft, golden, and well caramelized, about 20 minutes.

Meanwhile, preheat the oven to 325°F.

In a blender, combine the walnuts, pomegranate juice, pomegranate molasses, pepper, remaining 2 teaspoons (10 grams) salt, and ½ cup water and blend until smooth.

When the onions are caramelized, add the blended braising liquid to the pan, scraping the bottom with a wooden spoon to release any caramelization on the pan. Return the chicken thighs to the pan in a single layer, skin-side up. The liquid should just about cover the chicken.

Increase the heat to bring everything to a boil, then transfer the pan to the oven. Cook, uncovered, until the chicken is completely tender, about 1 hour.

Remove the chicken from the pan and skim any fat off the top of the sauce. Bring the sauce to a boil while whisking to emulsify it, then taste and adjust the seasoning. Return the chicken to the pan.

Garnish with the pomegranate arils and cilantro and serve hot, from the pan.

Pistachio Marzipan

I don't bother to use expensive peeled pistachios to make marzipan, and I never go through the trouble of peeling them myself. The slightly muted color from the pistachio skins is not an issue for me, as the rich, buttery taste of the nuts still comes through perfectly. But if you'd like a brilliant green marzipan, use peeled Sicilian pistachios. They'll need much less time in the food processor for the first step, about 5 minutes. Serve the sliced marzipan alone as a candy or snack, or as an accompaniment to tea or coffee.

Makes several dozen pieces

1¾ cups	pistachios (225 grams)
2 cups	powdered sugar (225 grams)
1 tablespoon	rose water (15 grams)

In a food processor, combine the pistachios and sugar. Run the machine, stopping to scrape down the bottom and sides often, until the mixture turns into a fine powder and is warm, 10 to 15 minutes.

Add the rose water and process just until the mixture becomes a paste, 1 to 2 minutes. If the mixture is still powdery at this point, add water 1 tablespoon (15 grams) at a time, stopping to scrape down the bowl often. As soon as the mixture becomes a paste, transfer it to a bowl and knead it until it becomes soft and flexible, 1 to 2 minutes. A little oil on your hands and the bowl is normal, but if the marzipan gets crumbly and starts exuding oil, knead in 1 or 2 tablespoons (15 or 30 grams) water until it's paste-like again.

Roll the marzipan into a thick log, wrap tightly in plastic wrap, and refrigerate until cool, at least 2 hours. Slice into bite-size pieces as needed right before serving.

Storage Directions
Keep the uncut and wrapped marzipan in an airtight container in the refrigerator for up to 3 weeks.

Baklava

Despite being one of the best-known desserts of the region, baklava is a slightly tricky recipe that requires time and precision. But rest assured, the homemade version is worth the effort. At La Boîte, we stock a smoked cinnamon I love using in baklava because it keeps the dish from being overly sweet, but any quality ground cinnamon will work. If you like, you can garnish it with very finely chopped pistachios and walnuts.

Makes about 32 pieces

Syrup

1 cup	sugar (200 grams)
½ cup	honey (170 grams)
2 tablespoons	freshly squeezed lemon juice (30 grams)
1 tablespoon	loosely packed dried rose petals (1 gram)
5	cardamom pods

Baklava

1 pound	(4 sticks) unsalted butter (454 grams)
1 tablespoon	ground ginger (6 grams)
8 ounces	hazelnuts (225 grams)
8 ounces	walnuts (225 grams)
1 tablespoon	ground smoked cinnamon or regular cinnamon (5 grams)
1	(16-ounce) package frozen phyllo dough (9 × 13- or 14-inch sheets), thawed according to the package directions

Storage Directions

Cover the baking dish with a clean kitchen towel and store the baklava at room temperature for up to 1 week.

Make the syrup: In a small saucepan, combine ¾ cup (160 grams) water, the sugar, honey, lemon juice, rose petals, and cardamom. Bring the mixture to a boil over medium-high heat, stirring occasionally to help dissolve the sugar. Reduce the heat so the mixture simmers and cook, undisturbed, for 4 minutes.

Strain the syrup through a fine-mesh sieve and discard the spices. Let the syrup cool completely. (The syrup must be completely cooled or the baklava will have a soggy, not crisp, final texture.)

Make the baklava: In a small saucepan, combine the butter and ginger and melt over low heat.

Preheat the oven to 325°F. Line the bottom of a 9 × 13-inch baking dish with parchment paper. Brush a thin layer of the butter mixture all over the inside of the pan.

In a food processor, pulse the hazelnuts just until coarsely ground. Transfer to a large bowl. Repeat with the walnuts. Add the cinnamon to the nuts and stir to combine.

Remove the phyllo from the package and count the sheets—there should be 36 to 40, which will determine how many layers you'll get. If the sheets are 14 inches long, trim them to fit the dish. Put 1 sheet on a clean work surface and stack the rest, keeping them covered with a slightly damp towel. Brush the sheet with a thin layer of the spiced butter and lay in the prepared pan. Repeat twice more for a total of 3 buttered sheets stacked in the pan. Sprinkle ¼ cup (30 grams) of the nut mixture evenly over the top.

Continue making layers with the remaining phyllo and nut mixture, buttering 3 sheets and topping with ¼ cup (30 grams) of filling for each layer. Finish with a final layer of 3 sheets of buttered phyllo. Brush the top with the remaining spiced butter.

Using a very sharp knife, cut the baklava the long way into 6 strips that are each 1½ inches wide. Cut another set of 1½-inch-wide strips at a 45-degree angle from the first to make diamonds.

Bake until the top is a deep golden brown, 1 hour 10 minutes to 1 hour 20 minutes. Transfer the dish to a wire rack and immediately drizzle all of the cooled syrup evenly over the hot baklava—it should sizzle. Leave the baklava to cool completely, uncovered, at least 4 hours. Serve at room temperature.

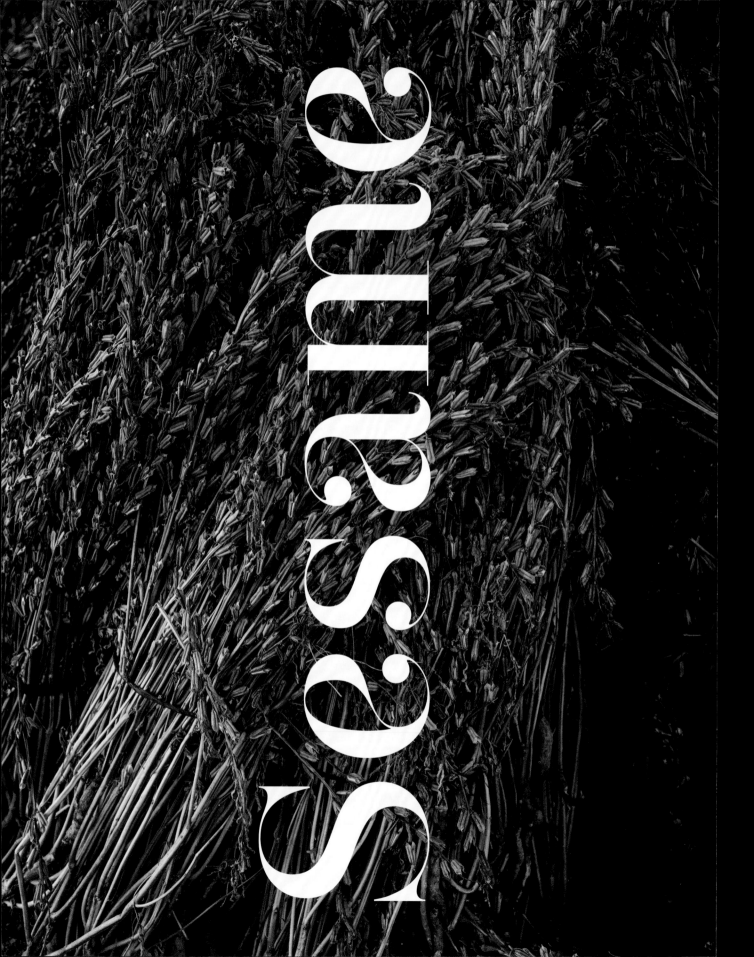

{ SESAME }

سمسم

susam

שׁוּמשׁוּם

كنجد

σουσάμι

քունջութ

Walk into a bakery, restaurant, or home kitchen in the Middle East and it's nearly impossible not to find at least one sesame-scented treat inside. These small, oil-rich seeds, used to garnish breads and pastries, are also the foundation of well-known staples like tahini and halva, and a key ingredient in spice mixes like za'atar (*see page 26*).

ORIGIN AND HISTORY

The word *sesame* originates from the ancient Egyptians, who called the seeds sesemet. Though not native to the Middle East, they have been there long enough as a food source, lighting fuel, and medicine to have been first documented as early as 1500 BC and to have been found in King Tut's tomb. Sesame was cultivated in the Fertile Crescent and North Africa, where it was used and traded extensively. In addition to pressing it for oil, many ancient civilizations mixed it with wheat and other grains to make flour, which is perhaps why it is still so closely associated with breads and pastries.

AGRICULTURAL DETAILS

The sesame plant is an annual in the Pedaliaceae family with white to pale pink flowers. Once the flowers are fertilized, they form pods, each containing fifty to eighty seeds. The seeds are 50 to 60 percent oil. In the ancient plant, the pods opened when dry (the origin of the phrase "open sesame"), an action that scattered the seeds everywhere and necessitated laborious hand harvesting. The plant is also drought-tolerant and able to grow in many types of soil (which helped spread its popularity). Modern scatter-resistant varieties allow for more mechanized, easier harvesting. After harvesting, sesame seeds are either dried or hulled to remove the outer skin (see Tahini, Production, *page 120*). Egypt is the biggest producer of sesame in the Middle East.

Tahini

The best tahini should be so mild and nutty you can eat it with no added seasonings, straight from the jar. If you've never been tempted to eat it that way, you probably haven't had quality tahini!

PRODUCTION

Tahini is perhaps the most famous use of sesame seeds in the Middle East. The name comes from the Arabic *tahana*, which means "to grind." Before grinding, the sesame seeds are first soaked in water, sometimes over twenty-four hours (some manufacturers use a hot lye treatment), and then crushed just enough to loosen the skins. Traditionally, they would be soaked again in highly salted water, which causes the skin to sink to the bottom so the now-hulled seeds can be easily skimmed off the surface of the water. These days, removing the softened skins is mostly handled by machine.

The hulled seeds are lightly roasted (or simply dried to make "raw tahini") and ground. Traditional producers may still use actual stone millstones to grind the seeds because the process is gentler, which many believe makes a smoother final product. Newer, industrialized producers have moved on to metal "stones," which are both more efficient and more affordable.

APPEARANCE AND FLAVOR

Tahini is a rich, nutty paste that can range from light beige to black, and from smooth and pourable to thick and spoonable. Some tahini may have an earthier taste or a slightly bitter edge, but ideally the taste is creamy and mild. Tahini made with black sesame seeds is more bitter and savory, though fairly rare. Lighter tahini is what is used most often in the Middle East and is not the same as Asian sesame pastes, which are darker and stronger-tasting because they are made with deeply toasted sesame seeds.

SOURCING AND STORING

Look for a product made from only sesame seeds (and perhaps salt). It is perfectly normal for tahini to separate—remember, sesame is up to 60 percent fat. To prevent a thick layer of solids at the bottom, store unopened jars upside down, then stir vigorously (or put in a blender) after opening to emulsify. Tahini does not need to be refrigerated, even after opening. Kept in its original container, and stored in a cool, dry place, it will last for quite some time.

Look for labels marked "stone-milled," as that is a sign of quality. Generally speaking, the best seeds are sourced from Ethiopia because of their optimal oil content for tahini. The tahini I sell in my store is the best tahini I've ever found (read more in Har Bracha Tahini, *page 123*).

TRADITIONAL USES

Hummus — *Levant and more* (see Hummus Tahina, *page 235*)
Siniya (meat or fish pie) — *Levant* (see recipe, *page 134*)
Tahinov hatz (filled bread) — *Armenia*
Tashi (dip) — *Cyprus*

Recipe Ideas

1. Drizzle over ice cream.

2. Stir into a meatball mixture for extra richness.

3. Use to replace some of the fat in cookie doughs, as in the Tahini Cookies (*page 136*).

Tahini

In my opinion, Har Bracha is the best tahini producer in the world. Despite containing just sesame seeds and being made with a simple three-step process, what distinguishes great tahini from average tahini is attention to detail. That's what now sets Yaakov Cohen's product apart from the rest.

Yaakov began his career working with his father, one of the biggest sesame traders in the West Bank and Israel. He was selling the seeds and other commodities around villages in the region when he decided to make his mark on tahini manufacturing in 2007. Yaakov had no knowledge of how to make tahini—just a dream of producing a high-quality ingredient in small, easy-to-control batches. So he bought a mill, set up shop in a small space lent by his uncle, sourced sesame seeds from his father, and got to work.

After his initial attempts (which were admittedly not great), Yaakov hired staff with extensive tahini production knowledge—as it turned out,

there was more to the process than simply crushing sesame seeds. That's when the business really took off. Today, they produce around ten tons of tahini per day and could produce twice that but choose not to in order to maintain their world-famous reputation for quality.

Production starts across the Red Sea, in Ethiopia, where Cohen exclusively sources rich and buttery Humera sesame seeds. Humera is both the variety and where most of the seeds are grown. The seeds have an oil content noticeably higher than other sesame seeds, making them ideal for tahini, and the plants thrive in the soils of Ethiopia.

When the seeds arrive from Ethiopia, they're unpacked and left out to dry for two days to remove moisture that may have seeped into them during transport. They're sorted to remove any subpar seeds—ones that are discolored or spoiled. Cohen estimates he discards about 10 percent of his shipment because the seeds are not up to his standard. (Those seeds are used as animal feed.)

After the sorting, the seeds are soaked in salt water and hulled (see Tahini, Production, *page 120*), then washed three times to remove any traces of salt. Cohen roasts the seeds not once like most companies but twice, for the richest possible flavor. The seeds are then processed twice, which helps make his tahini almost impossibly smooth. The final step is to send each batch to his quality control team, which makes sure the taste and texture are superb.

The Cohen family are Samaritans, a small religious group of about eight hundred people with both Jewish and Arab ties. The factory is located in Mount Gerizim, Nablus, in the West Bank, a location holy to them. His staff consists of Samaritans, Muslims, Christians, and Jews, and he sees the company as a small bridge between the communities in the region.

"I make peace every day with each jar of tahini we produce," Cohen says.

Hassan Fauzi harvests sesame, Sahl al-Battuf (Beit Netofa Valley), Lower Galilee, Israel

Halva

Derived from the Arabic word for "candy," this confection can be flour- or nut-based, and versions exist in countless cuisines, but the sesame halva most closely associated with the Levant is what I refer to here.

PRODUCTION

To make halva, sugar or honey syrup is heated to the soft- or hard-ball stage, then mixed with tahini and flavorings like cocoa powder, chopped nuts, or spices such as cardamom. It's kneaded and churned to get its unique flaky texture and formed into blocks to be sliced later.

It can also be made into a "floss," and though most halva flosses are wheat-based, I've sourced a quality sesame floss for La Boîte. The dough is extruded through a pipe to make thin wisps, which land on a heated surface and cook immediately. The end result is a cotton candy–like texture with a pure sesame flavor.

APPEARANCE AND FLAVOR

Halva is sweet, but also earthy and complex. The texture is what makes it so special: It's firm yet fudgy, with a flaky consistency that still slices easily. There is something reminiscent of cotton candy in the way it melts in your mouth.

The appearance depends on how the halva is flavored. It is often a light, sandy color but can be darker brown when mixed with cocoa or cinnamon, or marbled if a few flavors are mixed, and it may have chopped nuts or sesame seeds, which can also be swirled throughout.

SOURCING AND STORING

Suleiman the Magnificent, an Ottoman sultan, built a special halva-producing kitchen in the sixteenth century that was said to make some thirty varieties. If you're lucky, you might find that kind of selection today. One way to buy halva is to find a seller that slices it and sells by the pound—this halva is often much fresher, though good prepackaged varieties are plentiful. Shredded halva or halva floss is often only sold prepackaged. Look for a short ingredient list—sugar, sesame, perhaps a stabilizer or glucose—on the package.

All halva is shelf-stable, and as long as it's stored properly, it can last for months in a cool, dry place in an airtight container. A layer of oil may appear on the surface, but that is perfectly normal.

TRADITIONAL USES

Snack served with coffee or tea — *throughout the region*

Recipe Ideas

1. Add crumbled halva to cookie or cake doughs.

2. Use as a stuffing for pastries or babka.

3. Crumble over ice cream or toast.

4. Make your own Halva (*page 139*).

Sesame Oil

Most people think of the toasted oil used in Asian cuisines when they hear "sesame oil," but the lighter, all-purpose cooking oil has a long history in the Middle East.

PRODUCTION

All oils are produced two ways: through cold-pressing or hot-pressing. Cold-pressed oils (often referred to as "virgin" oils) have a better flavor, are higher quality, and are more expensive. The seeds are crushed at very high pressure until the oil is released and collected. The oil may need to be cooled because the friction of the pressing process raises the temperature of the oil. Expeller-pressed oils are made the same way, though the producer may also additionally heat the seeds in the process, which affects the flavor.

Hot-pressed oils aren't labeled as such, but any product without a "cold-pressed" label can be assumed to be hot-pressed. These oils are cheaper, use chemical solvent extraction, and are highly refined. This creates a blander, less flavorful oil.

APPEARANCE AND FLAVOR

The varieties used in the Middle East are light colored with a mild, though not entirely neutral, flavor. They are better for all-purpose cooking than dark sesame oil, which has a stronger, toasted flavor.

SOURCING AND STORING

Natural foods stores or Middle Eastern markets are the best source for sesame oil. Look for a light color and "cold-pressed" on the label. Store the oil in the refrigerator to prevent it from going rancid and becoming bitter and off-flavored.

TRADITIONAL USES

All-purpose cooking oil — *Egypt, Syria, and Iraq*

Recipe Ideas

1. Use sesame oil when you want a more interesting flavor from high-heat cooking than canola oil or vegetable oil.

2. Mix into salad dressings for a light sesame flavor, which works especially well for cabbage slaws.

3. Add a dash or two to a Bloody Mary.

Sesame Seeds

Whole sesame seeds are just as important for Middle Eastern cuisines as the products made from them.

APPEARANCE AND FLAVOR

The two types found in stores are white and black sesame seeds. The white seeds are more common in Middle Eastern cooking. The black seeds are oilier and more intense—I like and use both. Either variety can be purchased hulled or unhulled, but packaging won't always indicate. Unhulled white seeds are often darker in color—more of a beige than a white. I use unhulled since they have a deeper flavor and heartier texture.

SOURCING AND STORING

Besides hulled or unhulled, sesame seeds can also be purchased raw or toasted—but once heat is applied, the oil in the seeds will go rancid faster, meaning you have weeks instead of months to use toasted seeds. Your best bet is to buy them untoasted and toast them as needed (see below). Store both toasted and untoasted sesame seeds in an airtight container in a cool, dry place—same goes for any spice blends that contain sesame seeds. Stored this way, untoasted sesame seeds will last for months, toasted seeds several weeks.

TOASTING

To toast a small amount, put them in a skillet over low heat and cook, stirring often, until the seeds have darkened a few shades. To toast a larger amount, put them on a sheet pan in a 325°F oven (don't use convection mode or they'll fly around) and start with 2 to 3 minutes, adding more time as needed and stirring occasionally, until the seeds are golden and smell toasted. Cool completely before storing.

TRADITIONAL USES

Simit (bread) — *Turkey* (see recipe, *page 133*)
Semsemiyah (candy) — *Levant and more*
Boureka (savory pastry) — *Israel and more*
Za'atar — *Levant* (see recipe, *page 36*)

Recipe Ideas

1. Coat logs of fresh goat cheese with ground sesame seeds.

2. Ground sesame counters the sweetness in doughs wonderfully— try the Sesame Crackers (*page 131*) made with ground sesame.

3. Use sesame seeds to garnish rice and meat dishes.

Tahini Sauce

You can, of course, use tahini straight out of the jar and drizzle it over vegetables, cooked meat or fish, or just enjoy it with a piece of bread. But one of my favorite uses—and a Middle Eastern classic—is tahini sauce. It's a condiment that complements every meal with its rich and tart flavor. Some people like it thicker, some more runny, some add lots of garlic, others chopped herbs. However you like yours, it's simple to make, and a large batch can be kept in the refrigerator to use for multiple meals. Because tahini is sensitive to temperature, make sure you are using ice-cold water so your sauce does not curdle. If it does, slowly add more ice water and stir until it's emulsified and creamy again.

Makes 1 cup

Ice
½ cup   tahini
1   lemon, halved
Salt

In a measuring cup with a spout, mix ½ cup water with a handful of ice and stir until very cold. Remove the ice.

In a bowl, whisk together the tahini and juice of ½ lemon. Slowly drizzle in the water, whisking constantly, until the mixture is creamy and smooth. (If the sauce breaks, make another batch of ice water and add a few drops at a time until the sauce comes together.) Taste and season with salt and more lemon juice, if you like.

Variations
- Add ¼ cup finely chopped fresh herbs such as mint, cilantro, flat-leaf parsley, or a mix for an herbaceous green sauce.
- Whisk in 1 teaspoon finely chopped garlic.
- Replace ¼ cup of the water with an equal amount of pomegranate juice for a reddish, slightly sweet result.

Storage Directions
Keep the tahini sauce in an airtight container in the refrigerator for up to 3 days.

Sesame Crackers

For the real sesame lovers: These crunchy crackers have well over 1 cup of seeds in them, including ground seeds in the dough. The crackers are exceptional served with cheese, but with a bit of heat from Aleppo pepper and sweetness from aniseed, they stand on their own as a snack, too.

Makes several dozen

Dough

1¼ cups	sesame seeds (170 grams)
1¼ cups	whole wheat flour (150 grams), plus more for dusting
1½ teaspoons	aniseed (4 grams)
1 teaspoon	Aleppo pepper (2 grams)
1 teaspoon	fine sea salt (5 grams)
2 tablespoons	extra-virgin olive oil (25 grams)
1 tablespoon plus 1½ teaspoons	honey (30 grams)

Topping

2 tablespoons	extra-virgin olive oil (25 grams)
¼ cup	sesame seeds (35 grams)
	Coarse or flaky sea salt

Storage Directions

Keep the cooled crackers in an airtight container for up to 1 week.

Preheat the oven to 350°F.

Make the dough: Grind ½ cup (70 grams) of the sesame seeds in a spice grinder.

In a large bowl, whisk together the ground sesame seeds, whole wheat flour, remaining ¾ cup (100 grams) whole sesame seeds, aniseed, Aleppo pepper, and salt. Pour in the oil, honey, and ⅓ cup (80 grams) water and stir until a crumbly ball of dough forms. If your dough is dry, add more water 1 tablespoon (15 grams) at a time until all of the flour is incorporated into the dough, but add it sparingly to make sure your dough doesn't become soggy. Divide the dough into two equal pieces.

Lightly flour a large sheet of parchment paper or a silicone baking mat. Put one of the dough portions onto the parchment and roll into a large rectangle about 1/16 inch thick (the other dimensions don't matter as long as it fits on a sheet pan), dusting with more flour as necessary. Make sure your dough is evenly thin so all of the crackers are crisp when baked. Use a fork to dock the dough all over to help with crisping.

Top the crackers: Use a pastry brush to lightly brush the top with 1 tablespoon (13 grams) of the oil. Sprinkle 2 tablespoons (18 grams) of the sesame seeds evenly across the surface along with some coarse salt and firmly roll over the seeds a few more times with your rolling pin to push the seeds into the dough.

Score the dough into your desired cracker shape with a knife or pizza cutter. If you'd like your crackers to be perfect squares, you will need to trim the edges of your rectangle. Otherwise leave the odd edges.

Transfer the dough and parchment paper onto a sheet pan. Bake for 10 minutes, then check. Continue baking, rotating the pan front to back if the crackers are browning unevenly, until they are dark golden brown and smell toasted, up to another 5 to 10 minutes. Let the crackers cool completely on the pan.

While the first pan of crackers is baking, repeat the process with the remaining dough half, rolling it out directly on parchment paper, topping it with the remaining oil, sesame seeds, and salt, scoring the dough, then baking it.

Simit

One of the most common breads you'll find in Turkey is simit. Similar to the Jerusalem bagel in its shape and sesame topping but made from a richer dough twisted into enticing rings, it is light, crunchy, and also slightly sweet, thanks to a dip in diluted grape molasses before baking. Traditionally served for breakfast, simit can be enjoyed all day, as far as I'm concerned. This recipe is my own variation on a traditional one, using silan (date molasses) and olive oil as my sweetener and fat of choice, respectively.

Makes 8

Dough

1½ cups	lukewarm water (360 grams)
1 tablespoon	sugar (13 grams)
2 teaspoons	instant yeast (6 grams)
4 cups	all-purpose flour (560 grams), plus more as needed
¼ cup	extra-virgin olive oil (50 grams), plus more for the bowl
1 teaspoon	fine sea salt (5 grams)

Coating

¼ cup	silan (date molasses; 80 grams)
1½ cups	sesame seeds (210 grams)

Variations

• Substitute nigella seeds for half the sesame seeds.
• Replace the silan with maple syrup or the traditional grape molasses (see page 159).
• Add ¼ cup (32 grams) za'atar into the dough while kneading it.

Make the dough: In a small bowl, mix the lukewarm water, sugar, and yeast. Let sit until the yeast is foamy, about 10 minutes.

In a stand mixer fitted with the dough hook, combine the flour, oil, and salt. Add the yeast mixture and mix on low speed until a rough dough forms, about 2 minutes, scraping down the sides a few times. Increase the speed to medium and knead, pulling the dough off the hook if necessary, until the dough pulls away from the bowl and is smooth, 6 to 8 minutes. If the dough seems slightly sticky, add 1 or 2 tablespoons of flour and knead until smooth.

Lightly oil a large bowl, add the dough, and cover the bowl with plastic wrap. Set aside until the dough doubles in size, 1 to 1½ hours.

Turn the dough out onto your work surface and divide it into 16 equal portions (about 60 grams each). Work with one piece at a time and keep the others covered to prevent them from drying out. Shape each piece into a log 20 inches long.

Make the coating: In a wide, shallow dish, whisk together ½ cup (120 grams) water and the silan. Place the sesame seeds in another wide, shallow dish.

Preheat the oven to 400°F. Line two sheet pans with parchment paper.

Line up 2 logs together lengthwise so they're parallel and touching. Roll one end toward you and the other away from you on your work surface to twist them together (or twist them as demonstrated on page 132). Press the ends together to form a ring.

Dip the twisted dough ring in the water-silan mixture, followed by a dip in the sesame bowl so the simit is coated on all sides. Place the simit on the prepared pan. Repeat with the remaining dough, spacing 4 rings out evenly on each pan. Cover with a kitchen towel and set aside to rise until they've puffed up and are about one-third bigger, about 30 minutes.

Bake until golden brown, 20 to 25 minutes, rotating if necessary for even browning. Remove from the oven and transfer the simit from the pan to a wire rack to cool completely before serving. Simit are best the day they're made. Any remaining can be stored for another day in a paper bag or frozen in an airtight bag for a few weeks.

Siniya

"Siney" is the name that I've always known for the metal or clay pan used to bake siniya. The dish is made with lamb, beef, or vegetables, sometimes a layer of bulgur wheat, and topped with tahini sauce. (Some call it a casserole, while others describe it as being like shepherd's pie, both of which are close but not a perfect translation.) This recipe is inspired by a Gazan fisherman's version.

Serves 6

Spice Blend

1 teaspoon	ground cumin (2 grams)
1 teaspoon	ground sumac (3 grams)
½ teaspoon	Aleppo pepper (1 gram)

Fish Mixture

2 tablespoons	extra-virgin olive oil
2	medium yellow onions, halved and thinly sliced
1½ teaspoons	fine sea salt (8 grams)
1	medium bulb fennel, halved and thinly sliced
1	garlic clove, finely chopped
½	lemon
1½ pounds	cod fillet (1½ to 2 inches thick), cut into 6 equal pieces

For Serving

1 cup	Tahini Sauce (*page 129*)
¼ cup plus 1 tablespoon	roughly chopped fresh cilantro
1	small garlic clove, finely chopped
3 tablespoons	pine nuts, toasted (*see page 99*)

Preheat the oven to 400°F.

Make the spice blend: In a small bowl, mix the cumin, sumac, and Aleppo pepper together.

Prepare the fish: In a large heavy-bottomed skillet, heat the oil over medium heat. When the oil is hot, add the onions and 1 teaspoon (5 grams) of the salt, stir to combine, then cover and cook, stirring once or twice, until lightly browned and starting to become translucent, about 10 minutes.

Add the fennel, garlic, and half the spice blend (3 grams), stir to combine, then cover and cook until the fennel is crisp-tender, about 5 minutes. Remove the pan from the heat and squeeze the lemon over the mixture.

Transfer the fennel and onion mixture to the bottom of a siney, glass pie plate, or 10-inch cake pan, and spread into an even layer.

Season the cod with the remaining spice blend (3 grams) and remaining ½ teaspoon (3 grams) salt. Arrange the fish on top of the fennel and onions; if the fish pieces are 2 inches thick, put them on their side for more even cooking. Bake until the fish is about three-quarters of the way cooked (be careful not to overcook the fish at this point), about 8 minutes. Remove the pan from the oven and heat the broiler.

While the fish is baking, in a small bowl, mix the tahini sauce with ¼ cup of the cilantro and the garlic.

Spoon the tahini sauce in an even layer over the baked fish and vegetables. Set under the broiler and broil, turning the pan as necessary, until the sauce is browned in spots and the fish is cooked through, about 3 minutes.

Serve hot, sprinkled with the pine nuts and remaining 1 tablespoon cilantro.

Tahini Cookies

I am obsessed with cookies in every form and flavor. Many years ago, when I started La Boîte, it was a cookie company—the spices came later. This recipe was one of the first kinds of cookies that I sold and remains one of my favorites. The tahini binds the dough and creates a nutty cookie with an irresistible flaky texture—similar to shortbread but better.

Makes 15 cookies

8 tablespoons	(1 stick) cold unsalted butter (115 grams)
½ cup	sugar (100 grams)
¾ cup	tahini (210 grams)
1 teaspoon	vanilla extract (5 grams)
1¼ cups	all-purpose flour (175 grams)
2 teaspoons	ground ginger (4 grams)
1 teaspoon	baking powder (4 grams)
15	blanched almonds, for garnish (optional)

In a stand mixer fitted with the paddle, cream the butter and sugar on low speed until pale and fluffy, about 2 minutes. Add the tahini and vanilla and mix on low speed until fully incorporated, stopping to scrape down the sides as needed, 1 to 2 minutes.

Sift the flour, ginger, and baking powder together into a medium bowl, then stir to mix. Add the flour mixture to the tahini mixture. Continue mixing on low speed for just a few seconds, stopping to scrape down the sides once, until the dough comes together and no streaks of flour remain—the dough will overheat if mixed longer. (Alternatively, you can remove the bowl from the mixer and fold in the flour mixture by hand with a spatula.) Remove the dough from the bowl and gently press it together to form a ball.

Line a sheet pan with parchment paper. Divide the dough into 15 equal portions the size of golf balls (about 40 grams each) and place on the prepared pan. Gently press 1 blanched almond (if using) on top of each cookie. Transfer the pan to the refrigerator for at least 30 minutes and up to overnight.

Preheat the oven to 375°F.

Bake until the cookies are a dark golden color on the edges, about 14 minutes. Let the cookies cool completely on the pan before removing.

Variations

- Add ⅓ cup (50 grams) crumbled halva (*page 139*) into the dough with the dry ingredients for an even more intense sesame experience.
- Put 1 cup (140 grams) untoasted sesame seeds on a plate and gently roll each cookie dough ball in the seeds before baking.

Storage Directions

Store the cooled cookies in an airtight container for up to 4 days.

Halva

I've adored halva since I was a child. My favorite way to eat it now is simple: Slice off a thin wedge to have with a cup of coffee or tea. Making your own halva is surprisingly easy, fast, and rewarding. The texture is slightly different from the flaky store-bought kind—it's a little more dense and fudgy—but still with a pure, sweet sesame flavor. You can get creative by adding chopped dried fruits or different spices like ground ginger, dried chile, or Baharat (*page 36*). Try the impressive version layered with pistachios (see Variations, below).

Serves at least 6

1   (500-gram) container tahini (about 2 cups)

2 cups sugar (400 grams)

Line a standard 8½ × 4½-inch loaf pan with plastic wrap, then mist the plastic with cooking spray.

Pour the tahini into a large heatproof bowl.

Clip a candy thermometer to the side of a small heavy-bottomed pan. Pour in ½ cup (120 grams) water, then add the sugar (this allows the sugar to dissolve more easily)—but do not stir. Fill a small bowl with water and have a clean pastry brush ready.

Bring the sugar and water to a boil over high heat and cook, gently stirring to dissolve the sugar only if needed, and brushing the sides of the pot with water as necessary to prevent crystallization, until the mixture is between 245° and 248°F. The syrup should be thick and the bubbling slow.

Immediately pour the hot syrup onto the tahini and quickly mix with a heatproof silicone spatula to fully incorporate. This happens fast, so stir energetically to combine, as the mixture will turn fudgy in seconds. Pour the mixture into the prepared pan. Press it with the spatula to compact it into an even layer, and cover the top with plastic wrap.

Refrigerate until completely chilled, at least 8 hours or overnight. To serve, turn the pan over, slide out the halva, and peel away the plastic wrap. Slice the halva and serve.

Variations
- Add 1 cup (140 grams) roughly chopped raw or toasted pistachios to the syrup just before mixing it with the tahini.
- For a layered halva, sprinkle ½ cup (70 grams) roughly chopped pistachios on the bottom of the lined loaf pan, add half the halva, then repeat with another ½ cup (70 grams) pistachios and the remaining halva.

Storage Directions
Keep the halva tightly wrapped in plastic at room temperature or, for a firmer texture, store in the refrigerator for up to 1 week.

Dried Fruit

{ DRIED FRUIT }

مجففة

kurutulmuş meyve

פֵּרוֹת יְבֵשִׁים

برگه میوه

αποξηραμένα φρούτα

չիր

These simple preserved fruits are meant to be eaten as a snack or post-meal treat. In fact, a tray of dried fruit to accompany coffee or tea is a symbol of hospitality throughout the region. There is an abundance of dried fruit in the Middle East, but for this chapter, I've focused on the ones especially characteristic of the region—and my favorites: dates, figs, barberries, and fruit leather (which can be made from any type of fruit, though the apricot is most popular). I wish I could include all the types available!

ORIGIN AND HISTORY

The most popular fruits in the region, dates and figs, have been eaten since before recorded history and cultivated for thousands of years. Fruit is especially prone to fast spoilage, so there are many different fruit preservation methods used throughout the Middle East (for example, read about molasses on *page 157*). Drying is the oldest known technique, and evidence of dried foods dates back as far as 12,000 BC. Drying fruit is an incredibly easy process that requires no additives (as with jam making), jars or special containers (like fermenting), and uses an abundant and easily accessible form of heat: the sun.

Fruit leather (*see page 145*), also thought to have originated in the Middle East, requires just a few more steps beyond simply drying fruit. Any ripe fruit can be pureed, or cooked down to a pulp over a fire, then spread into a thin layer to dry in the sun. The first references to leather are much later, in the Middle Ages, but it was an established form of preservation by then.

SOURCING AND STORING

Look for uniformity, without color or size variation, and no spots or blemishes, which all indicate good sourcing. You want a little moisture and a soft texture. Some fruit, especially dates and figs, can be very dark and hard, which suggests they're old and should be passed over. And the more wrinkled a date is, the older it is. The color will be affected by sulfur dioxide, an additive used to prevent oxidizing and darkening, but dates, figs, and barberries are treated with sulfites less often than light-colored fruit like dried apricots. While I'm not necessarily against sulfur, I will go for dried fruit without it when I have the option. All of this also applies to fruit leather, but in that case preservatives are harder to avoid.

On the packaging, look for fruit with a specific varietal—Medjool dates or Smyrna figs, for example—rather than a generic name, as that also indicates better sourcing. "Sun dried" on a package is always a good sign for me since it points to less industrial methods.

Store your dried fruit in an airtight container, out of the sun and in a cool spot, to prevent further oxidation. I recommend keeping dried fruit for no more than 6 months.

Dates

For many cultures in the Middle East, dates are a symbol of hospitality, used to greet guests along with coffee or tea.

AGRICULTURAL DETAILS

Date palms, *Phoenix dactylifera*, have been an important crop since Neolithic times. The exact origin of the date palm isn't known, but it thrives in the desert because its deep root system reaches groundwater inaccessible to other plants. The trees have been known to grow over one hundred feet tall, though farmers usually prune them for manageable harvesting. The fruit grows in bunches that can contain up to one thousand dates, and a single tree produces anywhere from one to three hundred pounds of fruit in a year. Dates are harvested during the late summer and early fall.

There are an estimated six hundred varieties of dates, which are categorized by moisture content: soft dates (Bahri and Halawy, for example), semisoft (Deglet Noor and Medjool), and dry or "bread dates" (Thoory is a common variety). The fruit is also classified into five standard categories based on maturity. The fruit we buy is often the final, most mature category, called tamer or tamr. The biggest producers of dates in the world are Egypt, Saudi Arabia, and Iran.

APPEARANCE AND FLAVOR

Dates average about 2 inches long. They range from a deep red-brown color to almost black and can be semidried with some remaining moisture or almost completely dried. Some dates are more fibrous than others. They are up to 70 percent sugar by weight and thus are very sweet, almost caramelly. My favorite type is the Medjool date because it has a rich flavor with a hint of acidity.

TRADITIONAL USES

Ramadan break fast — *throughout the region*
Dipped into clarified butter — *Oman*
Sautéed in samneh (*see page 249*) — *Iraq*
Stuffed with almond paste and rose water — *throughout the region*
Batheeth (desert) — *Gulf countries*

Recipe Ideas

1. Stuff dates with cheese or nuts as an appetizer, or go the Spanish route and wrap with bacon and roast them.

2. For a main course, make the Braised Stuffed Apricots and Dates (*page 153*).

3. Add dates to stews, and as they fall apart, they'll sweeten the dish and thicken it.

4. Make a Date "Shake" (*page 155*).

5. If all you do with your dates is eat them while drinking coffee and tea, that is a great use of them.

Figs

When figs are in season, you can catch a whiff of their sweet perfume in the air. The smell instantly takes me back to picking them as a child, always surrounded by that honeyed scent.

AGRICULTURAL DETAILS

The domesticated fig tree, *Ficus carica*, is descended from the wild caprifig tree and is probably native to an area that includes Turkey, Iran, and Syria. Figs were first cultivated sometime between five and six thousand years ago in the Middle East. Early varieties needed to be pollinated in a complicated way by the tiny fig wasp, *Blastophaga psenes*. Luckily, a variety we call the "common fig" emerged during the Roman Empire (Romans consumed quite a lot of figs) that didn't require the insect to fruit. The wild caprifig and common fig, along with Smyrna and San Pedro, represent the four types, each with many more subvarieties and colors to try.

Harvest season is usually late summer, though some trees fruit twice a year. Figs do not continue to ripen off the tree, so they must be picked at peak ripeness. They are then dried in the sun until most moisture is gone, which can take up to ten days. Certain varieties, like Turkish Smyrna figs, have a white surface bloom, which results from their sugars rising to the surface and crystallizing in the heat.

APPEARANCE AND FLAVOR

Dried figs generally come in two types. There are the large, flat Turkish-style figs that are beige to light brown, and the Black Mission figs that are smaller and dark, nearly black in color. Most figs have a molasses-like sweetness with just a touch of pepperiness and a seedy texture. Smyrna figs—a large, plump white variety from Turkey—are considered by many to be the best dried figs, with their complex, fragrant sweetness and moist interior. Black Mission figs have a robust flavor with a hint of bitterness and a slightly dry interior.

TRADITIONAL USES

Charoset (Passover fruit compote) — *throughout the region*
Jam — *throughout the region*
Raki (alcohol) — *Turkey*

Recipe Ideas

1. Sauté dried figs with onions, a little bit of vinegar, and chicken livers for a quick appetizer.

2. Stuff large dried figs with ground lamb, beef, or goat cheese, all seasoned with herbs and spices, then bake them in seasoned liquid.

3. To make a sweet version of the braise described above, stuff the figs with ground nuts and bake in milk or cream mixed with honey.

4. Make Lebanese-Style Poached Dried Figs (*page 148*) and use as an accompaniment to meat and cheese.

Barberries

Known as zereshk in Iran, where they're most popular, barberries are another staple in my cooking, along with sumac (*see page 25*), for adding sour notes to almost any type of dish without additional liquid.

AGRICULTURAL DETAILS

There are many varieties of barberries that grow wild in Asia and Europe, where they are thought to be native. The species used for its edible sour berries in Iran and elsewhere is *Berberis vulgaris* and was first cultivated in Iran about two hundred years ago. Iran continues to be a top producer. Barberry plants were eradicated in many other countries (but not Iran) after the discovery that they host a fungus that can wipe out wheat crops.

They grow on a perennial bush that's eight to ten feet tall with yellow flowers. The berries are bright red, about the size of a small currant with an elongated shape, and hang in clusters. They ripen in the late summer or early fall and are harvested then. They're harvested on the branch by hand, then the stalks and leaves are separated. Barberries are traditionally dried in the sun or indirectly in the shade, although now more industrial dehydration methods are used.

APPEARANCE AND FLAVOR

Barberries have a tart, acidic flavor and a small, wrinkled appearance with a firm texture and a color that ranges from a bright reddish pink to dark red. Some discerning consumers won't buy them if they're a darker red color, as it's a sign of oxidation and, to them, poor quality. I don't mind dark barberries and haven't noticed any difference in taste.

TRADITIONAL USES

Zereshk polow (pilaf) — *Iran* (see recipe, *page 150*)
Tachin (rice cake) — *Iran*
Kuku sabzi (frittata) — *Iran*
Khoresh zereshk (stew) — *Iran*

Recipe Ideas

1. Use them whole, as is (I never sauté or rehydrate mine first, but you can if you prefer the texture), to garnish roasted vegetables or lamb chops.

2. Add them at the beginning of cooking when making a stew if you want them to soften and start to break apart, or midway through cooking a dish like roasted chicken to retain some of their texture.

3. Swap in any recipe that calls for unsweetened dried cranberries.

Leder

Fruit needn't be only dried whole to preserve it, and there's a long tradition of fruit leathers in the Middle East.

PRODUCTION

Fruit leather goes by many names in the region—lavashak in Farsi, basteigh or basteil in Armenian, and leder in Hebrew. In Arabic, it's mostly called amardeen or qamar al-din, which is a reference to leather made with apricots, by far the most popular type. Other common types include mulberry, plum, apple, grape, date, sour plum, sour cherry, kiwi, and pomegranate. Apple or other high-pectin fruits may be added to help supplement low-pectin fruit such as barberry or pomegranate. Turkey and Syria are big producers of fruit leather.

To make it, fresh fruit is washed (and pitted, if necessary), then either cooked down into a pulp or pureed raw. Sugar is optional, especially if the fruit is already sweet, like apricot. The fruit leather's flavor can be kept simple or it can be seasoned with spices and olive oil, or thickened with bulgur or flour. The puree is then spread very thinly onto trays and left to dry in the sun, in a dehydrator, or in a very low oven. If the leather is dried the traditional way, it must be brought in at night and can take several days to dry.

APPEARANCE AND FLAVOR

Dried leathers will vary in taste, of course, depending on what fruit they're made from, but generally speaking they are all quite tart (even if sugar is added) and with an intense fruit flavor, and all are a far cry from the commercial fruit roll-ups available for kids in the United States. The color is typically dark reddish, though apricot, which is usually the sweetest, is often a bright orange since it commonly contains sulfur. Fruit leather is sold in thin sheets, and the texture is chewy but shouldn't be tough. Look for a short ingredient list without sugar or any crazy preservatives, although sulfur or citric acid may be unavoidable.

TRADITIONAL USES

Qamar al-din (Ramadan beverage and pudding) — *throughout the region*
Snack — *throughout the region*

Recipe Ideas

1. Fruit leather can be used like molasses or dates in a savory stew to thicken and flavor the dish, as long as there is ample cooking time for the leather to break down (try pomegranate or barberry).

2. When reconstituted and pureed, fruit leather can be added to drinks, sorbets, and baked goods.

3. Finely chop and add to salads for a little bite and a sweet fruity flavor.

Lebanese-Style Poached Dried Figs

These spiced, slowly poached figs with walnuts and lemon zest are lovely served on a cheese board or to accompany roasted meats or charcuterie.

Makes about 2 cups

½ cup	honey
2 tablespoons	pomegranate molasses
2 teaspoons	ground ginger (4 grams)
2 teaspoons	ground star anise (3 grams)
½ teaspoon	freshly ground black pepper (1 gram)
⅛ teaspoon	fine sea salt (1 gram)
8 ounces	dried Mission figs, stems removed (about 1½ cups)
½ cup	walnuts, broken into quarters
1	lemon, zest peeled in strips, then juiced
1 tablespoon	sherry vinegar
1 tablespoon	rose water

In a heavy-bottomed saucepan (ideally a size that will fit the figs in a single layer or as close as possible), stir together 2 cups water, the honey, pomegranate molasses, ginger, star anise, pepper, and salt. Add the figs, walnuts, and strips of lemon zest.

Bring the liquid to a boil, then adjust the heat so it simmers gently. Cook, basting occasionally, until the figs are fully hydrated and the liquid has reduced by half, about 1 hour.

Remove the pot from the heat and add the lemon juice, vinegar, and rose water, swirling to mix the liquid and basting to coat the figs one final time. Serve warm or at room temperature.

Storage Directions
Cool the figs completely and store them covered in the refrigerator for up to 1 week. Let them return to room temperature before serving.

Zereshk Polow
(Persian Barberry Rice)

Barberries are not used enough outside of Persian cooking, sadly! I love their concentrated, tart taste and beautiful jewel tone. This dish showcases their sour and sweet taste with the addition of fragrant saffron and bright orange zest. The recipe's classic Persian steamed rice technique produces fluffy and completely separate grains.

Serves 6

3 tablespoons	extra-virgin olive oil
3 teaspoons	fine sea salt (15 grams), plus more as needed
½ cup	dried barberries
	Pinch of saffron threads (n/a)
1 tablespoon	warm water
2 teaspoons	sugar
2 cups	basmati rice
1	small yellow onion, halved and thinly sliced lengthwise
¼ cup	slivered almonds
	Grated zest of 1 small orange
1 tablespoon	loosely packed dried rose petals (optional; 1 gram)
1 teaspoon	rose water

In a large pot, bring 6 cups water, 1 tablespoon of the oil, and 2 teaspoons (10 grams) of the salt to a boil.

In a small bowl, cover the barberries with room-temperature water and let soak while you prepare the other ingredients. Put the saffron in a small bowl and mix with the warm water and sugar. Set aside.

Wash the rice in a large bowl of cold water by swirling it with your hand, then pour off the water while keeping the rice in the bowl. Repeat until the water runs clear.

When the water boils, add the drained rice and stir once, then reduce the heat to medium so the water simmers, and cook the rice until it's halfway cooked through (you can break a few grains in half and test), 8 to 12 minutes, depending on the rice. Drain in a sieve, rinse the rice to cool it, then drain thoroughly.

Return the pot to the stove. Add 1 tablespoon of the oil and ¼ cup water and mix well. Using a large spoon or spatula, spoon the rice into the middle of the pot, mounding each spoonful on top of the previous. Continue until all the rice is added and forms a pyramid-shaped mound in the middle of the pot.

Cover the pot with a clean kitchen towel or double layer of paper towels and then firmly press the pot lid on top. Fold the edges of the towel up and over the lid and away from the flame. Cook over low heat until the rice is fluffy and fully cooked, about 25 minutes.

Meanwhile, in a heavy-bottomed skillet, heat the remaining 1 tablespoon oil over medium heat until hot. Add the onion, season with the remaining 1 teaspoon (5 grams) salt, and cook until the onion is softened, about 10 minutes. Drain the barberries, add them to the skillet along with the almonds and orange zest, and cook for 2 minutes more, just to heat through. Add the saffron water, rose petals (if using), and rose water and stir to combine. Remove from the heat and set aside (make sure the mixture is ready before the rice is done).

As soon as the rice is ready, place one-third of the rice on a serving platter. Top with one-third of the barberry-almond mixture. Repeat the layering two more times with the remaining rice and barberry mixture. Serve right away.

Braised Stuffed Apricots and Dates

Dried fruits are the real star of this impressive dish. Filled with ground beef and rice, the apricots and dates soften in the oven and absorb the savory, spiced braising liquid. The bigger the dried fruits are, the easier they will be to stuff, but really any dried fruit will work—they can be butterflied open and molded around the filling.

Serves 6

½ cup	basmati rice

Spice Blend

2 teaspoons	ground allspice (4 grams)
2 teaspoons	ground coriander (4 grams)
2 teaspoons	ground turmeric (5 grams)
1 teaspoon	freshly ground black pepper (2 grams)

Stuffed Fruit

1 pound	ground beef
1	small onion, finely diced
½ cup	roughly chopped fresh flat-leaf parsley
3	garlic cloves, finely chopped
1	large egg
1 tablespoon	fine sea salt (16 grams)
20	large whole dried apricots
20	large dates, split open and pitted

Braising Mixture

2 tablespoons	extra-virgin olive oil
1	medium onion, halved and thinly sliced lengthwise
	Salt
1 cup	French green lentils
¼ cup	tomato paste

Wash the rice in a large bowl of cold water by swirling it with your hand, then pour off the water while keeping the rice in the bowl. Repeat until the water runs clear. Cover the rice with room-temperature water and soak for 1 hour, then drain.

Make the spice blend: In a small bowl, mix the allspice, coriander, turmeric, and pepper until thoroughly combined.

Prepare the stuffed fruit: In a large bowl, combine the drained rice, ground beef, onion, parsley, garlic, egg, salt, and half of the spice blend (7.5 grams) until just combined. Do not overwork the mixture.

Divide the filling into 40 portions (about 1 tablespoon or 20 grams each) and roll each into a ball. If necessary, split the apricots open more to fit around the filling (most apricots are sold split). To assemble, wrap a split apricot or date around each portion and press gently to hold everything together. Repeat until you've stuffed all of the dried fruit. Preheat the oven to 350°F.

Make the braising mixture: In a deep heavy-bottomed 12-inch skillet or Dutch oven, heat the oil over medium-low heat until hot. Add the onion, season with salt, and cook, stirring occasionally, until the onion is very soft, golden, and well caramelized, about 40 minutes. Stir in the lentils, tomato paste, and remaining spice blend (7.5 grams) and spread into an even layer. Turn off the heat.

Alternating between adding apricots and dates, cover the surface of the pan with fruit in concentric circles in a single layer. Carefully pour 6 cups water around the edges of the pan and between the fruit (avoiding pouring on the filling) to submerge the fruit. Bring the liquid to a boil, then reduce the heat so it simmers gently, and cover.

Transfer the pan to the oven (put it on a sheet pan, if necessary, to catch any spillover) and cook for 30 minutes, checking to make sure the water is simmering (if not, turn the oven up to 375°F). After 30 minutes, test the filling. If the rice is not yet tender, continue cooking, covered, until it is. Uncover the pan and continue to cook until the meat, lentils, and rice are tender and the liquid has reduced to a saucy consistency, about 30 minutes more. Serve hot.

Date "Shake"

I discovered date shakes when I traveled to Palm Springs, California, as an adult—but I wish I had known about them much sooner, as they combine two of my childhood favorites: sweet dates and rich milkshakes. This is my sophisticated version made with classic Middle Eastern ingredients like tart labne and fragrant orange blossom water. It's a lighter shake made without ice cream and naturally sweet from both dates and concentrated date molasses. The recipe can easily be doubled to serve four.

Serves 2

1 cup	pitted dates
1 cup	boiling water
1 cup	cold water
½ cup	labne or Greek yogurt
2 tablespoons	silan (date molasses)
2 tablespoons	tahini
½ teaspoon	orange blossom water
1 cup	ice

Put the dates in a heatproof medium bowl, cover with the boiling water, and set aside for 5 minutes to soften. Drain the dates, discarding the water.

Transfer the dates to a blender and add the water, the labne, silan, tahini, and orange blossom water. Blend until smooth.

Add the ice and blend again until smooth and thick. Serve immediately.

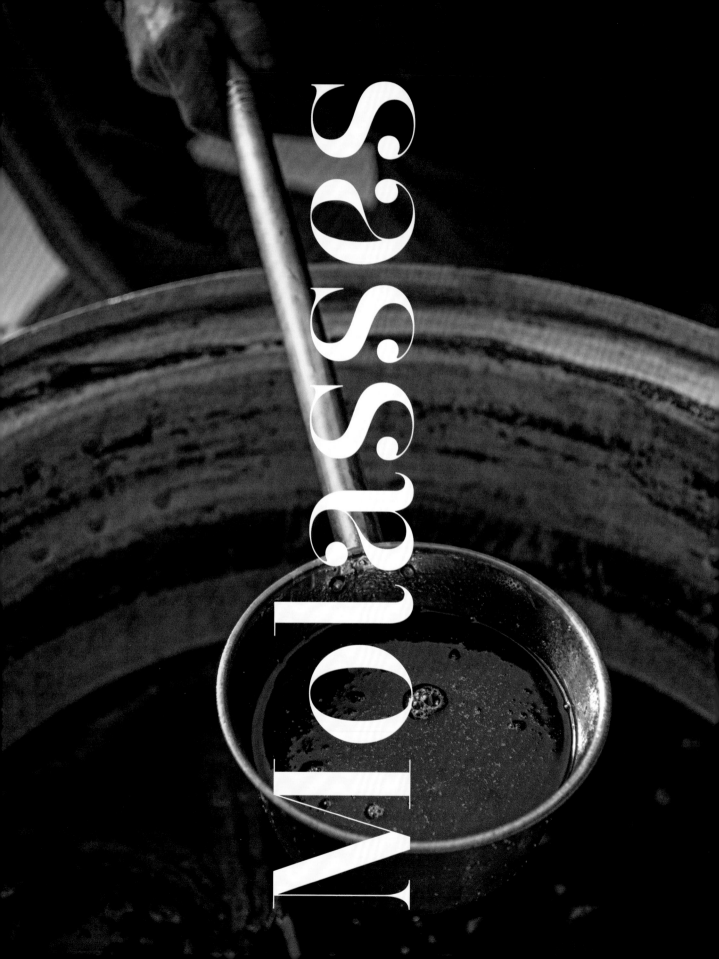

Molasses

{ MOLASSES }

دبس

pekmez

דְּבְשָׁה

רב

μέλασσα

ηη2ωρ

What makes molasses such a versatile ingredient is that it was meant to act like sugar but adds so much more to a dish than just one-note sweetness. It's sometimes tart, nearly savory, or even slightly smoky. Molasses made from pomegranates and dates (called silan) have both become popular around the world. In addition to those two, the other most common types of molasses in the Middle East are made from carob and grape, though they can actually be made from nearly any fruit: mulberry, orange, fig, apple,

and cactus fruit molasses exist. Next time you think a dish needs honey or sugar, try using fruit molasses instead for a sweet and concentrated fruit flavor that complements a surprising range of ingredients.

ORIGIN AND HISTORY

Before the arrival of cane sugar in the Middle East—and long before it became affordable—there was fruit molasses, which was made as a way to preserve fresh fruit and filled a need for sweetness beyond the harvest season. Some historians now believe the "honey" referred to in the Old Testament was not from bees but rather was silan, made from dates. It's probably no coincidence that the most common types of molasses are made from three of the biblical seven species meant to demonstrate the agricultural fertility of the region: grapes, dates, and pomegranate. The hieroglyph for the carob pod is ancient Egyptian for "sweet."

SOURCING AND STORING

For all fruit molasses, look for an ingredient list that consists of just the fruit and perhaps water. I look for a thick viscosity and pronounced flavor. The appeal of molasses is in its complex sweetness that can have hints of clove-like spice, umami savoriness, or intense tartness (depending on the type), so you're looking for something more than just "sugary." A darker color will generally mean a more concentrated product, unless caramel coloring (which is best avoided) is listed in the ingredients.

Store molasses in a cool, dry place away from sunlight. Kept tightly sealed this way, it should last for more than a year (in fact, for many years). If you have molasses that's starting to solidify, submerge the bottle in warm water to thin it out. As long as there is no sign of mold, it's good to use.

Silan

Date molasses, sometimes called date honey or date syrup, is silan in Hebrew (which is how I refer to it) and rub or dibs in Arabic. It's a millennia-old sweetener that's a little acidic, with a hint of fruitiness and a chocolate-like complexity.

PRODUCTION

The ancient recipe remains essentially the same for silan made today. Traditionally, silan is produced after the date harvest, which runs from late August to October. The dates are soaked, cooked until they turn into a pulp, and pressed, and the resulting liquid is simmered and reduced to a thick, viscous liquid. Sometimes the partially reduced liquid is poured into trays and left to finish reducing in the sun.

Old-style pressing methods were often elaborate. One involved putting the pulp in strainer baskets, which were then put between two boards that people stood and jumped on to extract as much of the juice as possible. These days, commercial makers often steam the dates before pressing them into a syrup using mechanical presses—a much simpler process.

APPEARANCE AND FLAVOR

Date molasses has a rich, caramel-like flavor with none of the burnt notes of actual caramel. There's a hint of fruit and acid, similar to good chocolate, and an almost savory aroma. The texture is silky and smooth and a little lighter than honey. It should be a deep, dark brown.

TRADITIONAL USES

Dibs bi tahini (sweet dip) — *throughout the region*
Salgham helu (stewed turnips) — *Iraq*
Muhammar (rice dish) — *Gulf countries*
Luqamaat (sweet fritters) — *UAE*

Recipe Ideas

1. Spread bread with tahini and then drizzle with silan.

2. Use in marinades for grilled or roasted poultry and vegetables.

3. Use in place of honey in salad dressings.

4. Make a Date "Shake" (*page 155*) with dates and silan.

5. Make Spiced Silan Carrots (*page 167*).

Grape Molasses

The rich, sweet flavor of this molasses comes not from fine grape varietals but rather from whatever grapes are available at harvesttime. The product is so popular that about one-fifth of Turkey's annual grape crop is used to make molasses.

PRODUCTION

The production of grape molasses follows much the same rhythm as other types of molasses in that it is traditionally made in the early fall after the harvest. Any type of grape can be used (green grapes are most common), and the deep color comes from caramelizing the sugars over the length of cooking.

Much like for making wine after harvest, freshly picked grapes are crushed to release their liquid. The resulting mixture of solids and liquid is known as must. The must is mixed with a natural mineral compound (referred to as soil or molasses soil) that is mostly calcium carbonate, which clarifies the must and alkalinizes it. After sitting for a few hours, some soil rises to the top and creates a foam that is skimmed off, and the remaining juice is carefully transferred to a pot, leaving the rest of the soil that settled to the bottom behind. The mixture is then cooked down. As with silan (*see page 158*), some small makers will finish the process in the sun.

APPEARANCE AND FLAVOR

Very sweet with slightly bitter undertones, grape molasses has a hint of clove and a pungent aroma. It's a deep, dark purple color, with a runnier consistency than pomegranate molasses.

TRADITIONAL USES

Simit (bread) — *Turkey*
Cevizli sucuk or soutzioukos (walnut candy) — *Turkey, Cyprus*
Diluted as a drink — *Turkey, Levant* (see Jallab, *page 173*)

Recipe Ideas

1. Mix with tahini and spread on bread for breakfast or a snack.

2. Finish seared halloumi with it—the combination of treacly grape and salty cheese is superb.

3. Mix with vinegar as a sweet and sour sauce for meat or vegetables.

4. Make Goat Cheese, Grape, and Walnut Salad with Grape Molasses Dressing (*page 165*).

5. Try your hand at Homemade Grape Dibs (Molasses) on *page 163*.

Pomegranate Molasses

While all molasses falls firmly into the "sweet" category of flavors, and many are interchangeable, pomegranate molasses is known for its intense, pucker-inducing taste that many of the cuisines in the region cherish. For instance, *rumman* is Arabic for "pomegranate," and the famous Palestinian dish *rummaniyeh*, amply flavored by the molasses, simply translates to "pomegranate-y."

PRODUCTION

The juice of sour varieties of pomegranates is used to make molasses. Perhaps surprisingly, the sour types have a higher sugar content than the pomegranates that are eaten out of hand (which may explain why many homemade pomegranate molasses recipes call for added sugar). To make molasses, the arils—the seeds and surrounding flesh—are crushed or pureed and then strained, and the bright red juice is boiled down until it becomes a dark, viscous liquid with no hint of its former jewel tone.

APPEARANCE AND FLAVOR

Pomegranate molasses is the most acidic and fruity of the molasses varieties, with an intensely concentrated flavor. The balance of sweet to sour can vary by brand and country of origin, but all are bracingly tart. The viscosity is thicker than that of date or grape molasses but less thick than that of carob. It's a very dark brown, almost black color.

TRADITIONAL USES

Fesenjan (stew) — *Iran* (see recipe, *page 113*)
Muhammara (dip) — *Syria, Lebanon, Turkey* (see recipe, *page 110*)
Dolmas — *throughout the region*

Recipe Ideas

1. Add to a barbecue sauce for a brighter flavor.

2. Pair it with lamb chops prepared your preferred way—in a marinade or as part of a sauce—or make Pomegranate-Roasted Leg of Lamb (*page 170*).

3. Drizzle over rich desserts like roasted figs or vanilla ice cream.

4. Pair with eggplant and tomato, prepared nearly every way.

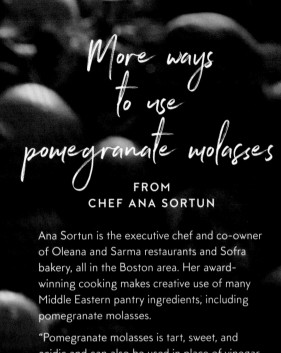

More ways to use pomegranate molasses

FROM CHEF ANA SORTUN

Ana Sortun is the executive chef and co-owner of Oleana and Sarma restaurants and Sofra bakery, all in the Boston area. Her award-winning cooking makes creative use of many Middle Eastern pantry ingredients, including pomegranate molasses.

"Pomegranate molasses is tart, sweet, and acidic and can also be used in place of vinegar or lemon. Making it is very labor-intensive, and unfortunately there are many commercial brands that add too much sugar and coloring to offset the cost of labor and fruit. Make sure you use a quality product.

"I use this pantry gem to add brightness to a rich stew after it has been braised all day. A spoonful at the end of cooking takes something rich and blends in intensity and acidity. The same goes for any and all cooked vegetable dishes—use it as you would a splash of vinegar in pepper relishes, chopped salads, gazpachos, and roasted eggplant dishes. It makes a wonderful dressing for fattoush and a great glaze for roasted lamb or chicken wings. I love to mix a spoonful of molasses with about the same amount of melted butter and drizzle it over hummus."

Carob Molasses

This ancient sweetener's complexity can overpower many other ingredients, but when added to long-cooked dishes with other strong ingredients like lamb or chocolate (it works *with* chocolate, not just as a substitute), its pungent qualities mellow, and the jammy, roasted fruit flavors shine.

PRODUCTION

The molasses is made from the 6- to 12-inch-long pods from the carob tree. They are picked when dark and ripe, the bitter seeds are discarded, and the pods are used to make molasses. The cracked pods are soaked for a few hours to dissolve the natural sugars, then the water is strained and reused to soak a fresh batch of pods. This is repeated multiple times. The resulting liquid is boiled until it becomes thick and concentrated, at which point it is traditionally removed from the heat and continually stirred until it cools.

In Cyprus, carob is known as black gold because it was once the island's main export.

APPEARANCE AND FLAVOR

This is a heavy, dark molasses with a smoky, chocolaty, sometimes fruity flavor that packs a powerful punch. It has layers of caramel and dried fruit notes like prunes or raisins and is slightly bitter and nuanced like chocolate.

TRADITIONAL USES

Sfouf b'debs (molasses cake) — *Lebanon*
Pastelli (toffee) — *Cyprus*
Dibs bi tahini (sweet dip) — *throughout the region*

Recipe Ideas

1. Add it to chocolate desserts to play up chocolate's bitter complexity.

2. Use in a marinade for long-roasted meat like leg of lamb and braised meats like beef or rabbit.

3. Make Carob Molasses Roast Chicken (*page 168*).

Homemade Grape Dibs
(Molasses)

The word *dibs* means "molasses" (or "concentrate") in Arabic and applies to a boiled-down syrup made with any type of fruit. I think grape dibs is a perfectly easy and simple introduction to the process of making your own molasses. The amount of time it will take varies greatly, depending on the dimensions of your pot and strength of your stove, so stay close and look for the visual cues described in the recipe. The end product may not be as perfectly smooth as a store-bought molasses, but it's just as delicious as an ice cream sundae topping, drizzled onto pancakes or waffles, added to a cheese plate, or in a salad dressing (see Goat Cheese, Grape, and Walnut Salad with Grape Molasses Dressing, *page 165*).

Makes about 2 cups

10 pounds black grapes

Pick through the grapes, removing any spoiled or excessively bruised ones. Remove the stems and wash the grapes.

Put the medium disk into a food mill and fit the mill over a large bowl. Process the grapes in small batches until all grapes have been juiced and no fruit is left on the skin. Discard the solids.

Pour the juice through a fine-mesh sieve into a large heavy-bottomed pot. Bring the juice to a boil, skimming away any foam or impurities as they rise. Continue cooking, adjusting the heat as necessary to keep the juice at a steady boil and occasionally scraping the bottom and sides with a silicone spatula to prevent burning, until the juice begins to thicken and look shiny, about 1 hour (but the time can vary greatly).

Reduce the heat so the juice is at a low-to-medium simmer and continue cooking until it has reduced to the consistency of honey (the final amount of dibs varies depending on the grapes you started with, so you may have a bit more or less than 2 cups). Pour the molasses into a clean 1-quart container and let cool to room temperature before covering. When cool, the molasses will be very thick and may possibly crystallize.

Storage Directions
The molasses will keep for several months, covered, in the refrigerator. If the molasses begins to crystallize, submerge the container in warm water to loosen it.

Goat Cheese, Grape, and Walnut Salad

with Grape Molasses Dressing

Grapes are used in three different forms in this colorful salad to really drive home their versatility: grape molasses to make caramelized walnuts, verjus as the acidic component of the dressing, *and* fresh grapes, which complement the creamy fresh goat cheese.

Serves 4

Caramelized Walnuts

1 cup	walnuts
1 tablespoon	grape molasses, homemade (*page 163*) or store-bought
	Salt
	Aleppo pepper

Dressing

2 teaspoons	grape molasses, homemade (*page 163*) or store-bought
1 teaspoon	extra-virgin olive oil
1 teaspoon	verjus, homemade (*page 56*) or store-bought
	Salt
	Aleppo pepper

Salad

1½ cups	red grapes, halved
4	sprigs fresh mint, leaves picked and chopped
5 ounces	fresh goat cheese, crumbled
1 tablespoon	nigella seeds (8 grams)
	Extra-virgin olive oil, for serving

Make the caramelized walnuts: Preheat the oven to 350°F. Line a sheet pan with parchment paper.

In a medium bowl, toss the walnuts with the grape molasses and season to taste with salt and Aleppo pepper. Transfer the walnuts to the prepared pan, reserving the bowl. Bake until the walnuts look and smell caramelized, about 15 minutes. Set the walnuts aside to cool.

Make the dressing: In the same bowl used to mix the nuts, whisk together the grape molasses, oil, and verjus. Season to taste with salt and Aleppo pepper.

Assemble the salad: Add the grapes and half of the mint to the dressing and gently stir to combine. Arrange the cheese on a serving platter, then top with the grape mixture, followed by the caramelized walnuts, nigella seeds, and remaining mint. Finish with a drizzle of oil and serve.

Spiced Silan Carrots

I often roast carrots, always with an ever-changing mix of spices and seasonings that play up their earthy flavor. In this dish, the silan adds sweetness, of course, but also an unexpected savory note. The cumin and paprika create a nearly meat-like flavor. I prefer oil-cured olives to cook with, but use whichever olives you can find or like best. The resulting caramelized carrots can be served at any temperature, as a side dish or added to a grain salad.

Serves 4

8	medium carrots, scrubbed but not peeled, and trimmed
2 tablespoons	extra-virgin olive oil
2 tablespoons	silan (date molasses)
1½ teaspoons	ground cumin (3 grams)
1½ teaspoons	hot or sweet paprika (4 grams)
	Salt
½ cup	pitted black olives, preferably oil-cured, halved
1	lemon, cut into 6 wedges

Preheat the oven to 400°F. Line a sheet pan with parchment paper.

Cut the carrots into 2-inch pieces and any particularly thick sections in half, if necessary. In a large bowl, combine the carrots with the oil, silan, cumin, and paprika and season with salt. Fold in the olives and lemon wedges. Transfer the mixture to the prepared pan and spread into a single layer.

Roast until the carrots are nicely caramelized and easily pierced with a knife, flipping the carrots every 10 minutes, 25 to 30 minutes total. Serve warm or cold.

Carob Molasses Roast Chicken

Carob molasses adds a multifaceted, roasted undertone to the flavor of chicken, plus it helps the skin brown beautifully. There's no substitute for it, and if you are at all intrigued by carob molasses, I highly recommend sourcing a jar and trying this dish. Carob deserves to be seen as so much more than just a chocolate substitute. It's one of my secrets for a perfectly roasted chicken, along with very generously seasoning the poultry with salt. If you don't want to remove the backbone from the chicken yourself (called spatchcocking), have your butcher do it for you.

Serves 4

1	whole chicken (3½ pounds)
½ cup	extra-virgin olive oil
1 cup	broken vermicelli (½-inch pieces)
2	medium yellow onions, halved and sliced lengthwise
1	medium bulb fennel, halved and sliced lengthwise
2	garlic cloves, finely chopped
1 teaspoon	fine sea salt (5 grams), plus more as needed
1 teaspoon	ground coriander (2 grams)
1 teaspoon	ground sumac (3 grams)
1 teaspoon	crumbled dried za'atar leaves (0.5 grams)
½ teaspoon	Aleppo pepper (1 gram)
½ teaspoon	ground cumin (1 gram)
2 tablespoons	carob molasses

Preheat the oven to 375°F.

To spatchcock the chicken, place the chicken breast-side down on a cutting board. Using kitchen shears or a sharp knife, cut along both sides of the backbone and remove it. Flip the chicken breast-side up and firmly press on the breastbone until the chicken lies flat.

Heat a heavy-bottomed 12-inch skillet over medium heat. When the pan is hot, add the olive oil and vermicelli. Toast the noodles, stirring often, until the pieces are evenly golden brown, about 5 minutes. Add the onions, fennel, garlic, and 1 teaspoon (5 grams) salt and stir to combine. Remove from the heat.

In a small bowl, stir together the coriander, sumac, za'atar leaves, Aleppo pepper, and cumin and season very generously with salt. Rub the chicken all over, front and back, with the carob molasses, then season with the spice mix.

Lay the chicken flat on top of the vermicelli-vegetable mixture and bake, basting occasionally, for 1 hour.

Reduce the oven temperature to 350°F and continue to bake until a thermometer inserted into the thickest part of the breast registers 165°F, another 10 to 25 minutes. Remove from the oven and let the chicken rest for 15 minutes before carving and serving warm.

Pomegranate-Roasted Leg of Lamb

Slow-roasted leg of lamb gets not only a deep, rich color from the pomegranate molasses but also plenty of sour accents and fruit flavor—from both the molasses and the pomegranate juice—that counteract the meat's richness. Remember to take the meat out of the refrigerator 45 minutes to 1 hour before roasting, to ensure even cooking. Cold meat, or larger, tougher legs can add an hour or more to cooking time. Serve this with Zereshk Polow (Persian Barberry Rice, *page 150*) to play up the sweet-tart flavor even more.

Serves 8

- 1 medium onion, halved and sliced lengthwise
- 4 medium red beets, peeled and cut into 1-inch wedges
- 6 garlic cloves, unpeeled
- 1 tablespoon ground cardamom (6 grams)
- 1 tablespoon ground coriander (6 grams)
- 1 tablespoon ground cumin (7 grams)
- 1 tablespoon fine sea salt (16 grams)
- 1 tablespoon Urfa chile (7 grams)
- 1 whole bone-in leg of lamb (6 to 7 pounds)
- 2 tablespoons pomegranate molasses
- 1 quart pomegranate juice

Preheat the oven to 375°F.

In the bottom of a large roasting pan, spread the onion, beets, and garlic in a single layer.

In a small bowl, stir together the cardamom, coriander, cumin, salt, and Urfa chile. Rub the lamb all over with the pomegranate molasses, then with the spice mixture. Place the lamb on top of the bed of vegetables and pour the pomegranate juice over the vegetables (avoiding the lamb so as not to rinse off the seasoning). Roast for 1 hour.

Reduce the oven temperature to 325°F, pour 2 cups water over only the vegetables, and baste the lamb. Continuing roasting until the lamb is completely tender, about 4 more hours, basting every hour. To test, grip the leg bone and twist it. If the bone is exposed and twists easily (as if you were removing the bone), the roast is ready.

Remove from the oven and let the lamb rest for 15 minutes before carving. Serve warm.

Jallab

This intensely flavorful, incredibly refreshing drink is popular in the Levant during the hottest days of summer. It's usually made from a mix of molasses and rose water, and I recommend finding your perfect balance of fragrant grape, tart pomegranate, and savory date molasses—or even strong carob molasses. In some establishments, before serving the jallab, the glasses are held upside down over burning incense to capture the smoky musk, then are filled with plenty of ice, their signature mix of molasses, and a generous topping of pine nuts, blanched almonds, pistachios, and/or golden raisins.

Serves 2

1 cup	boiling water
2 tablespoons	grape, pomegranate, or date molasses (or a mix)
1 teaspoon	honey
1 cup	cold water
¼ teaspoon	rose water or orange blossom water, or more to taste (optional)
4 cups	ice
1 tablespoon	pine nuts, for garnish

In a heatproof bowl or measuring cup, whisk together the boiling water, molasses, and honey until thoroughly combined and the molasses has dissolved. Stir in the water to cool the mixture. Add the flower water (if using).

Divide the ice between two large glasses, divide the jallab between the glasses, and garnish with the pine nuts. Serve right away.

Variation
For a (nontraditional) cocktail, add about 1½ ounces vodka to each glass.

Flowers

{ FLOWERS }

زهور

çiçekler

פְּרָחִים

گل‌ها

λουλούδια

ծաղիկներ

Scent and smell play an incredibly important part in how you experience a meal. Roses and orange blossom water don't really add much taste at all—but their aroma can take a dish to an ethereal level. Whether distilled into a concentrated condiment, dried and added to a spice mix, sprinkled as a garnish, or used fresh to make a jam, flowers contribute to classic Middle Eastern flavor profiles that have been refined for generations.

ORIGIN AND HISTORY

The cuisines of the ancient societies of the Middle East made use of many flowers, but roses and orange blossoms are two of the most popular flowers still used in cooking today. Both are thought to be native to China and first cultivated widely in ancient Persia. For thousands of years, they have been used as a breath freshener and in beverages, perfumes, pickles, soaps, sweets, and more. The petals were infused into any number of other ingredients to impart their scent—wine, sugar, milk, honey, and water—and used for both edible and olfactory reasons.

There is some debate about when distillation was discovered and how long it's been used, but the first written formula for rose water is generally traced back to the tenth-century Persian doctor and philosopher known as Avicenna, who used sweet cabbage rose to make rose water. The process converts a liquid (in this case water mixed with flower petals) into a vapor and then condenses it back into liquid in an alembic still. This creates a more concentrated taste and aroma that will last longer than simply infusing water. It also gives the final product a fresh, clean taste.

Once distillation was widespread, flower waters became an integral part of Middle Eastern cooking. Many pastries today are soaked in a sugar syrup after baking, and the sugar syrup is very often scented with rose water, orange blossom water, or a combination of the two. Puddings and cakes are frequently garnished with flower petals just to drive home the association between floral scents and sweet treats.

Rose

You probably associate roses with sweetness—desserts, holidays, floral scents—but they work beautifully in savory cooking, too, especially with meats and roasted vegetables.

AGRICULTURAL DETAILS

The rosebush is a perennial plant that blooms each spring. The flowers are harvested in the late spring and summer in the early morning, when rose's oil content is highest and the flower has opened but the oils have not yet been burnt off by the sun. The rose varieties most used in cooking are the cabbage rose, the damask (or Damascus) rose, and the musk rose. Roses are cultivated and farmed in Iran and Turkey.

Once harvested, fresh petals are sold as is, distilled to make rose water, or turned into jam; or the petals, buds, and leaves are dried and then sold whole or ground. Drying roses never happens in the sun because of the sun's effect on the delicate oils. Rose water is traditionally distilled only during a two-month window when roses bloom (*see page 175* for more on the distilling process).

APPEARANCE AND FLAVOR

Rosebuds and leaves are floral, sweet, and slightly acidic. The buds are a little more pungent than the leaves, which I also use. Rose jam is, of course, very sweet as well as floral, with a pleasant toothsome texture from the petals. Rose water has very little taste—it's just lightly bitter—but it adds a lovely sweet aroma to food. The "soapy" taste that some associate with roses is from overuse. In moderation, the taste and fragrance play a delightful background note to whatever else the dish has going on. Heat fades the aroma, so always add rose water at the end of cooking.

SOURCING AND STORING

When buying rose petals or buds, it is very important to purchase flowers that haven't been sprayed with chemicals. Make sure there aren't stems and rocks mixed in with the dried leaves and buds. Store them out of direct sunlight in an airtight container, since the flowers are sensitive to light and attractive to bugs.

For rose water, strength varies from brand to brand; try a few until you find one you like. My favorite brand is Mymouné from Lebanon. Look for "distilled rose water" in the ingredient list to make sure it's not just rose-flavored water or that the rose water hasn't been diluted with other ingredients. Rose water will keep for quite a while in your pantry. If kept over a year, though, the aroma will start to fade.

TRADITIONAL USES

Sholeh zerd (rice pudding) — *Iran*
Loukum — *Turkey* (see Rose Loukum, *page 184*)
Biryani — *Oman*
Balaleet (vermicelli dish) — *Gulf countries*
Salep (drink) — *Turkey, Iran*

Recipe Ideas

1. Splash rose water onto fresh fruit or berries as a simple dessert.

2. Used alone or in a blend, rose petals are fantastic crumbled or sprinkled over roasted vegetables.

3. Season chicken soup with the dried buds or petals.

4. Add a few drops of rose water to coffee or tea.

5. Fill cakes or top ice cream with rose jam.

Orange Blossom Water

Unless you have access to a Seville orange tree, you have probably only encountered orange blossoms in the strong, sweetly scented distilled ingredient commonly used in desserts, though the dried petals are another wonderful ingredient to add to your cooking. Use them to make your own orange blossom water with the Flower Water recipe on *page 178*.

AGRICULTURAL DETAILS

Orange trees are most likely native to China and northern India and were brought farther west first by ancient Persians, then later by the Romans. The trees currently grow in many areas throughout the Middle East because of the favorable climate. Egypt, Turkey, and Iran grow the most, commercially, in the region.

Also known as sour orange or bitter orange, the fruit from Seville orange trees, *Citrus × aurantium*, is a cross between a pomelo and a mandarin and is perhaps best known in the US as the main ingredient in marmalade. The small, white, fragrant flowers are harvested in the spring when they bloom. Only the petals are distilled (*see page 175* for more on the distilling process) into orange blossom water.

APPEARANCE AND FLAVOR

Orange blossom water is a clear liquid with an intensely sweet, fresh fragrance and only a slightly bitter taste. Compared to rose water, it is stronger in scent and should be applied the same way: with a very light touch at the end of cooking.

SOURCING AND STORING

Look for pure distilled orange blossom water with no other ingredients on the label. Try a few brands until you find one with an aroma that's the right strength for you. Store out of direct sunlight, which can cause the lingering traces of essential oil in it to yellow.

TRADITIONAL USES

White coffee — *Lebanon, Turkey, and more* (see Flower White Coffee, *page 179*)
Ater (sugar syrup for pastries) — *throughout the region*

Recipe Ideas

1. It's magnificent when used to accentuate the floral flavors of fresh stone fruit or tomatoes.

2. A few drops can make fresh oranges taste even more like themselves—as in the Orange Salad with Orange Blossom Dressing (*page 181*).

3. Add it to a clean, simple broth made from chicken or beef.

4. Use delicately as a seasoning for raw fish and seafood.

Flower Water

I don't expect that many people own an alembic still, but I wanted to share a version of flower water that could be easily made at home. This steeped version doesn't have the same strength as commercial distillations, so you may need to add more to taste if using it in a recipe.

Makes 3½ cups

3½ cups	distilled water (don't use tap water)
1 cup	loosely packed dried rose petals (12 grams), 1 cup dried jasmine blossoms (23 grams), or ½ cup dried orange blossom petals (13 grams)

In a sterilized 1-quart jar or similar size of container, combine the distilled water and flower of your choice. Stir and cover. Steep the flowers overnight at room temperature. The following morning, transfer the jar to the refrigerator and continue to steep for 1 week. Strain the mixture through a fine-mesh sieve and discard the flowers.

Storage Directions
Store the flower water in a clean container in the refrigerator for up to 2 weeks.

Flower White Coffee

Another drink known as white coffee (the other, on *page 47*, is made from spices and very lightly roasted coffee beans) from the region, this one is a perfect after-dinner version with zero caffeine and all the soothing digestive properties of flower water.

Serves 1

1 cup	boiling water
1 teaspoon	honey
1 teaspoon	orange blossom water or rose water
	Dried orange blossoms or rose petals, for garnish (optional)

In a mug, combine the boiling water, honey, and flower water and stir until the honey dissolves. Garnish with the flower petals (if using) and serve immediately.

Orange Salad
with Orange Blossom Dressing

Orange blossom water is mainly used in the Middle East for desserts and sweets, but it's great in savory dishes as well. Mixed into a salad dressing with a diverse blend of spices, it enhances the flavor of the citrus that here is paired with crunchy cucumbers, sharp radishes, and fresh herbs.

Serves 6

Oranges

3	large navel oranges
3	blood oranges

Dressing

¼ cup	extra-virgin olive oil
2 tablespoons	freshly squeezed lemon juice
2 tablespoons	orange blossom water
½ teaspoon	Espelette pepper (1 gram)
½ teaspoon	fine sea salt (3 grams)
½ teaspoon	freshly ground black pepper (1 gram)
½ teaspoon	onion powder (2 grams)
½ teaspoon	ground sumac (2 grams)

Salad

5	medium radishes, thinly sliced
2	medium Persian (mini) cucumbers, thinly sliced
¼ cup	fresh cilantro
¼ cup	fresh mint, large leaves torn
¼ cup	pistachios, toasted (see page 99) and roughly chopped

Prep the oranges: Zest the navel oranges with a Microplane until you have 2 tablespoons zest and set the zest aside in a small bowl. Trim the top and bottom of one of the navel oranges so that it sits flat on your cutting board. Peel the orange by following the round shape with a knife, cutting from top to bottom and discarding strips of pith. Slice the orange crosswise into ¼-inch-thick rounds. Peel and slice the remaining navel and blood oranges the same way.

Make the dressing: To the bowl with the reserved orange zest, add the oil, lemon juice, orange blossom water, Espelette pepper, salt, black pepper, onion powder, and sumac. Whisk until well combined.

Assemble the salad: On a large serving platter, arrange a single layer of navel and blood orange slices, followed by radishes, cucumbers, cilantro, mint, and pistachios, repeating until all of the ingredients have been used.

Just before serving, drizzle on the dressing.

Malabi

Street food isn't just savory in the Middle East. You can also get desserts, baked goods, and other sugary treats. One of the most famous sweet offerings is malabi, which is similar to panna cotta. I have fond memories of buying it from a street cart on the hottest days of summer, topped with cherry syrup and chopped nuts. It's lightly sweet and perfect for scorching-hot temperatures. These days, I like to top mine with pomegranate molasses and chopped pistachios, fresh cherries or figs, or caramelized nuts.

Serves 8

3 cups	whole milk (720 grams)
⅓ cup	sugar (65 grams)
¼ cup	cornstarch (35 grams)
1 tablespoon	rose water (15 grams)

In a small saucepan, mix 2½ cups (600 grams) of the milk with the sugar. Bring to a simmer over medium-high heat, whisking occasionally to help dissolve the sugar.

Meanwhile, put the cornstarch in a small bowl and whisk in the remaining ½ cup (120 grams) milk and the rose water until smooth.

When the milk simmers, stir the cornstarch mixture again to incorporate anything that may have settled at the bottom of the bowl, then slowly add it to the simmering milk while whisking constantly to prevent lumps. Reduce the heat so the mixture simmers gently and cook, whisking constantly so the bottom doesn't burn, until the mixture thickens and coats the back of the spoon, 1 to 2 minutes.

Pour the mixture into eight 4-ounce ramekins or other small serving dishes or glasses. When the custard is no longer steaming, gently cover the surface of each with plastic wrap (no need to press down). Refrigerate until the malabi has set but is still gently wobbly in the center, at least 4 hours. Serve cold.

Storage Directions
The malabi will keep, covered, in the refrigerator for up to 3 days.

Rose Loukum

Rahat loukum, or simply loukum, is a popular confection in the region (you may know it as Turkish delight) that is soft and chewy and can sometimes be cloyingly sweet, but I love it. I developed a greater appreciation for loukum working in France, where I was asked to make them at a Michelin three-star restaurant as part of the dessert program. The recipe is simple, calling for very few ingredients. The creative part is in using different flavorings like hard cider and sparkling wines to customize them. I've included the traditional rose water in my recipe, but once you've made them and have the technique down, try your own customized additions.

Makes 64 pieces

Loukum

	Neutral vegetable oil, for the pan
3 cups	granulated sugar (600 grams)
1 tablespoon	freshly squeezed lemon juice (15 grams)
¾ cup	cornstarch (105 grams)
½ teaspoon	cream of tartar (2 grams)
2 tablespoons	rose water (30 grams)

Coating

½ cup	powdered sugar (50 grams)
¼ cup	cornstarch (35 grams)

Variation
Add ½ cup (70 grams) roughly chopped pistachios to the mixture with the rose water.

Make the loukum: Grease an 8- or 9-inch square baking pan with oil. Line with parchment paper, then grease the parchment.

Clip a candy thermometer to the side of a medium saucepan. Add the granulated sugar, lemon juice, and 1 cup plus 2 tablespoons (270 grams) water. Cook the mixture over medium heat, stirring occasionally only if needed to help the sugar dissolve, then bring to a boil, undisturbed. When the mixture boils, reduce the heat so the syrup simmers and cook until the mixture reaches 235° to 240°F (soft-ball stage). Remove from the heat and set the syrup aside.

In a large saucepan, combine the cornstarch, cream of tartar, and 2¼ cups (540 grams) water. Stir until no lumps remain. Set the pan over medium heat and bring to a boil while stirring. Cook until the mixture has a glue-like consistency, about 5 minutes.

Gradually drizzle the reserved syrup into the cornstarch mixture while stirring constantly. Continue cooking and stirring until the mixture has thickened and is slightly milky, about 5 minutes. Reduce the heat so the mixture simmers, and cook, stirring frequently, until it has thickened, is slightly shiny, and turns lightly golden, 45 minutes to 1 hour.

Remove from the heat and stir in the rose water, then pour the mixture into the prepared pan. Spread into an even layer and cool completely to room temperature, at least 4 hours.

Make the coating: In a wide, shallow dish, mix together the powdered sugar and cornstarch.

Sprinkle some of the mixture over a clean work surface. Turn the cooled loukum out onto the surface and cut into an 8 × 8 grid of squares (or any size you like). Working a few at a time, toss each square in the cornstarch mixture to coat. Repeat until all the squares are coated, and serve.

Storage Directions
Coat any loukum not eaten
immediately in the remaining
cornstarch mixture, then keep
them in an airtight container
in a cool, dry place for up to
1 week. The loukum may absorb
the coating, but if any is left,
gently tap off the excess before
serving.

Aysh el-Saraya
(Lebanese Bread Pudding)

This is a sophisticated way to use up leftover bread. Some recipes call for bread crumbs, but I opt for whole slices to soak up the rose-infused syrup—and I prefer cheap, store-bought bread over a quality homemade loaf. Unlike many other types of bread pudding, this version is not baked. It's a great make-ahead dessert for warm weather.

Serves 12

Rose Water Syrup

½ cup	boiling water (120 grams)
½ cup	sugar (100 grams)
¼ cup	freshly squeezed lemon juice (60 grams)
2 tablespoons	rose water (30 grams)

Milk Custard

2½ cups	whole milk (600 grams)
2 cups	heavy cream (475 grams)
½ cup	sugar (100 grams)
6 tablespoons	cornstarch (54 grams)
2 tablespoons	grated lemon zest (12 grams)
2 tablespoons	rose water (30 grams)

Assembly

12	slices white sandwich bread, crusts removed and lightly toasted
½ cup	pistachios, chopped (65 grams)

Storage Directions
The pudding will keep, covered, in the refrigerator for up to 3 days.

Make the rose water syrup: In a small heatproof bowl, whisk the boiling water and sugar together until the sugar has dissolved. Allow the syrup to cool to room temperature, then stir in the lemon juice and rose water.

Make the milk custard: In a heavy-bottomed medium saucepan, combine 2 cups (480 grams) of the milk, the cream, and sugar and warm over medium heat, stirring occasionally to help dissolve the sugar, until steaming but not boiling.

Meanwhile, in a small bowl, whisk the remaining ½ cup (120 grams) milk with the cornstarch until smooth. When the cream mixture steams, slowly drizzle the cornstarch slurry into the pot, whisking constantly to prevent lumps.

Continue cooking and whisking, scraping the sides and corners of the pot with a silicone spatula as needed to prevent burning, until the mixture bubbles and thickens, about 10 minutes. The custard should look smooth and thick but still be pourable (it will thicken as it cools). Remove from the heat and stir in the lemon zest and rose water.

Assemble the bread pudding: Spread ½ cup (125 grams) of the hot custard onto the bottom of an 8- or 9-inch square baking dish.

Arrange 4 slices of bread in a single even layer so there is no overlap. Drizzle 6 tablespoons (90 grams) of the syrup onto the bread and allow it to soak in for a few seconds. Spread 1 cup (250 grams) of the custard over the soaked bread.

Add another layer of bread and drizzle with ½ cup (140 grams) of the syrup, allowing it to soak in for a few seconds. Spread 1 cup (250 grams) of the custard over the bread.

Add the remaining 4 slices of bread and remaining syrup, letting it soak in again. Pour the remaining custard over the top, then gently tap the dish on the counter to knock out any air pockets and even out the top. The custard should completely cover the bread and fill in the pan between the bread layers.

Evenly sprinkle the pistachios over the top (you may not need them all, depending on the size of your pan). Cover the dish with plastic wrap and refrigerate overnight to set. Slice into squares and serve chilled.

Honey

{ HONEY }

عسل

bal

דְּבַשׁ

عسل

μέλι

մեղր

In Israel, my family never bought honey. Not because we didn't eat it but because the kibbutz had a thriving honey business (and still does; see Dan-Galil Honey, *page 193*). We'd go to the bee-keeper's hut with our empty jars and fill them up with whatever the honey of the moment was. If we were lucky, the beekeeper would give us kids a piece of honeycomb as a treat. I have vivid memories of being there, surrounded by bees and the warm, intoxicating smell of honey.

It was magical roaming around the fields as a kid and seeing the hives everywhere. Perhaps because of my fond memories, I have quite the soft spot for honey. I enjoy all honey, as long as it's a real, pure product, and to this day, one of my favorite ways of consuming it is simply by the spoonful.

ORIGIN AND HISTORY

Humans have been eating honey for tens of thousands of years—some historians believe since the very beginning of our history. For much of

this time, honey was considered a gift directly from the gods—Aristotle claimed that bees had divine qualities. Many pots of honey were found in Egyptian tombs to accompany the dead in the afterlife. The oldest written reference to honey is Egyptian, from about 5500 BC (Lower Egypt was once known as Bee Land). Sometime about three thousand years after that, Egyptians discovered smoke's taming effect on bees and that wild swarms could be convinced (or forced) to build their honeycombs in man-made hives.

Not much about the basics of beekeeping changed until the mid-nineteenth century, when Lorenzo Langstroth designed the collateral hive. It had removable frames that bees used to build individual combs and allowed for movement and air circulation inside the hive. This revolutionized beekeeping, as until this point, the entire hive would often have to be smashed or otherwise destroyed to get to and remove the comb to harvest the honey. Now, a hive can be used season after season, with much less disruption for the bees and easy harvesting for beekeepers.

PRODUCTION

Honeybees travel from flower to flower collecting liquid nectar, and when a bee has filled up its dedicated nectar stomach, it flies back to the hive to deposit its haul into a honeycomb. Worker bees in the hive fan the nectar to evaporate much of the water, and when the consistency is reduced enough to their liking (or perhaps more accurately, their instincts), the honey is ready. The bees cap each cell in the honeycomb with wax to store the honey.

Human intervention can happen at every stage. Creating enticing hives for wild swarms of honeybees makes collection much easier, and moving the hives close to a field or grove of one type of plant or flower during its blooming period yields a single (or *mostly* single) varietal honey. A honeybee can visit thousands of flowers in a single day, so the best way to ensure a single-flower honey is to make sure they don't have too many tempting options.

To harvest honey, beekeepers use the original method discovered millennia ago: wafting smoke into the hives to calm the bees for a long enough period to collect the honey, usually ten to twenty minutes. The smoke works two ways: It causes the bees to gorge on honey for their hasty exit from the "burning" hive to find a new home, which weighs them down, and prevents bees from picking up on danger pheromones produced by other bees. While the bees are subdued, the honeycomb is removed and the honey is collected.

APPEARANCE AND FLAVOR

Honey is, of course, sweet, but also incredibly complex. It is naturally sweeter than cane sugar, but because there are so many other flavoring components from flowers in honey, we don't perceive it that way. The taste also will vary by season. For example, during the summer, honey is much more concentrated and stronger because plants retain less water.

How honey looks and pours depends on the source flower: The colors range due to the pigments in the flowers, and the texture varies because of the different ratios of sucrose to simple sugar in the nectars. Thus, you can get a runny, nearly clear honey or a dark, viscous variety almost like molasses, and any gradation in between.

SOURCING AND STORING

I can't tell you what exact types to seek out, as one of the most exciting things about honey is that it is a product of the local environment. I might not get the avocado blossom honey of my youth in New York City, but I can purchase dark and rich buckwheat honey or full-bodied blueberry blossom honey. Go to a farmers' market and see the diversity available in your area. To find a quality product, look for information on the bees' territory or indication of what the bees were feeding on. Avoid products labeled simply "honey" with no sense of where it was made and what flowers the bees visited. This honey will not have the terroir that makes this food so special. Good honey should have a strong, warm scent and lots of character.

Honey will never spoil as long as bacteria and water are kept out of the jar. Keep it in a well-sealed jar and out of direct sunlight. Contrary to what many people believe, crystallization does not mean the honey has gone bad. It's actually the sign of a quality, pure product. If your honey crystallizes or turns cloudy, simply submerge the jar in warm water and it will liquefy and clear.

TRADITIONAL USES

Briwat bi loz (pastry) — *Turkey*
Feteer meshalet (pancake) — *Egypt*
Baklava (pastry) — *throughout the region* (see recipe, *page 117*)
Basbousa (semolina cake) — *throughout the region*

Recipe Ideas

1. Labne or tahini mixed with honey is a morning go-to for me.

2. Mix honey, any fat, and spices (the combinations are endless and you really can't go wrong) and use the mixture to season vegetables or poultry before roasting.

3. Make Honey-Glazed Beets with Orange (*page 197*).

Honey

Started in the 1960s by Kibbutz Dan members, the Dan-Galil honey company has five thousand hives disbursed around Galilee and Golan producing between 100 and 140 tons of honey per year. Their goal is to sell out within a year of harvesting—which is never a problem.

To run a quality honey production operation, beekeepers must be in perfect tune with nature. Every year, Zohar Rudolph and his team monitor the winter rainfall, which helps them plan where the best flowers and highest yields will be and thus where to move their hives. The honey season starts around April, when they begin harvesting and packaging as they go, and ends in late September.

Most of the honey Dan-Galil produces is a blended wildflower honey that changes color and flavor from year to year, as no two seasons are ever the same. And because Israel is so small, it's difficult to have 100 percent single-varietal honey. The bees will roam wherever they please, collecting any and every nectar they encounter. Dan-Galil is, however, able to make a few types of honey that are predominantly one type of flower.

EUCALYPTUS HONEY

There is a large concentration of eucalyptus trees in the area, and so Zohar makes a mostly eucalyptus blend. It's a thick amber honey with the tree's famous camphor and mint aroma.

CHRIST'S THORN JUJUBE HONEY

This tree blooms three times per year, which allows Zohar to collect enough of this robust honey to sell.

CLOVER HONEY

Some springs, Zohar is able to produce mild, sweet clover honey because there are such large areas of clover in northern Israel, but it all depends on plentiful rainfall, which nature doesn't always provide.

AVOCADO BLOSSOM HONEY

The company offers its hives to farmers and growers who need the pollinators. Many of the plants yield very little nectar, so they don't collect honey from these bees. The one exception is avocado—the flowers produce a good volume of nectar, and the plots are usually quite big, and Zohar is able to harvest and sell the deep, dark, slightly savory honey.

Honey will go bad if it's heated, so unlike larger producers who apply heat to their honey to prevent crystallization, Zohar never heats his honey to more than 100°F (some heat is required to kill yeast that can cause fermentation), and the honey preserves its nutritional benefits, such as its antibacterial properties. (Interestingly, honeybees keep their hives at exactly 93°F.)

Global warming, less rainfall, and unpredictable yields are concerning for beekeepers. As is the Varroa mite, a parasite that kills honeybees globally (also known as Varroa destructor). Additionally, as much as technology improves and new equipment becomes available, the bulk of the work of making honey has not changed since ancient times—it's still very hard manual labor, and workers are always in short supply. Challenges like these, and collapsing honeybee populations, mean it's more important than ever to support your local beekeepers.

Zohar Rudolph and his beehives, Upper Galilee, Israel

Honey-Glazed Beets with Orange

Beets lend themselves to so many flavors and cooking techniques. Here they are braised and then glazed in the same pan with a favorite spice combination of mine (cardamom and Aleppo) plus tart vinegar and plenty of sweet honey. Pair them with a long-cooking main, such as roast chicken (try Carob Molasses Roast Chicken, *page 168*), as the beets need ample cooking time to become tender.

Serves 2 to 4 as a side dish

1	medium orange
1 pound	beets, peeled and cut into ½-inch wedges
¼ cup	honey
3	cardamom pods, cracked
½ teaspoon	Aleppo pepper (1 gram)
½ teaspoon	fine sea salt (3 grams)
1	garlic clove, smashed
2 tablespoons	cider vinegar
¼ cup	fresh cilantro leaves

Use a vegetable peeler to remove the zest of the orange in large strips; set aside. Trim the top and bottom of the orange so that it sits flat on the cutting board. Remove the pith by following the round shape of the orange with a knife, cutting from top to bottom. Finely dice the orange; discard any seeds.

In a large heavy-bottomed skillet or Dutch oven, arrange the beet wedges in a single layer and add the honey, cardamom, Aleppo pepper, salt, garlic, and reserved orange zest. Fill the skillet with enough water to cover the beets by 1 inch. Bring the water to a boil, then adjust the heat so the water simmers. Cover and cook until the beets are tender, about 10 minutes.

Remove the cardamom pods and garlic. Add the vinegar and increase the heat to high. Reduce the liquid until it glazes the beets, swirling the pan as the liquid thickens so the beets are coated evenly. The time will vary depending on the dimensions of your pan and how much water was needed, but it may take up to 45 minutes or longer.

Garnish with the diced orange and cilantro and serve warm.

Lokma with Honey-Saffron Syrup

These small fritters are popular in nearly every country in the region. They do not need to be perfectly round and, in fact, *should* be a little rustic and rough. The uneven dough adds more texture to each bite. The soak in honey syrup and final coating of chopped pistachios make for a perfect dessert.

Serves 6

Dough

1 to 1¼ cups	lukewarm water (240 to 300 grams)
1 teaspoon	instant yeast (3 grams)
1 teaspoon	sugar (5 grams)
2 cups plus 2 tablespoons	all-purpose flour (300 grams)
3 tablespoons	cornstarch (27 grams)
½ teaspoon	fine sea salt (3 grams)

Syrup

¾ cup	sugar (150 grams)
½ cup	honey (170 grams)
3 tablespoons	freshly squeezed lemon juice (45 grams)
	Pinch of saffron threads (n/a)

To Finish

Neutral vegetable oil, for frying

Crushed pistachios, for garnish

Make the dough: In a small bowl, stir together ½ cup (120 grams) of the lukewarm water with the yeast and sugar and let sit until the yeast is foamy, about 10 minutes.

In a medium bowl, whisk together the flour, cornstarch, and salt. Form a well in the middle and pour in the yeast mixture and ½ cup (120 grams) of the lukewarm water. Whisk vigorously until the dough is sticky, stretchy, and loose, 3 to 5 minutes. If the dough is dry and stiff (like a bread dough), slowly add up to another ¼ cup (60 grams) of the remaining lukewarm water. Cover the bowl with plastic wrap and proof until the dough has doubled in size, about 1 hour.

Meanwhile, make the syrup: In a small saucepan, combine the sugar, honey, lemon juice, saffron, and ¾ cup (180 grams) water. Bring the mixture to a boil, stirring occasionally just to dissolve the sugar, then adjust the heat so it simmers gently. Cook for 3 minutes. Remove from the heat and cool to room temperature.

Finish: When you're ready to fry the lokma, clip a deep-fry thermometer to the side of a small or medium Dutch oven or other heavy-bottomed pot. Pour in 2 inches of oil (or halfway if your pot is less than 4 inches tall). Bring the oil to 350°F. Fill a small bowl with water and keep it by the stove. Line a sheet pan with paper towels. Have the cooled syrup nearby as well.

Give the dough a quick stir to knock out some of the air. Dip a teaspoon into the water, then scoop out 1 rounded teaspoon of the dough, using the side of the bowl to help shape the ball (they don't need to be perfectly shaped). Drop the dough into the oil and repeat with a few more dough balls, taking care not to crowd the pot.

Fry the dough until evenly golden brown, flipping once, 6 to 8 minutes per batch. Once the lokma are cooked, use a spider or slotted spoon to transfer them to the paper towels. After the excess oil has drained off, transfer the hot lokma to the syrup and soak for 5 minutes, then transfer to a colander to drain. Repeat with the remaining dough, making sure the oil comes back up to temperature between batches.

To serve the lokma, toss them with some of the remaining syrup, sprinkle with the pistachios, and serve warm.

Kunafe

My all-time favorite dessert, kunafe, consists of shatteringly crisp kataifi pastry (shredded phyllo) filled with cheese, all soaked in honey syrup. It has become a mission of mine to find the perfect version of it outside of the Middle East. One challenge is sourcing the traditional Nabulsi cheese. I came up with a combination that gets pretty close to its uniquely salty brined flavor and soft texture by combining three cheeses. Kunafe is also usually made entirely on the stovetop, but I find it's easier to bake it most of the way in the oven. This helps the shredded pastry crisp and brown deeply and evenly—as does ghee, which won't burn at the higher temperature used.

Serves 8

Filling

1 pound	creamy farmer cheese (or substitute cottage cheese)
¾ cup	grated halloumi cheese (80 grams)
½ cup	grated whole-milk mozzarella cheese (50 grams)
1 tablespoon	honey

Pastry

1	(1-pound) box frozen kataifi, thawed according to the package directions
1 cup plus 2 tablespoons	ghee (225 grams), melted
½ cup	powdered sugar (50 grams)

To Finish

¾ cup	honey (355 grams)
1 teaspoon	orange blossom water (5 grams)
½ cup	roughly chopped pistachios (70 grams), for garnish

Preheat the oven to 400°F.

Make the filling: In a small bowl, mix the farmer cheese, halloumi, mozzarella, and honey until thoroughly combined. Keep at room temperature.

Make the pastry: Cut the kataifi into 2- to 3-inch pieces. In a large bowl, mix the kataifi, 1 cup (200 grams) of the ghee, and the powdered sugar and stir, fluffing and tossing the kataifi to separate and coat each strand well.

Brush the bottom and sides of a 10-inch nonstick ovenproof skillet with the remaining 2 tablespoons (25 grams) ghee.

Spread half of the kataifi mixture in an even layer in the prepared pan. Spread the cheese mixture evenly on top, leaving a ½-inch border around the edge, then top with the remaining kataifi mixture, making sure it encloses the filling.

Set the skillet over low heat. As the kataifi starts to sizzle, cook for 5 minutes, giving the pan a light shake to make sure the kunafe is moving freely in the pan.

Transfer the skillet to the oven and bake until golden brown on top and warmed through, about 25 minutes.

Cover the skillet with a larger, flat plate. Hold the plate firmly against the pan with one hand and grip the handle (using a towel or oven mitt) with the other. In one swift movement, turn the skillet and plate over together. Slide the kunafe back into the skillet with the bottom now facing up and put it back on the stove over low heat to crisp the other side until golden brown, about 5 minutes. You want the kunafe to be nicely browned on the top and bottom and warmed through. (If either side is not as golden as you like, repeat the flipping and browning.) Transfer to the plate you used to flip the kunafe, leaving the ghee in the pan.

Finish: In a small saucepan, warm the honey over low heat just until it's runny. Remove from the heat and stir in the orange blossom water. Drizzle the warm syrup over the hot kunafe and garnish with the chopped pistachios. Slice and serve warm.

Storage Directions
Kept covered and refrigerated,
the kunafe will be good for
3 days.

Bint el Sahn

With its layers of flaky dough soaked in butter and honey and baked until golden, this traditional Yemeni cake is one to add to your repertoire. The toasted sesame oil and nigella seeds keep it from being cloyingly sweet and add intriguing, savory flavor. The cake is best eaten warm just out of the oven and does not keep well.

Serves 8

Dough

1 cup plus 1 tablespoon	lukewarm water (250 grams), plus more as needed
2 tablespoons	sugar (25 grams)
1 tablespoon	instant yeast (10 grams)
2 cups	bread flour (250 grams)
1¾ cups	all-purpose flour (250 grams), plus more for rolling
1½ teaspoons	fine sea salt (8 grams)
⅓ cup	lukewarm milk (70 grams)

Assembly

8 ounces	(2 sticks) unsalted butter (220 grams), melted, plus more for the pan
¼ cup	toasted sesame oil (55 grams)
1⅓ cups	honey (450 grams)
¼ cup plus 1½ teaspoons	nigella seeds (35 grams)
1	large egg yolk

Make the dough: Put the lukewarm water into a small bowl or measuring cup and stir in the sugar and yeast until dissolved. Let sit until the yeast is foamy, about 10 minutes.

In a large bowl, stir together the bread flour, all-purpose flour, and salt. Make a well in the center and pour in the lukewarm milk and the yeast mixture. Slowly stir until a tacky, soft bread dough forms. Knead the dough in the bowl until it's soft, stretchy, and still tacky, 10 to 12 minutes. If the dough is dry and isn't sticking a bit to the bowl and your hands, add 1 to 2 tablespoons (15 to 30 grams) water to help get a soft texture. Cover with a dry cloth and proof until the dough doubles in size, about 1 hour.

Divide the dough into 12 equal portions (about 72 grams each) and shape them into balls. Cover with a damp cloth and let rest for 15 minutes.

Assemble the cake: Preheat the oven to 350°F. Generously butter the bottom and sides of a 10-inch springform pan.

In a small bowl, stir together the melted butter and the sesame oil.

Using a rolling pin and very little flour (the dough sticking a bit to your work surface helps stretch it out), roll one of the dough balls into a thin 10-inch round that's nearly see-through. When rolling, give the dough a quarter-turn after a few rolls to keep the shape even, and if the dough shrinks after you remove it from your work surface, let it rest for a few minutes and try again.

Place the round of dough in the springform pan. Using a brush, generously drizzle about 1 tablespoon of the melted butter mixture over this layer of dough. Drizzle with 1 tablespoon (22 grams) of the honey.

Roll out another dough ball the same way. Stack it on top of the dough round in the pan, drizzle with the butter mixture, then sprinkle with 1½ teaspoons (5 grams) of the nigella seeds.

Repeat this process with all but one of the dough balls, drizzling honey on every odd layer and nigella seeds on every even layer. Reserve the remaining butter mixture, nigella seeds, and ample honey for finishing the cake.

For the final layer using the last ball of dough, roll it out to 11 inches. Place the dough on the top and tuck in the sides. In a small bowl, beat the egg yolk with 1 tablespoon (16 grams) of the butter mixture, 1 tablespoon (22 grams) of the honey, and 1 tablespoon (15 grams) water, then brush it over the top of the dough. Sprinkle evenly with the remaining nigella seeds.

Bake until the top of the cake is a deep golden color and the interior is light and spongy, about 40 minutes. If the top darkens too quickly, cover the pan with foil halfway through the baking time and reduce the oven temperature to 325°F.

Remove the pan from the oven and immediately drizzle the remaining butter mixture and the remaining honey on top of the cake. Let it soak in for at least 10 minutes. Serve the cake warm.

Honey Sekanjabin
(Vinegar Drink)

If you're skeptical of vinegar as a drink ingredient, this recipe will convert you. Sekanjabin is a centuries-old, highly refreshing Persian drink usually made with a concentrated honey-vinegar syrup mixed with fresh produce. Think of it as a virgin cucumber-margarita-meets-a-mojito, with a delightful crisp acid profile from the vinegar. If you're looking for an actual cocktail, add vodka.

Serves 4 as a nonalcoholic drink or 6 to 8 as a cocktail

2 cups	boiling water
1 cup	honey
⅛ teaspoon	fine sea salt (1 gram)
1	small bunch fresh mint, a few leaves reserved for garnish
½ cup	distilled white vinegar
2	medium Persian (mini) cucumbers, cut into 1-inch pieces
1 tablespoon	grated lime zest (from about 2 limes)
1 tablespoon	freshly squeezed lime juice
8 ounces	vodka (optional)
	Ice, for serving

In a heatproof medium bowl or pitcher, whisk the boiling water, honey, and salt until the honey has dissolved. Stir in the mint sprigs and vinegar and cool to room temperature. Cover and chill in the refrigerator overnight to infuse the mint into the syrup.

When ready to serve, remove the mint, gently squeezing it to return every drop of flavored syrup to the bowl. Transfer the mixture to a blender and add the cucumbers, lime zest, and lime juice. Blend until smooth. If using vodka, blend it in now.

Add ice to each glass, then evenly divide the sekanjabin. Garnish with mint leaves and serve immediately.

Grain

حبوب

tahıllar

דְּגָנִים

غلات

σιτηρά

հացահատիկներ

Along with legumes and vegetables, grains make up the bulk of the Middle Eastern diet. Both long- and short-grain rice are used in the Middle East, and I cook both at home. I always have freekeh, bulgur, semolina flour, wheat berries, and vermicelli in my pantry. After reading this chapter, I hope you'll agree that simple staples like grains should not be treated as an afterthought—and that choosing superior products is always worth the effort to source them.

SOURCING AND STORING

For rice, basmati is the best substitute for the long-grain rice used in the region (the varietals used there are rarely exported), and any type of short-grain white rice is good for stuffings and sweets. Please skip buying shortcut quick-cooking or pre-cooked rice—the few minutes saved is not worth the compromise in taste and texture. Good-quality rice has a richer, nuttier taste and separate, fluffy grains when cooked. By good-quality, I mean branching out beyond the typical, cheap supermarket options and looking for brands that acknowledge the terroir of the rice, sort their product consistently (which makes for even cooking), pay attention to the way the rice is polished, and more. When you start looking for this level of detail, you'll see not all rice is created equal.

There are plenty of great high-quality wheat berries, freekeh, bulgur, semolina flour, and vermicelli available today. For these products, there should be no additives, the color should be uniform, and you should see no broken or crumbling pieces (or in the case of bulgur, dust), which may indicate the product is old. When choosing a specific brand, packaging with the varietal and country of origin lets you know the producer cares about details. A "best before" date minimizes the risk of oxidation. Bulgur and semolina come in different grinds, so pay attention to the labeling. Recipes will usually specify coarse, medium (only bulgur), or fine for semolina and bulgur.

Store wheat and rice in an airtight jar in a cool, dark place for no more than a year. Wheat oxidizes and starts to break apart, and flour will start to lose its gluten. Rice can in theory keep for years, but my recommendation is to keep what you need for two or three months, then replenish.

Rice

I think rice is often taken for granted, but by sourcing high-quality rice, and cooking it with the techniques that have been developed over centuries, such as the crispy Persian method for Tahdig on *page 218*, you'll know just how special rice can be.

ORIGIN AND HISTORY

The rice consumed in the Middle East—and much of the rest of the world today—evolved from a wild grass probably native to the Himalayas (there are also types of rice native to Africa and North America). This Himalayan rice was first grown in India, China, and other parts of Asia. As humans domesticated rice at least ten thousand years ago, they realized the best yields came from rice that thrived in shallow, but not stagnant, water.

Rice was probably not cultivated in the Middle East before the fourth century BC, most likely by the Babylonians first, then in Persia and Arabia, and eventually in Egypt by the seventh century AD. It didn't become a major crop in the region until the Islamic conquests of the first millennium AD. After invasions by the already rice-growing Arabs and the development of elaborate irrigation systems, rice was grown in all Muslim territories by the year 1000 AD. Later, during Ottoman rule, the demand grew so high that rice had to be imported from India.

AGRICULTURAL DETAILS

Oryza sativa, the strain of rice from Asia, is a labor-intensive crop with yields that are generally higher than that of wheat. Rice is an annual plant, a grass, that grows tall stalks topped with dense clusters of flowers that when pollinated become grains of rice. Most rice is grown in shallow water. The field, called a paddy, is submerged in a few inches of water for the length of the growing period.

Rice is harvested when the grains are a golden-yellow color. The stalks are cut and the husk of the rice kernel and the other remaining parts of the plant (the chaff) must be removed, which often happens in milling. What's left is brown rice. White rice is made by removing the outer layer of the rice (the bran) and the nutrient-dense part of the grain that spoils quickly called the germ. The grains may then be polished with glucose or talc and are dried for storage.

Rice is grown in Iraq, Egypt, Iran, and Turkey, but much is imported. Iranians tend to grow and use long-grain rice, while Egyptians grow a variety of short-grain rice most commonly used there.

APPEARANCE AND FLAVOR

I recommend basmati rice, preferably from India, as it's the best long-grain rice you can find in the United States, and any quality short-grain white rice will do as a substitute for Egyptian rice. Basmati is an aromatic, floral grain that's nutty and sweet with a firm texture when cooked properly. The grains are long and slender, and good basmati rice may be a very light golden color when dried. Short-grain rice is squatter and rounder in shape. The color is usually white and the flavor mild and slightly sweet.

Rice pudding — *throughout the region* (see Turkish Rice Pudding, *page 224*)
Tahdig (crispy rice) — *Iran* (see recipe, *page 218*)
Mushbuss (meat or seafood dish) — *Gulf countries* (see Mushbuss Rubyan, *page 62*)
Arseeyah (savory rice porridge) — *throughout the region*
Tachin (rice cake) — *Iran*

Recipe Ideas

1. I don't think you need to do much to rice to improve on it, but I do like to add saffron or turmeric to the cooking water for yellow rice, tomato paste to the pot when making a pilaf for red rice, or pomegranate molasses for pink rice.

2. Mix cooked rice with chopped herbs for a side dish.

3. Top any type of cooked rice with toasted nuts for added crunch.

4. Make Dolmas (*page 79*) stuffed with rice.

Wheat

I've grouped all the important wheat products in the Middle Eastern pantry—wheat berries, freekeh, bulgur, vermicelli, and semolina flour—into one section because they are all so closely tied to the agricultural product they come from. There's relatively little processing but so many ways to use one of humanity's first staple crops.

ORIGIN AND HISTORY

Wheat is most likely native to the Middle East and North Africa. Barley and wheat were the first cereals grown by humans, and over the course of many thousands of years, we selected wheat that grew large grains with easier-to-remove hulls, creating the crop we know today. Early wheat varieties were probably first cultivated in the Fertile Crescent, a swath of land that stretched from the Nile Delta, along the Euphrates and Tigris rivers to the Persian Gulf, over twelve thousand years ago. Durum wheat, a harder variety than common wheat (see Agricultural Details, below), was probably grown much later, around the first century BC.

AGRICULTURAL DETAILS

Wheat is a large genus of grasses. The most widely grown is *Triticum aestivum*, or common wheat, followed by durum wheat, *Triticum durum*. Emmer, *Triticum dicoccum*, an ancient wheat with a lower gluten content than common and durum wheats, was a more popular crop in the past, though is becoming easier to find now. All wheat grows in a thin stalk several feet tall, with a cluster of flowers at the top. Each self-pollinating plant has anywhere from twenty to one hundred flowers, depending on the species, each of which becomes a kernel of wheat. Depending on the strain of wheat, it's either sown in the spring for a fall harvest (known as spring wheat) or hardier varieties are planted in the fall for a spring harvest (known as winter wheat). Spring wheat varieties take about four months to mature, as does durum, while winter wheat takes up to twice as long.

When the wheat is golden and the ears of kernels are heavy, the wheat is harvested. The stalks are cut, grains are removed from the plant (called threshing), then the hull and any remaining parts of the plant known as chaff are removed (called winnowing). What's left is the whole kernel (the wheat berry) with all parts of the seed—endosperm, bran, and germ—intact. The wheat is then dried to extend its shelf life for storage. Turkey and Iran grow the most wheat in the region.

PRODUCTION

The process described above results in wheat berries that are ready to be consumed. If they are destined to be another product, the process is slightly different.

Freekeh is believed to have been first "discovered" about four thousand years ago, perhaps after farmers tried to salvage their young wheat crop after a fire. They most likely sorted through the burned chaff to discover the immature, moist wheat berries were unharmed. Now the stalks are purposefully burned to create a prized toasted, earthy taste. To do so, "green" or underripe durum wheat stalks are harvested and piled in the fields to dry in the sun for a short period. The wheat is set on fire to burn only the chaff, not the young berries. Next, it's threshed and winnowed and sun-dried again. The berries may be left whole or cracked like bulgur (see below).

Bulgur is made from several types of wheat, including durum. It is believed to be about the same age as freekeh, originating in southeastern Turkey, though we have fewer details about how the process was developed. There are three

grades: Medium and coarse are used for tabbouleh and similar dishes, and fine bulgur is used to make doughs, such as for kibbeh. The wheat berries are boiled until they split, fully dried, and the bran removed. They are then ground in a mill into one of the three grades, which are separated by sifting. Nowadays most bulgur is kiln-dried as opposed to the traditional sun-drying.

"Noodles" appear in Arabic dictionaries in the fourteenth century AD and were presumably made from durum wheat. Because durum, which dries very well, was grown in the Middle East before Italy, there is even speculation that it was the Arabs who made early versions of dried pasta that were later introduced to Italy (with fresh noodles most likely originating in China). Vermicelli is often made from durum wheat flour. It's mixed with water and perhaps salt, then extruded through a special tool to make the thin noodles. They're fully dried—either in the sun or in an oven—making them ready for storage.

Semolina flour, used for pastries, puddings, pasta, and breads, is made from durum wheat. The threshed and winnowed grains are milled to remove the bran and germ, leaving just the starchy center, and ground into coarse or fine flour.

APPEARANCE AND FLAVOR

Wheat has a mild nutty taste with a slight savoriness, the only outlier being freekeh, which has a more prominent toasted flavor. Some freekeh tastes more smoky than others.

Bulgur, wheat berries, vermicelli, and semolina all have a golden color. The semolina is a bit whiter in the Middle East than the almost-yellow flour you'll find in the US. Freekeh has a green tinge and is slightly darker than the rest.

When cooked, wheat has a soft and chewy texture. Semolina flour is coarser than all-purpose flour, with a texture like fine sand. Vermicelli retains a nice bite when toasted before cooking and is often used this way in rice pilafs throughout the region.

TRADITIONAL USES

Freekeh or bulgur pilaf — *throughout the region*
Koubeh (semolina dumplings) — *Israel, Iraq, and more* (see Koubeh Soup, *page 221*)
Tabbouleh (bulgur salad) — *Levant and more* (see recipe, *page 215*)
Kibbeh (bulgur fritters) — *Levant and more* (see Kibbeh with Pine Nuts, *page 106*)
Balaleet (sweetened vermicelli) — *Gulf countries*
Hariss, h'riss, haleem (wheat berry stew) — *throughout the region*

Recipe Ideas

1. Cook freekeh (or wheat berries) in stock or water, then use for stuffings or in a salad.

2. Bulgur is perfect for stuffing anything from vegetables to chicken, and is excellent paired with ground beef.

3. Toast vermicelli in fat until well browned, then simmer in water or stock. Try the method in Toasted Freekeh and Vermicelli with Eggplant (*page 216*).

4. Wheat berries lend themselves well to a long-cooking meat dish or stew, as they retain a satisfying texture.

5. Make Lavash (*page 213*).

Lavash

It was important to me to include one bread made with just all-purpose flour. Even if there's nothing particularly special to the region about this ingredient, bread is, of course, a staple! When you don't feel like turning on the oven, make this flatbread that's popular in Armenia, Turkey, and Iran. Lavash requires only a little kneading and no rounds of proofing, just an hour of resting to let the gluten relax. Serve it with spreads (try Cevizli Biber, *page 60*, or Olive Spread, *page 92*), scoop up bites of roasted meat with it, or use it as a sandwich wrap.

Makes 20 flatbreads

¾ cup	lukewarm water (180 grams)
¾ cup	warm milk (180 grams)
1 tablespoon	instant yeast (10 grams)
1½ teaspoons	sugar (7 grams)
3½ cups	all-purpose flour (490 grams), plus more as needed
1 teaspoon	fine sea salt (5 grams)
1 tablespoon	extra-virgin olive oil (13 grams), plus more for the bowl

In a small bowl, stir together the lukewarm water, warm milk, yeast, and sugar. Let sit until the yeast is foamy, about 10 minutes.

In a stand mixer fitted with the dough hook, mix the flour and salt together just until combined. Add the yeast mixture and the oil and mix on medium-low speed until the ingredients come together to form a rough ball of dough, 1 to 2 minutes. Continue to knead, scraping down the sides as necessary and dusting with flour as needed if the dough is sticky to the touch, until the dough is smooth and elastic, 8 to 10 minutes.

Lightly oil a large bowl. Transfer the dough to the bowl, cover, and let the dough rest for 1 hour.

Divide the dough into 20 equal portions (about 44 grams each) and roll each into a ball. Cover the balls with plastic wrap to prevent drying. (The dough can also be frozen at this point. See Storage Directions, below.)

Heat a 10-inch nonstick skillet over medium heat. Working with one dough ball at a time, use a rolling pin to roll it into an 8-inch round, flouring the dough as needed. Lay the dough in the hot pan and cook until it is lightly browned, flip, then repeat until the other side is lightly browned, 30 to 45 seconds per side (if browning is taking longer than 45 seconds, increase the heat). Remove the bread from the pan to a plate and cover with a towel to keep warm.

Repeat with the remaining dough, rolling and cooking one lavash at a time, and stacking them one on top of the other after they're finished cooking.

Storage Directions

Lavash is best the day it's made. If you don't eat them all (or don't want to cook all of them at once), the cooked lavash or dough balls can be frozen. To freeze dough balls, place them on a parchment-lined sheet pan so they are not touching and freeze until solid. Transfer the dough balls to a sealed bag and freeze for up to 2 months. To thaw, leave as many dough balls as you like out on the counter until they are room temperature and pliable, about 1½ hours, then proceed with the rolling and cooking.

Tabbouleh

I'm sure you've had tabbouleh—it is one of the most recognizable and famous salads of the region, comprising bulgur wheat and heaps of chopped herbs—but if you've never made it yourself, I highly recommend you do. It's important to give the tomatoes a squeeze to make sure all the excess moisture is gone so you have a light salad with none of the ingredients weighed down by extra liquid.

Serves 4

½ cup	coarse bulgur wheat
1½ cups	warm water
½ cup	extra-virgin olive oil
3 tablespoons	freshly squeezed lemon juice
1	garlic clove, grated with a Microplane
1 teaspoon	fine sea salt (5 grams)
1 teaspoon	freshly ground black pepper (2 grams)
1 cup	fresh mint, roughly chopped
1 cup	fresh flat-leaf parsley, roughly chopped
¾ cup	finely diced Persian (mini) cucumbers (about 3)
¾ cup	finely diced seeded plum tomatoes (about 3)
½ cup	fresh cilantro, roughly chopped
4	scallions, thinly sliced

Put the bulgur in a small bowl and cover with the warm water, making sure the grains are submerged. Soak until the bulgur is tender with a nut-like texture but not mushy, about 20 minutes but possibly up to 1 hour, depending on the brand. Pour into a fine-mesh sieve and set aside to drain completely.

In a small bowl, whisk together the oil, lemon juice, garlic, salt, and pepper.

In a large bowl, combine the mint, parsley, cucumbers, tomatoes, cilantro, scallions, and drained bulgur. Drizzle on the dressing to taste and mix to combine all the ingredients, fluffing the mixture so everything is evenly distributed. Taste and adjust the seasoning. Serve at room temperature.

Toasted Freekeh and Vermicelli with Eggplant

Using vermicelli gives this freekeh dish even more nutty layers than the toasted green wheat would have alone. Be sure to take your time and really brown each piece of pasta and all the freekeh before cooking, so they retain their texture in the oven. The pepper paste and browned eggplant make it a very hearty meal that only needs one side dish (try the salad on *page 90* or the olives on *page 95*).

Serves 6

1	medium Chinese eggplant, sliced into 1-inch-thick rounds
1 teaspoon	fine sea salt (5 grams), plus more for the eggplant
½ to ¾ cup	extra-virgin olive oil, as needed
1¾ cups	freekeh
2 ounces	vermicelli, broken into 1-inch pieces (about ½ cup)
2	medium yellow onions, finely diced
4	garlic cloves, sliced
2 tablespoons	sweet Turkish pepper paste
¼ teaspoon	Aleppo pepper (0.5 grams)
½ teaspoon	freshly ground black pepper (1 gram)
3	medium plum tomatoes, cored and halved crosswise

Preheat the oven to 400°F.

Lightly season the eggplant with salt. In a large, deep, heavy-bottomed ovenproof skillet, heat ¼ cup of the oil over high heat. When the oil is hot, add the eggplant and brown it on both sides, adding another ¼ cup of the oil if the eggplant absorbs all of the first amount, 6 to 10 minutes total. Remove the eggplant and set aside.

Reduce the heat to medium. Add the remaining ¼ cup oil to the pan along with the freekeh and vermicelli. Toast, stirring often, until all the pasta and freekeh are nicely browned, about 10 minutes.

Add the onions, garlic, and ½ teaspoon (3 grams) of the salt and continue cooking until the onions are translucent, about 10 minutes.

Stir in the pepper paste, Aleppo pepper, and black pepper and sauté, without browning the onions, for 2 more minutes to cook the pepper paste.

Add 4 cups water—the grains should just be covered; if not, add more water—and arrange the eggplant and tomato halves around the pan cut-side up. Sprinkle the remaining ½ teaspoon (2 grams) salt over everything.

Increase the heat to bring the liquid to a boil, then transfer the pan to the oven to bake, checking occasionally to make sure the liquid maintains a simmer (if it isn't simmering, increase the oven temperature to 425°F), until the freekeh is tender with a bit of nutty bite and the liquid is absorbed, 20 to 40 minutes. Serve hot.

Tahdig (Persian Crispy Rice)

This famous Persian preparation celebrates crispy and golden toasted rice, inverted onto a plate to show it off. To make it even more special, half of the parcooked rice is mixed with yogurt and saffron, which ensures a beautifully enriched, toasted bottom. A perfect crust is the sign of an accomplished cook, and if you're a beginner, know that your technique will only improve with experience.

Serves 6 to 8

2 cups	basmati rice
½ teaspoon	saffron threads (n/a)
2 tablespoons	hot water
¼ cup	labne
3 tablespoons	unsalted butter
1 teaspoon	fine sea salt (5 grams)
2 tablespoons	extra-virgin olive oil

Wash the rice in a large bowl of cold water by swirling it with your hand, then pour off the water while keeping the rice in the bowl. Repeat until the water runs clear. Cover the rice with room-temperature water and soak for 1 hour. Drain in a fine-mesh sieve.

In a large pot, bring 16 cups water to a boil. In a medium bowl, steep the saffron in the 2 tablespoons of hot water for 5 minutes, then stir in the labne. Meanwhile, melt 2 tablespoons of the butter.

Once the water boils, add the rice and cook until about one-third of the way cooked through (break a few grains to test), about 5 minutes. Drain in a fine-mesh sieve and rinse the rice under cold water until completely cool. Leave to drain for 10 minutes.

Transfer the drained rice to a large bowl and fold in the melted butter and salt. Add 2 cups of the rice to the bowl with the saffron-labne mixture and stir well to combine.

To assemble, use a 10-inch nonstick skillet with a tight-fitting lid. Add the remaining 1 tablespoon butter and the oil to the skillet and heat over medium-low heat, uncovered, just until the butter melts. Turn off the heat.

Very gently put the saffron-rice mixture into the skillet in a flat, even layer. Avoid packing and pressing the rice so the end result is fluffy and crisp, not dense and tough.

Add the remaining rice on top and gently smooth it into a flat, even layer, taking care not to pat or compact the rice. Poke five deep holes in the rice with the end of a wooden spoon to allow steam to escape (but avoid poking holes all the way to the bottom). Wrap the lid with a clean towel, tying the ends on top.

Turn the heat to medium-low and cover the pan. Cook, giving the skillet a half-turn (180 degrees) halfway through to ensure even browning, until the crust is golden brown and the rice is cooked through, 20 to 25 minutes.

Remove from the heat and uncover. Hold a larger, flat plate firmly against the skillet with one hand and grip the handle with the other hand. In one swift movement, turn the skillet and plate over together. Set the platter down to reveal the golden crust. (If your crust is not very golden, return it to the pan to cook for another 5 minutes, then check again.) Serve immediately.

Koubeh Soup

The beet-stained, meat-filled dumplings called koubeh in this Iraqi dish usually feature a much heartier, chewier dough. I adapted the classic and made it with a bit of baking powder for lightness but kept the flavorings and assembly somewhat traditional.

Serves 4 to 6

Soup

2 tablespoons	extra-virgin olive oil
1	medium onion, diced
2	garlic cloves, finely chopped
8 cups	chicken stock or water
1 pound	beets (about 4), peeled and cut in ½-inch wedges
¼ cup	tomato paste
2 tablespoons	sweet paprika (16 grams)

Dumpling Dough

2 cups	fine semolina flour (300 grams)
1 teaspoon	fine sea salt (5 grams)
½ teaspoon	baking powder (2 grams)
1¼ cups	boiling water (300 grams)

Dumpling Filling

8 ounces	ground beef
½	medium onion, finely diced
2 tablespoons	roughly chopped fresh cilantro
2	garlic cloves, finely chopped
2 tablespoons	extra-virgin olive oil
	Salt and freshly ground black pepper

To Finish

2 tablespoons	sugar
	Juice of 1 lemon
	Salt and freshly ground black pepper

Make the soup: In a large heavy-bottomed pot, heat the oil over medium heat until hot. Add the onion and garlic and cook until translucent, about 5 minutes. Add the stock, beets, tomato paste, and paprika and bring to a boil. Reduce the heat so the mixture simmers, and cook until the beets are tender and the flavors have come together, about 30 minutes. Cover and keep warm.

Meanwhile, make the dumpling dough: In a large heatproof bowl, mix the semolina, salt, and baking powder together. Add the boiling water and stir quickly to thoroughly combine. Knead the dough for 30 to 60 seconds, just to bring it together and form a ball (if the dough is very hot, use a wooden spoon). Cover the bowl and let sit until the dough cools to room temperature, about 45 minutes.

Make the filling: In a large bowl, mix the beef, onion, cilantro, garlic, and oil until thoroughly combined. Season with salt and pepper and lightly mix again. Set aside.

When the dough is cool, divide it into 1-tablespoon portions (about 19 grams each) and cover with plastic wrap to keep them from drying out.

To shape the koubeh, it helps to have wet hands. Place a small bowl of water next to your work surface. Wet your hands and working with one dough ball at a time, gently flatten it to make a disk 2½ inches across and about ¼ inch thick. Push 1 teaspoon (6 grams) of the filling into the center of the dough. Bring the edges of the dough together over the filling to form a rough ball and pinch them together to seal. Gently roll the dumpling between your hands so it is sealed, round, and smooth. Cover the dumplings as you complete them so they don't dry out. It may take a few tries to get the filling and shaping down, but work gently and continue with the remaining dough and filling.

When the dumplings are ready, return the soup to a simmer. Gently add all the dumplings to the soup. Poach the koubeh, uncovered and maintaining a gentle simmer, until the dough and filling are cooked through, about 30 minutes.

Finish: Stir the sugar and lemon juice into the soup. Season with salt and pepper. Divide the dumplings evenly among bowls, ladle over the soup, and serve right away.

Basbousa (Semolina Cake)

There are many similar versions of the popular soft and tender semolina cake from nearly every country in the region (some may know it as namoura, shamali, harïsa, or revani). Made with tangy yogurt, it gets even better after you pour the aromatic orange blossom syrup on top and let it soak through. Coconut flakes make a perfect topping with their crunchy contrast, though other versions push a blanched almond into every piece or sprinkle the cake with chopped pistachios. Note that the syrup must be cooled before being poured over the warm cake, and cooling takes longer than the cake needs to bake—so give yourself enough lead time.

Makes about 16 pieces

Syrup

2 cups	sugar (400 grams)
1 tablespoon	freshly squeezed lemon juice (15 grams)
3 tablespoons	orange blossom water (45 grams)

Cake

3	large eggs
½ cup	sugar (100 grams)
1 cup	labne or Greek yogurt (230 grams)
¾ cup	extra-virgin olive oil (150 grams)
	Grated zest of 1 lemon
1 teaspoon	vanilla extract (5 grams)
1 cup	fine semolina flour (150 grams)
5 tablespoons	all-purpose flour (45 grams)
¼ cup	almond flour (30 grams)
2 teaspoons	baking powder (8 grams)
½ teaspoon	baking soda (2 grams)
	Coconut flakes, for garnish (optional)

Position a rack in the center of the oven and preheat the oven to 350°F. Mist a 10-inch round cake pan with cooking spray.

Make the syrup: In a small saucepan, combine the sugar and ½ cup (120 grams) water. Bring to a boil over high heat while stirring constantly. Once boiling, reduce the heat so the mixture simmers, and cook, without stirring, for 2 minutes to slightly reduce the syrup. Stir in the lemon juice, remove from the heat, and set aside to cool to room temperature. When the syrup is completely cool, stir in the orange blossom water.

Meanwhile, make the cake: In a large bowl, combine the eggs and sugar and whisk until the mixture is aerated and the sugar dissolved, about 2 minutes.

Add the labne, oil, lemon zest, and vanilla and whisk just until well combined, less than a minute. Add the semolina flour, all-purpose flour, almond flour, baking powder, and baking soda and whisk together until no lumps remain. Pour the batter into the prepared cake pan and smooth out the top.

Bake until a toothpick inserted in the center comes out clean and the top has browned, 25 to 30 minutes. Transfer to a wire rack and let the cake cool in the pan for 5 minutes.

Slice the cake (still in the pan) into 1½-inch-wide strips, then turn the pan 45 degrees and cut another set of 1½-inch-wide strips to make diamonds.

Slowly (so the syrup doesn't pool at the bottom) spoon all of the syrup over the warm cake. Cover the pan with foil and refrigerate it so the texture becomes denser, at least 2 hours and up to overnight.

To serve, garnish each slice with coconut, if desired.

Storage Directions
Store the cake wrapped
tightly with plastic wrap in the
refrigerator for up to 2 days.

Soutlek (Turkish Rice Pudding)

Unlike many other rice pudding recipes, this beloved Turkish version made with short-grain rice is baked so it develops a wonderful caramelized top layer in the oven. I've used both sushi and Arborio rice to make it (both of which are easy to find), which results in the ideal creamy, slightly runny texture. This is one recipe where you don't want to completely wash the rice, as a little starch helps thicken the pudding.

Serves 8

½	vanilla bean (2 grams)
¾ cup	sugar (150 grams)
½ cup	sushi or Arborio rice (100 grams)
4½ to 5½ cups	whole milk (1.1 to 1.32 kilograms)
2 tablespoons	cornstarch (18 grams)
1	large egg yolk
	Ground cinnamon, for garnish

Storage Directions
The pudding will keep covered in the refrigerator for 2 days.

Position one oven rack in the center and one just below it and preheat the oven to 350°F. Line a sheet pan with foil.

Halve the vanilla bean lengthwise, leaving the tip intact, and scrape out the seeds into a small bowl. In the bowl, mix the seeds and bean pod with the sugar. Set aside.

Wash the rice in a small bowl of cold water by swirling it a few times with your hand, then pour off the water while keeping the rice in the bowl. Repeat once more (the water will not be totally clear).

In a medium heavy-bottomed saucepan, combine the rice and 1 cup (240 grams) water. Bring the water to a boil over medium-high heat and cook, whisking frequently to avoid burning or sticking on the bottom, until most of the water evaporates, 5 to 10 minutes.

To the same pot, add 4 cups (960 grams) of the milk and bring to a boil, whisking frequently to prevent boiling over. Once the milk comes to a boil, add the sugar and vanilla mixture, including the pod, and whisk to combine. Adjust the heat so the mixture simmers very gently. Cook for 15 minutes, whisking often to prevent burning on the bottom of the pot and scraping down the sides.

In a small bowl, dissolve the cornstarch in ¼ cup (60 grams) of the milk. Add the cornstarch slurry to the rice pudding while whisking constantly—the mixture should thicken quickly. Cook until the liquid is the consistency of heavy cream, 1 to 2 minutes. Depending on the rice, it may be thicker than cream. If so, add ½ cup (120 grams) of the milk and stir, then add up to another ½ cup (120 grams) as needed to get a consistency like heavy cream. Pour the mixture into a 9-inch square baking dish. (Remove the vanilla pod now, if you like.)

In a small bowl, use a fork to beat the egg yolk with the remaining ¼ cup (60 grams) milk until combined. Carefully drizzle the mixture all over the top of the rice pudding just before baking and *do not stir.*

Set the rice pudding on the center rack and set the lined sheet pan on the lower rack for any spillover. Bake until a caramelized, almost burnt-looking skin forms on the top, 40 to 45 minutes. If the top is still pale after 40 minutes, switch your oven to the highest broiler setting and broil for 3 to 5 minutes, watching constantly and turning the pan to evenly brown the top—it will darken quickly.

Transfer the pudding to a wire rack and let cool to room temperature. Once cool, refrigerate until the pudding is dense and topped with a thick layer of creamy custard, at least 4 hours. Serve chilled, dusted with cinnamon.

Legumes

{ LEGUMES }

خضروات

baklagiller

קִטְנִיּוֹת

حبوبات

όσπρια

լոբազգիներ

Dried legumes are a magnificent source of nutrition that can be stored for many months and are much more affordable than proteins like meat. You can season them with almost anything, they are delicious hot or cold, and are just as good for a quick and easy meal as they are in a long-simmered soup or stew. In short: They're a perfect ingredient. The cuisines of the Middle East have never taken beans for granted. They may have been regarded as a poor person's food but were universally enjoyed. As the Arab saying goes, "Beans have even satisfied the pharaohs."

ORIGIN AND HISTORY

Most of the popular legumes used in the region—chickpeas, fava beans, and lentils—are native to the Middle East. And then there is the white bean, which is a broad category that includes many types grown around the world. The history of foraging and consuming legumes goes back further than the advent of agricultural societies, and so evidence of legumes in societies in the Middle East, and their crucial role in the diet, is plentiful. Fava beans are believed to be the oldest legume consumed by humans, and charred remains have been found in Israel dating back to the eighth century BC. Favas grew abundantly around Central Asia, the Middle East, and the Mediterranean and were eventually domesticated in the Fertile Crescent, along with lentils and chickpeas.

SOURCING AND STORING

You can't make good food with bad legumes. When shopping for dried beans and lentils, make sure they're whole, intact, and the skin isn't bruised or broken. Look for uniform color, as inconsistency can indicate bad sourcing. It's good to have a "best before" date or date of packaging too. Shop from a store you know has a high turnover to ensure the beans haven't been on a shelf for years. Old beans can take many hours to cook or might never get soft (in which case you're out of luck).

It's great if you have the time and inclination to cook your own beans (see Preparation, *page 228*), but how many people can predict a hummus craving twenty-four hours in advance? I can't, so I always keep canned beans in my pantry as well. I like organic options when it comes to canned, but for dried beans, I don't think it makes much of a difference. Canned beans should list nothing beyond the bean, water, and salt.

Dried beans should be used up within a year, and follow the expiration date on canned beans.

PREPARATION

For many centuries, beans were cooked for hours in a special wide-bottomed, narrow-necked pot over coals called a damassa in Arabic. Today a slow cooker, a carefully watched pot, or the oven will suffice. Pressure cookers are a convenient option, though I like to be able to check my beans while cooking, and that's hard to do with a pressure cooker.

To start, pick out and discard broken, discolored, or shriveled beans, then rinse the rest. Soaking beans helps them cook evenly, and I always soak beans (but not lentils). To soak, put the beans in a bowl large enough to fit them when they swell to about twice their size, and cover with water by at least 2 inches. Soak for 4 to 6 hours at room temperature or in the refrigerator overnight. Add ½ teaspoon baking soda per 1 pound of legumes to help soften the beans if you plan on pureeing them (and you *have* anticipated your hummus craving in advance).

When ready to cook, drain and rinse the beans and cook them in fresh water. I season my cooking liquid at this point with salt and spices. I know many believe salting at the beginning can make the skin tough, but I find the difference is negligible, and salting early in the cooking process means the flavor penetrates the whole bean. If using whole spices, make sure they're big enough to easily fish out, or put them in a cheesecloth sachet. I'll use spice blends or ground spices when I don't mind the cooking liquid being darker and cloudy. If I'm making hummus, I'll add another ½ teaspoon baking soda per 1 pound of beans to the cooking water to help soften the chickpeas.

I like to bake my beans in the oven, because movement, like circulating around in boiling water, causes the beans to break up as they hit the sides of the pot and each other repeatedly. To bake beans, place them in a heavy-bottomed ovenproof pot like a Dutch oven and add enough cooking liquid to come 2 inches above the beans. Cover and bake at 325°F until tender. If you cook on the stovetop, adjust the heat as low as possible so there is just a bubble or two at a time. Cooking time varies based on the type of bean, age, and how long they've been soaked, so check often until they're as tender as you like. If I'm using the cooking liquid in the final dish, I'll check the seasoning when the beans are ready, but the beans are as seasoned as they'll get at this point.

For canned beans, rinse them before serving. Add them to another dish to be cooked further or warm them up if you like, but simply rinsed and drained is fine for cold salads.

After cooking, beans can be cooled completely and stored in their cooking liquid in the refrigerator for up to 1 week, or in the freezer for up to 3 months.

Chickpeas

I adore chickpeas. Hummus is the first thing that might come to mind, but they're also fantastic fried, roasted, added to salads, used to bulk up soups and stews, and ground into flour.

AGRICULTURAL DETAILS

The domesticated plants we know today, *Cicer arietinum*, are small, bushy, self-pollinating, and grow pods that contain two or three seeds—the chickpeas. There are two varieties grown and consumed: a smaller one called desi and a larger called kabuli.

Chickpeas take three to seven months to mature, with a short harvest season for fresh chickpeas in late spring and early summer, then they are left to dry in the field. When the leaves dry and turn brownish yellow, they are ready to harvest. The chickpeas are removed from the dried pods and then left to finish drying in the sun. Turkey grows the most chickpeas in the region.

APPEARANCE AND FLAVOR

Dried chickpeas come in a variety of colors, though green (also found fresh or frozen) and black chickpeas are more often used outside of the Middle East. The smaller desi chickpeas are darker and more colorful, and the large kabuli type are the pale tan variety found most often in Middle Eastern cuisines. They are very hard and have a skin that is basically invisible when dried and can separate from the seed during soaking or cooking (I never bother to peel cooked chickpeas). When cooked, they have a wonderfully mild flavor and meaty texture.

TRADITIONAL USES

Hummus — *throughout the region* (see Hummus Tahina, *page 235*)
Falafel — *throughout the region* (see recipe, *page 241*)
Topik (stuffed dumpling) — *Armenia, Turkey*
Dango (spiced chickpeas) — *UAE, Oman*
Halabessa (soup) — *Egypt*
Nan-e nokhodchi (cookies) — *Iran*

Recipe Ideas

1. Chickpeas puree wonderfully in soups or to make dips (besides the obvious hummus). If planning on pureeing them, add ½ teaspoon baking soda per 1 pound of beans to both the soaking and cooking waters to help soften them.

2. Pan-fry chickpeas in oil until crisp and use as a garnish for savory dishes.

3. Add them to salads, soups, and stews for protein and meaty texture.

Fava Beans

My Tunisian grandfather made a simple, exquisite appetizer with fava beans: He'd soak and then boil dried favas until tender and serve them with olive oil seasoned with salt and cumin. To eat, we'd pinch the skin of the bean to hold it, dip the whole thing into the oil, eat the seasoning and the tender bean, then discard the skin.

AGRICULTURAL DETAILS

Vicia faba, fava bean bushes, produce twenty-five to fifty pods per plant and up to nine seeds per pod, depending on the variety. Fava beans are a cool-weather crop that has a brief window for the fresh young beans in the spring. They're then left on the plant to dry and are usually harvested in the fall. The pods are removed; the skin on each bean may also be removed in processing. Egypt grows the most in the region.

APPEARANCE AND FLAVOR

You can purchase two types of dried favas: small fava beans are rounder and often darker than the larger variety (also called broad beans), which are flatter. The smaller beans have a soft skin, while the large broad beans have a tougher skin that is edible but often removed. Both types are brown unless the skin has been removed, and split favas are pale yellow, green, or white. Canned fava beans are plump and brown. All favas have an earthy taste and texture similar to chickpeas. The young, fresh favas are tender and slightly sweet and sold at farmers' markets in the spring or frozen at some Middle Eastern grocers.

TRADITIONAL USES

Ful medames (stew) — *Egypt, Levant, and more* (see recipe, *page 236*)
Bagilla bil-dihin (stew) — *Iraq*
Ta'ameya (fritter) — *Egypt*
Bissara (dip) — *Egypt*

Recipe Ideas

1. Just as my grandfather did, boil them and serve simply with a dip made of olive oil, salt, cumin, and—my addition—lemon juice.

2. Peel the skins from any type of fava bean and puree the beans in soups or into dips.

3. Add small fava beans, unpeeled, to soups and stews with a long cooking time.

Lentils

These small pulses don't require soaking to cook quickly and evenly, making them a perfect choice for weeknight dinners. They absorb spices and seasonings beautifully and work as a simple side dish, as a main course, in salads, or mixed with stock to thicken soups and sauces.

AGRICULTURAL DETAILS

Lentils are an annual plant, *Lens culinaris*, that can grow over two feet tall and is self-pollinating. The plants grow seedpods that each contain about two seeds (the lentils). The lentil pods dry on the plant in the field and are ready in the late summer. The dried pods are harvested, threshed (meaning the pods are removed), and either sold whole (brown, green, or black) or hulled and split (red, yellow, or orange). Turkey is the biggest producer of lentils in the Middle East and one of the top five producers in the world.

APPEARANCE AND FLAVOR

The most common lentils used in the Middle East are large greenish tan or tiny red. The former are bigger than the French le Puy lentils (which I prefer) and don't hold their shape quite as well, though with attentive cooking they will be fine. Lentils have an earthy, sometimes peppery or sprout-like flavor. They have a firm, toothsome texture.

TRADITIONAL USES

Mujadara (rice dish) — *throughout the region*
(see recipe, *page 239*)
Adas polow (rice dish) — *Iran*
Kushari (rice dish) — *Egypt*
Shourba bilsen (stew) — *Yemen*
Marak dal (stew) — *Oman*
Vegetarian kibbeh — *Turkey*

Recipe Ideas

1. Fry cooked lentils in oil until crisp as a garnish for salads or grain dishes (do not overcook them, or they'll disintegrate).

2. Mix cooked lentils into fritter batters.

3. Blend cooked lentils with chicken or vegetable stock for a simple creamy soup.

White Beans

The creamiest bean of all the legumes in this chapter is a group of beans and not one specific variety. You're mostly likely to find the standard American and European options even at Middle Eastern grocers: navy (haricot) beans, baby lima (butter) beans, Great Northern beans, and cannellini (white kidney) beans.

AGRICULTURAL DETAILS

White beans are harvested when the pods and seeds are almost completely dried in the field in the late summer or fall. They are threshed to remove the pods and, since they are dry when harvested, may be ready to sell immediately or need a short additional stint in the sun to finish drying.

APPEARANCE AND FLAVOR

The available varieties range from small navy beans to large butter beans and white kidney beans. All are, of course, white, though some varieties have a slight greenish tinge. White beans tend to retain their shape well when cooked. They are mild and nutty in flavor and have textures that range from soft and creamy to firm and slightly mealy—in a pleasant way.

TRADITIONAL USES

Fassoulia (stew) — *Iraq, Levant* (see recipe, *page 242*)
Fasolada (stew) — *Cyprus*
Fasulye ezmesi (puree) — *Turkey*

Recipe Ideas

1. Add cold cooked beans, or rinsed canned beans, to salads.

2. Serve long-braised dishes, especially meat, with a side of seasoned white beans.

3. Bulk up soups and stews with precooked white beans (or soaked beans if there is enough time for them to soften).

Hummus Tahina

Hummus means "chickpea" in Arabic and is also the name of the most famous dish you make with the legume. It is, unsurprisingly, very popular in the region and found nearly everywhere. In the Middle East, hummus is a breakfast dish served slightly warm with a few optional toppings to make it a meal. It's usually eaten in small specialty restaurants that are open for just the morning meal and only serve hummus. Although it is so simple to make and has very few ingredients, the taste differs greatly from one restaurant to another—and most people feel passionately about their favorite. At home, I often make hummus with canned chickpeas, because I have a hard time waiting a day for dried beans to soak. Tahini is used here both as a paste straight from the jar and as a sauce to serve over the hummus.

Makes 2 cups

1½ cups	cooked chickpeas (see Preparation, *page 228*) or canned, preferably organic, rinsed and drained
½ cup	tahini
½ cup	ice water
1 tablespoon	freshly squeezed lemon juice
¼ teaspoon	ground cumin (0.5 grams), plus more to taste
	Salt
2 tablespoons	Tahini Sauce (*page 129*), or more to taste, for serving
	Extra-virgin olive oil, for serving
	Paprika, for garnish (optional)

In a food processor, combine the chickpeas, tahini, ice water, lemon juice, cumin, and a pinch of salt. Process until completely smooth. Taste and adjust the seasoning with more salt and/or cumin if necessary.

To serve, spoon some or all of the hummus into a serving bowl. Spread and swoosh the hummus to the sides, creating a well in the center. Spoon as much of the tahini sauce in the center as you like. Drizzle with oil and dust with more cumin and/or paprika (if using).

Storage Directions
Store any extra hummus in an airtight container in the refrigerator for up to 3 days.

Ful Medames

Dried fava beans are rarely used outside of the region for some mysterious reason—but *inside* the region, this Egyptian stew is the most famous way to eat them. A big part of the appeal is the variety of toppings and mix-ins to customize your ful. I love hard-boiled eggs, tahini, and chiles on mine.

Serves 6

2 cups	small dried fava beans, picked over
2 tablespoons	extra-virgin olive oil
1	medium red onion, finely diced
3	garlic cloves, finely chopped
2 teaspoons	ground cumin (4 grams)
1 teaspoon	fine sea salt (5 grams), plus more as needed
	Freshly ground black pepper

Suggested Garnishes

Hard-boiled eggs, cut into quarters

Diced fresh tomato

Roughly chopped fresh flat-leaf parsley

Finely diced red onion

Chopped fresh chiles

Extra-virgin olive oil

Lemon wedges

Tahini

Warm pita

In a large bowl, cover the beans with water by at least 2 inches. Let soak overnight. The next day, the beans should have roughly doubled in size. Drain the beans.

In a large pot, heat the oil over medium heat until hot. Add the onion, garlic, and cumin and cook until the onion and garlic are softened and fragrant but not yet starting to brown, about 10 minutes.

Add the soaked beans, salt, and 8 cups water. Increase the heat to high and bring to a boil, then adjust the heat so the mixture simmers. Cook, uncovered, until the beans are tender and the liquid has reduced so that it just covers the beans, about 1 hour.

Remove the pot from the heat and pulse with an immersion blender until the stew is thick and chunky with a good mix of whole and broken beans in a thick liquid (it will also thicken quite a bit as it cools). Taste and add pepper and/or more salt if necessary.

Serve hot with as many of the suggested garnishes as you like.

Mujadara

The simple and hearty combination of rice and lentils, which is popular in many countries, is taken to new heights with the addition of fried onions, which is really what this classic dish is all about. I prefer the textural contrast (and ease) of the premade fried shallots you're more likely to find in an Asian market than a Middle Eastern one. If you can't find them or want to keep things conventional, set some of the browned onions meant for stirring into the dish aside to use as a topping (even consider doubling the amount).

Serves 6 to 8

½ cup	extra-virgin olive oil
2 cups	thinly sliced yellow onion (about 1 medium)
½ cup	raisins
2 tablespoons	freshly squeezed lemon juice
2 tablespoons	hot water
1 cup	French green lentils, rinsed and drained
1 cup	basmati rice
1 tablespoon	ground coriander (6 grams)
1 tablespoon	ground cumin (7 grams)
1 teaspoon	freshly ground black pepper (2 grams)
½ teaspoon	ground cinnamon (1 gram)
2	bay leaves
4	garlic cloves, sliced
2 teaspoons	fine sea salt (10 grams)

For Serving

½ cup	store-bought fried shallots (or use the reserved ¼ cup browned onion from the first step)
½ cup	roughly chopped fresh cilantro
½ cup	sliced scallions
	Labne

In a large heavy-bottomed pot, heat the oil over medium heat until hot. Add the onion and cook, covered and stirring occasionally, for 10 minutes, to soften. Uncover and cook, adjusting the heat as needed to prevent the onion from burning, until well browned, about another 15 minutes.

Meanwhile, in a small bowl, mix the raisins with the lemon juice and hot water and set aside to hydrate.

In a small saucepan, cover the lentils with plenty of water and bring to a boil. Adjust the heat so the water simmers, and cook until the lentils are tender, about 8 minutes. Remove the pot from the heat but do not drain the lentils until right before you add them to the rice mixture (the sudden temperature change will cause the lentils to split).

Wash the rice in a medium bowl of cold water by swirling it with your hand, then pour off the water while keeping the rice in the bowl. Repeat until the water runs clear. Set aside to drain.

When the onion is ready, add the coriander, cumin, pepper, and cinnamon and stir to coat the onion. (If you're not using store-bought fried shallots, set aside ¼ cup of the onion for garnish.)

Add the raisins and their soaking liquid to the onion, scraping the bottom of the pot with a wooden spoon to deglaze it. Add the cooked lentils, drained rice, bay leaves, garlic, salt, and 1½ cups water. Bring to a boil, then adjust the heat so the mixture simmers. Cook, covered, until the rice is tender and the liquid has evaporated, stirring gently halfway through to ensure the rice cooks evenly, about 10 minutes. Remove from the heat and leave to steam, covered, for 10 more minutes. Fluff up the rice and lentils.

Serve: Top with fried shallots (or reserved onions), cilantro, and scallions. Finish with a spoonful of labne. Serve hot.

Falafel

Like hummus, falafel elicits strong opinions from everyone in the Middle East about the best place to buy it. But they're also simple to make at home, and this version with fresh herbs and an easy spice blend is the perfect excuse to stuff your pita with it and add as many condiments (try Amba, *page 59*, and Tahini Sauce, *page 129*) and toppings as you can fit. Note that falafel must be made with uncooked chickpeas to get the right texture.

Serves 4

Chickpeas

2 teaspoons	baking soda
¾ cup	dried chickpeas

Falafel Spice Blend

2 teaspoons	ground cumin (4 grams)
1 teaspoon	garlic powder (3 grams)
1 teaspoon	onion powder (3 grams)
1 teaspoon	fine sea salt (5 grams)
½ teaspoon	sweet paprika (1 gram)

Falafel

½ cup	fresh flat-leaf parsley leaves and tender stems, very roughly chopped
½ cup	fresh cilantro leaves and tender stems, very roughly chopped
½ teaspoon	baking powder
	Neutral vegetable oil, for frying

Prepare the chickpeas: In a large bowl, dissolve the baking soda in 4 cups water, then add the chickpeas. Soak the chickpeas overnight. (They can be soaked up to 2 days in advance in the refrigerator.) The following day, drain the chickpeas.

Make the spice blend: In a small bowl, mix the cumin, garlic powder, onion powder, salt, and paprika. Set aside. (You could also double or triple the spice blend for future falafel batches. Keep it stored in an airtight container.)

Prepare the falafel: In a food processor, combine the parsley, cilantro, and drained chickpeas and pulse until the herbs are roughly chopped. Add the baking powder, 1 tablespoon water, and all of the spice blend and continue pulsing until the mixture resembles gritty, coarse sand. To test the mixture, gently press a handful. You want the mixture to hold together but still retain some texture so that the falafel will be crunchy. If it doesn't hold together, pulse a few more times and test again.

Divide the mixture into 16 equal portions (about 30 grams or a spoonful each) and shape into balls.

Clip a deep-fry thermometer to the side of a large heavy-bottomed pot. Pour in 3 inches of oil (or half the depth of the pot if your pot is less than 6 inches deep) and bring the oil to 350°F. Line a plate or sheet pan with paper towels.

Working in batches so the oil temperature doesn't drop, carefully put a few falafel into the heated oil and fry until golden brown and crunchy, 4 to 6 minutes total. Transfer to the paper towels to drain and repeat with the remaining falafel. Serve right away.

Storage Directions
The falafel can be cooked in advance and reheated in the oven, but they really do taste best fresh out of the oil. Refrigerate for up to 5 days if you like.

Fassoulia

This comforting white bean and meat stew is served all over the Middle East. When I make it at home, I use white navy beans, although baby lima (butter) beans could also work well. Serve it with steamed rice and yogurt drizzled on top, plus a salad on the side to make a complete meal.

Serves 8 to 10

2 cups	dried white beans, picked over
1 pound	veal stew meat, cubed
2¼ teaspoons	fine sea salt (13 grams)
¾ teaspoon	freshly ground black pepper (1.5 grams)
½ teaspoon	ground cumin (1 gram)
2 tablespoons	extra-virgin olive oil
2 cups	finely diced onions (about 2 medium)
2	garlic cloves, finely chopped
¼ cup	tomato paste
1	(14.5-ounce) can diced tomatoes, undrained
	Chopped fresh cilantro, for garnish

In a large bowl, combine the beans with water to cover by at least 2 inches. Let soak overnight. The next day, the beans should have roughly doubled in size. Drain the beans.

Season the veal with ½ teaspoon (3 grams) of the salt, ½ teaspoon (1 gram) of the pepper, and the cumin.

In a large Dutch oven, heat the oil over high heat until hot. Working in batches if necessary, to avoid crowding, add the meat and cook, turning as needed, until browned on all sides, 5 to 6 minutes. Transfer the first batch of browned meat to a plate, then repeat with the remaining veal.

Return all the meat to the pot and reduce the heat to medium. Add the onions, garlic, and ½ teaspoon (3 grams) of the salt and cook until the onions are soft and translucent, about 5 minutes. Stir in the tomato paste and cook, stirring often, until the paste is caramelized, 2 to 3 minutes.

Add the drained beans, diced tomatoes and their juices, the remaining 1¼ teaspoons (7 grams) salt, remaining ¼ teaspoon (0.5 grams) pepper, and 5½ cups water. Mix everything together.

Increase the heat to bring to a boil, then adjust the heat so the mixture simmers gently, cover, and cook until the meat and beans are tender, 1 to 1½ hours. Check the water level every 20 minutes or so and add more water to keep it consistent throughout the cooking time.

Taste and adjust the seasoning. Serve hot, garnished with cilantro.

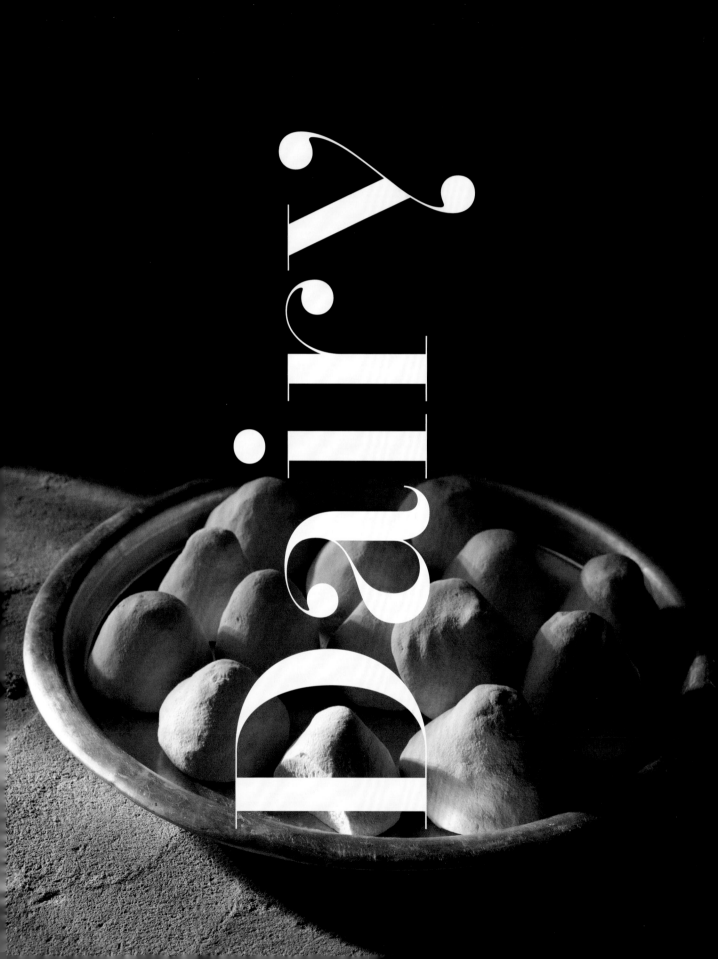

Dairy

{ DAIRY }

ألبان

süt ürünleri

מוּצְרֵי חָלָב

لبنيات

γαλακτοκομείο

կաթնամթերք

Our ancestors used almost all the preservation techniques at their disposal to make fresh milk last out the year. Milk was reduced, strained, dried, fermented, brined, and preserved in oil. It's how we can have kishk and jameen (*see page 246*), which can last for years, or yogurt with a shelf life of several months (*see page 248*) without refrigeration. Not a single drop of goat or sheep (or increasingly cow's) milk is wasted to make the traditional dairy products in this chapter.

ORIGIN AND HISTORY

Many historians believe that milking animals began in the Middle East probably about seven thousand years ago (humans have been herding for about ten thousand years). Some of the first evidence of milking appears in a mural from the ancient Mesopotamian city of Ur in modern-day Iraq that dates back about five thousand years. Sheep, donkeys, goats, and horses were all domesticated and milked before the dairy cow. The earliest dairy products in the Middle East were most likely from goats and sheep.

Modern dairy products were probably discovered by accident. The oft-repeated theory is that vessels for carrying fresh milk were made from animal stomachs, and the bacteria and enzymes naturally present in the lining of the stomach probably fermented the milk. If the bag jostled while walking or riding, or if it was very hot, solids formed. Thus the milk soured and thickened, or separated into solids and liquids, creating something close to yogurt, butter, and fresh cheese.

A whole slew of preservation techniques developed around this discovery. Most of the traditional dairy products start with culturing milk (introducing bacteria to ferment it). They can be eaten immediately, as with yogurt, preserved, as with cheese, or the fat can be separated from the liquid to create cultured butter and buttermilk. Butter is eaten fresh or turned into samneh (*see page 249*), a type of clarified butter that keeps for months, and the buttermilk can be drunk immediately or separated again into curds and whey, with the curds being preserved and pressed into cheese. Whey, the liquid separated from the solids, isn't preserved but can be served as a drink or used for other purposes, like pickling.

Kishk and Jameen

I crave the tangy, sour note these products add to food and highly recommend seeking them out. They might not be as common as labne or feta here in the United States, but they are equally important ingredients in the Middle East.

ABOUT

Kishk, kashk, and kishek are all names for a very hard, completely dried cheese made from yogurt and bulgur wheat that brings a rich, fermented note to food when fresh yogurt isn't available. (Kashk is also, confusingly, dried whey used in Iranian cooking.) Kishk brings together two major crops of agrarian societies: dairy and wheat. It's unclear whether the two were combined to save time or to stretch out limited milk, but the taste is pure soured yogurt. It's used by Lebanese, Syrian, Palestinian, Turkish, and Armenian cooks, who live in areas where wheat grows.

Jameen or jameed (or, rarely, it can also be called kishk) is a similar product without the bulgur. It's most closely associated with the Bedouin and used throughout the Levant, especially in Jordan, as well as in Iraq and the Arabian Peninsula countries. The name means "hardened" and they are literally that: completely dried balls of salted yogurt. The nomadic Bedouin tribes, who herded goats and sheep in the desert, needed to keep milk from spoiling in a very hot climate. They have many different dairy products, and jameen is the longest lasting. The dried yogurt balls just needed to be soaked in water or ground into a powder before cooking.

PRODUCTION

Kishk is made from goat, sheep, or cow's milk in the late summer or early fall. After the wheat is processed into bulgur, it's mixed with plain yogurt, drained salted yogurt, a combination of the two, or buttermilk. The wheat and dairy mixture is fermented for several days. As the bulgur absorbs the liquid, it's kneaded or rubbed daily. When the mixture is firm, it's formed into balls and dried in indirect sunlight—direct sunlight will turn them yellow—until all the moisture is gone. Some is ground into powder instead of stored as balls, which makes it easier to use smaller amounts.

Making jameen starts with goat, sheep, or cow's milk yogurt or buttermilk. Yogurt is salted and drained in cheesecloth for several days, the outside of the cloth is rinsed to help remove the whey as it drains, and once the yogurt is dense, it's formed into balls. If the jameen is made from buttermilk, which is the traditional Bedouin way, it starts with culturing the milk and separating out the fat and liquid (buttermilk). The buttermilk is heated and cooled again to separate out the solids, which are also drained in cheesecloth. The thick cheese is shaped into balls or cones and sundried for several days, until all of the moisture is removed. The Bedouin would dry the balls in the sun, and most producers nowadays dry them in indirect sunlight or in an oven.

APPEARANCE AND FLAVOR

Both kishk and jameen taste like a strong, sour yogurt with an extra layer of flavor if they're made from goat or sheep milk. Both are a uniform ivory color. The balls look like large pieces of round or cone-shaped chalk (*see the photo on page 244*), and the consistency of ground kishk resembles flour.

SOURCING AND STORING

The ingredients should be just yogurt, salt, and bulgur (for kishk). If buying balls, they should not have dents, cracks, or any dust in the packaging, which could be a sign that they're very old or weren't made properly. You can also buy kishk as a powder, which should be bright white. Commercially available jameen products, like smaller cubes and "soup starter" mix, are of unclear origin and may contain additional yogurt, stabilizers, and fillers. I stick with the pure product. Store both in a cool, dry place away from sunlight and in an airtight container for up to 2 years.

TRADITIONAL USES

Meeykeh (salad) — *Lebanon*
Soup and stew seasoning — *throughout the region*
Mansaf (lamb and rice dish) — *Levant, Kuwait, Saudi Arabia* (see recipe, *page 262*)
Manquish (flatbread) — *Levant*

Recipe Ideas

1. Grate kishk (no need to soak) over pasta, the same way you might grate Parmesan.

2. Toast or warm bread, drizzle with olive oil, then top with grated kishk.

3. Soak balls of either type in water until it's soft enough to crumble (overnight is ideal), then add it to stewed legume dishes—especially chickpeas or fava beans.

4. Rehydrate jameen and mix with water to make a sauce for kibbeh.

More ways to use kishk

FROM MICHAEL SOLOMONOV

The chef behind multiple Philadelphia restaurants, including the award-winning Zahav, and author of three cookbooks, Michael is a longtime friend who has a similarly deep appreciation for using traditional ingredients, no matter when he discovered them in his cooking career.

"I was introduced to kishk by my good friend Reem Kassis, who always has some in her Palestinian household. Kishk is often used to make sauces because you can boil it without worrying it will break like other milk products. My favorite way to use it, though, is to grate it over the top of a dish: over fresh vegetables or salads, or really almost any cooked dish for garnish. When it's used this way, it's just a great introduction for people to this very special ingredient. It's a lot like using crumbled goat cheese but with a more robust flavor."

Labne Balls

Drained (or "strained") yogurt, labne is one of the most popular ingredients of the Levant, and our ancestors discovered a rather ingenious way to preserve it without the help of refrigeration: submerging labne balls in oil.

ABOUT

Labne is derived from the Arabic word *laban*, which means "white" or "milk." It's a drained, sometimes salted, yogurt with a thick, rich, creamy consistency. It's very popular in the Levant and requires refrigeration. Labne balls, however, can be preserved in oil for months. The oil—usually olive—keeps out air, and the labne is acidic, both of which prevent most bacteria from thriving and spoiling the dairy.

PRODUCTION

Labne starts with milking the cow, sheep, or goat. The fresh milk may be boiled to cook off some of the water. It's then mixed with a yogurt starter and left to sit at room temperature for several hours to thicken and sour. The yogurt may be salted and is then drained through cheesecloth. Usually, it takes a day or two to thicken, and the final consistency is a matter of personal preference.

The thickened labne is rolled into balls and can either be preserved right away or left to dry for another day or two. The balls are packed into a jar and covered in olive oil. They can also be rolled in spices before preserving or rolled in spices after removing from the jar and before serving.

APPEARANCE AND FLAVOR

Labne is very creamy and less tangy than yogurt because draining removes the acidic whey. The goat and sheep varieties tend to be sourer and cow's milk labne milder. The balls are slightly crumbly yet spreadable, like a fresh goat cheese, and bright white in color.

SOURCING AND STORING

I like goat and sheep milk labne balls, which naturally have more character, and prefer to buy them in high-quality olive oil without any added spices. When looking at a jar, the balls should be white and pristine (even in the golden oil) and the oil should be clear, unless it's flavored with spices or herbs. There shouldn't be any bits of labne on the bottom of the container and any milk staining the oil. Stored in a cool, dark place, the labne balls will keep for several months if fully submerged in the oil. After opening, use a clean utensil to fish out a labne ball every time to avoid introducing bacteria.

TRADITIONAL USES

Mezze dish — *throughout the region*

Recipe Ideas

1. I enjoy them straight from the jar, perhaps with only a piece of bread.

2. Roll plain labne balls in za'atar, sesame seeds, or nigella seeds and serve them with bread.

3. Make your own Oil-Cured Labne Balls (*page 251*).

4. Make Yogurt and Greens Soup (*page 252*).

Samneh

This cooking fat, similar to ghee, is my go-to when I want the flavor benefits of butter for high-heat cooking. The main differences between samneh and ghee are the spices used and that samneh is traditionally made with goat or sheep milk, or a mixture, and ghee is made from cow's milk.

ABOUT

Samneh, samn, samna, or sadeyag in Turkish are the names for this clarified butter, which has been cooked to slightly toast the milk solids before straining them out, that is used in the Middle East. Traditionally it was made from sheep, goat, and water buffalo milk, and now cow samneh is available, too.

Butter making is traditionally the first step to preserving any fresh dairy: It is first separated out into butter fats (see Production, below) and buttermilk, which is then used to make products like kishk and jameen (*see page 246*). Clarification was the butter preservation of choice in the Middle East, and pots used to store samneh were found in an Egyptian tomb from 3200 BC. In Yemen (and several North African countries), clarified butter is fermented into stronger-tasting smen.

PRODUCTION

Samneh is traditionally made in the spring, when milk is the richest. Cream from the milk is shaken or churned until the fat clumps together to form butter. The butter is then cooked with rice, bulgur wheat, or flour, which absorb the milk solids and water (the grains or flour may be omitted). Spices can be added—cumin and coriander seeds are common in Oman, fenugreek in Yemen, and a mix called "samneh spice" is used in the Levant. The mixture is boiled until the fat is transparent, then the grains and spices are strained out. The pure fat is ready for storage, and the grains are served to whoever is lucky enough to be present.

APPEARANCE AND FLAVOR

The flavor is like a lighter butter with a slight toasted flavor from cooking. Goat or sheep samneh has a slightly stronger taste than one made from cow's milk. If spices have been added, they'll provide a very faint flavor. It should be a pure golden color and clear if liquid (some may solidify).

SOURCING AND STORING

Look for the shortest ingredient list possible: butter and perhaps spices. There should be nothing in the liquid and no coloration. An opened container of samneh will keep for many months unrefrigerated, and unopened it will keep for a year or more.

TRADITIONAL USES

Fatoot samneh (egg dish) — *Yemen*
Burek (savory pastry) — *Turkey*

Recipe Ideas

1. Heat with dried Urfa chile and drizzle the mixture over hummus.

2. Fry pine nuts or almonds in samneh to garnish both sweet and savory dishes.

3. Use samneh instead of the ghee in the Kunafe (*page 200*) or the melted butter in the Baklava (*page 117*). These dishes have traditionally used samneh to brown the pastry.

Oil-Cured Labne Balls

Growing up we would often drive to the Druze villages near our kibbutz. As we entered the town, we'd come upon stands selling produce as well as rows and rows of glass jars stuffed with labne balls. They're great for a snack or sandwich filling, and the oil is fantastic for tossing into salads and drizzling over cooked vegetables, making them a two-for-one deal, really.

Makes 15 to 20 pieces

1 quart whole-milk yogurt

Good-quality extra-virgin olive oil, as needed

Put the yogurt in a clean kitchen towel or cheesecloth, tie it on a wooden spoon, and hang it over a bowl or tall pitcher with enough space so the cheesecloth doesn't touch the whey that will collect below it. Let the yogurt drain at room temperature or in the refrigerator until you can shape a small ball without it coating your hands (a little sticking is fine), about 24 hours.

Open the towel or cheesecloth. Wet your hands and form the labne into tablespoon-size balls. If the labne is too soft to make firm balls, refrigerate it for 1 hour to set up. If the labne starts sticking too much to your hands, rinse and rewet your hands and continue. The final amount of balls will depend on the yogurt used.

Loosely layer a clean 1-quart container with the balls, taking care to not compact them. Pour in enough oil to cover them completely. Cover the jar.

They are ready to eat right away or can be stored in the refrigerator for up to 1 month (the oil will solidify, but that's okay).

Variations
- Add fresh or dried herbs, such as thyme or rosemary, to the oil.
- Roll the balls in Za'atar (*page* 36), shake off any excess, then cover them in oil.

Yogurt and Greens Soup

What looks like a simple soup made with some greens and spices is actually a rich and complex dish. The labne balls act as little dumplings, delivering sour and creamy hits in every bite.

Serves 4 to 6

12	Oil-Cured Labne Balls (*page 251*), drained, plus some oil from the jar for serving
2 tablespoons	extra-virgin olive oil
2	medium yellow onions, halved and sliced lengthwise
4	garlic cloves, finely chopped
2 teaspoons	ground coriander (4 grams)
1 teaspoon	fine sea salt (5 grams), plus more as needed
¼ teaspoon	freshly ground black pepper (0.5 grams)
1 bunch	green Swiss chard, leaves and stems separated and cut into 1-inch pieces
1	medium Yukon Gold potato, unpeeled and cut into ½-inch cubes
6 cups	chicken stock
2 teaspoons	dried dill (2 grams)
2 tablespoons	freshly squeezed lemon juice

Remove the labne balls from the refrigerator to come to room temperature while you make the soup.

Heat a large heavy-bottomed pot over low heat. When the pan is hot, add the oil, onions, garlic, coriander, salt, and pepper and stir. Cover and cook, stirring a few times, until the onions are translucent, about 5 minutes. Stir in the Swiss chard leaves and stems, cover, and cook for 5 more minutes to soften them.

Add the potato, chicken stock, and dill and increase the heat to bring to a boil. Adjust the heat so the mixture simmers, cover, and cook until the potatoes and chard stems are tender, 10 to 15 minutes. Stir in the lemon juice. Taste and adjust the seasoning.

Warm the soup bowls. Put 2 or 3 labne balls into each bowl (depending on the number of portions), then ladle the hot soup over to warm the labne. Drizzle with some of the oil from the labne balls and serve immediately.

Chickpea Tarhana

Tarhana is a Turkish pantry ingredient I couldn't leave out of this book. It's very similar to kishk but with tomatoes and other vegetables added to the yogurt and bulgur mixture. It is used mainly like a bouillon powder to flavor soups throughout the year (try it in the very easy Chickpea Tarhana Soup on *page 257*) and is another amazing example of how clever and efficient Middle Eastern preserving is: Fresh vegetables, grains, *and* dairy are fermented, dried, and preserved together. In my version of tarhana, I replace the bulgur with chickpeas for added flavor.

Makes about 3 cups

8 ounces	red bell peppers, seeded and cut into 2-inch pieces
8 ounces	yellow onions, cut into 2-inch pieces
8 ounces	plum tomatoes, cut into 2-inch pieces
1¼ cups	cooked chickpeas (see Preparation, *page 228*) or canned, preferably organic, rinsed and drained
3¼ cups	all-purpose flour (450 grams)
1 cup	plain yogurt
1 tablespoon	extra-virgin olive oil
1½ teaspoons	fine sea salt (8 grams)
1½ teaspoons	freshly ground black pepper (3 grams)
1 teaspoon	instant yeast (3 grams)
½ teaspoon	red chile flakes (1 gram)

Storage Directions

The tarhana will keep in an airtight container in a cool, dark place for up to 1 year.

In a large pot, combine the bell peppers, onions, tomatoes, chickpeas, and 2 cups water. Bring to a boil, then reduce the heat so the water simmers. Cook, uncovered and stirring occasionally, until the bell peppers and onions are tender and the liquid has reduced to ½ cup, about 1 hour.

Working in batches, transfer the cooked vegetables and remaining liquid to a blender and blend until completely smooth. As each batch is blended, transfer to a large, wide, lidded container that will hold at least 3 quarts. Once all the vegetables are blended, let the mixture cool to room temperature.

Mix in the flour, yogurt, oil, salt, pepper, yeast, and chile flakes into the cooled vegetables and thoroughly combine, making sure there are no pockets of dry flour.

Cover the container and leave at room temperature to ferment, stirring daily. The mixture is ready when it stops actively bubbling (some small bubbles are fine) and no longer smells yeasty, 5 to 7 days, or possibly longer depending on the yeast.

To dry at room temperature: Line two sheet pans with silicone baking mats or parchment paper. Divide the mixture between the pans and spread into very thin, even layers. Leave out at room temperature until completely dried, 1 to 2 weeks (depending on weather and climate), flipping the tarhana when it's about halfway done.

To dry in a dehydrator: Preheat the dehydrator to 122°F. Line as many dehydrator trays as you can fit in your machine with parchment or mats. Spread the mixture into thin, even layers and heat until completely dried, 1 to 2 days, but it could vary greatly by machine and how many trays are used, so check every few hours.

Once the mixture has completely dried, break it into smaller pieces and grind them in batches in a coffee grinder (or a food processor, but the coffee grinder does a much better job). As each batch is ground, transfer to a fine-mesh sieve and sift out any larger pieces. Continue processing each sheet and any pieces until you have a fine powder with no lumps (this helps the tarhana rehydrate faster and more evenly).

Chickpea Tarhana Soup

This is a quick and comforting weeknight soup that's a perfect use for your homemade tarhana. I don't recommend using a store-bought option, as the strength and flavor may be quite different. Taking the time to properly toast all the orzo to a nice golden brown color will give it a pleasantly nutty taste and texture, so do not skip—or rush—that step.

Makes 6 cups

¼ cup	extra-virgin olive oil
1	small yellow onion, finely diced
¼ cup	orzo pasta
2	garlic cloves, thinly sliced
1 tablespoon	tomato paste
2 tablespoons	Chickpea Tarhana (*page 255*)
1 cup	cooked chickpeas (see Preparation, *page 228*) or canned, preferably organic, rinsed and drained
2	medium plum tomatoes, finely diced
1 tablespoon	unsalted butter
2 teaspoons	fine sea salt (10 grams), plus more as needed
½ teaspoon	freshly ground black pepper (1 gram), plus more as needed
½ teaspoon	dried mint (0.5 grams)
½ teaspoon	dried oregano (0.5 grams)

In a large heavy-bottomed saucepan, heat the oil over medium heat until hot. Add the onion and orzo and cook gently until the pasta is golden, stirring often, about 15 minutes. Add the garlic and tomato paste and stir to coat the pasta. Cook, stirring often and watching the pasta and paste closely so they don't burn, until the pasta is golden brown, about 5 minutes more.

Add the tarhana and 5 cups water. Increase the heat to bring the soup to a boil, then adjust the heat so the water simmers and cook until the pasta is tender, about 10 minutes.

Add the chickpeas, tomatoes, butter, salt, pepper, mint, and oregano and simmer for another 5 minutes to heat everything through and let the flavors combine. Taste and adjust the seasoning as necessary. Serve hot.

Shish Barak with Yogurt Sauce

The best way to describe this dish is to call it a Middle Eastern ravioli. The meat filling is richly seasoned with cumin, allspice, and Aleppo pepper, and the duo of sauces adds even more flavor. Once you've stuffed the shish barak, the rest is easy, as the quick labne pan sauce comes together while the dumplings simmer. Note that you will have to start the sauce as soon as you drop the dumplings into the water, so have all your ingredients ready.

Serves 4

Dumpling Dough

1 cup	all-purpose flour (140 grams), plus more for dusting
½ cup	boiling water (120 grams)
2 teaspoons	extra-virgin olive oil (10 grams)
	Fine sea salt

Dumpling Filling

8 ounces	ground beef
1 tablespoon	sweet Turkish pepper paste
1 tablespoon	roughly chopped fresh cilantro
½ teaspoon	ground allspice (1 gram)
½ teaspoon	ground cumin (1 gram)
½ teaspoon	fine sea salt (3 grams)
¼ teaspoon	Aleppo pepper (0.5 grams)

Make the dumpling dough: In a medium bowl, mix together the flour, boiling water, oil, and a pinch of salt until everything comes together to form a rough dough. Turn the dough out onto a work surface and knead until smooth, about 5 minutes, dusting with flour as needed if the dough is sticky.

Divide the dough into 2 equal portions and roll each into a 1-inch-thick rope. Using a 1-teaspoon measuring spoon, push the dough into the spoon and cut the dough on the edges of the spoon to make level teaspoon-size portions of dough. Keep the dough balls on the counter covered to prevent drying as you work.

Make the dumpling filling: In a medium bowl, combine the beef, pepper paste, cilantro, allspice, cumin, salt, and Aleppo pepper and mix until thoroughly combined, taking care not to overwork the mixture.

Fill a small bowl with water and keep it by your work surface. Lightly flour a sheet pan.

Flatten 1 dough ball into a ⅛-inch-thick disk, then push 1 teaspoon (6 grams) of filling into the center of the dough. Wrap the dough around the filling and carefully pinch the opposite edges closed in a half-moon shape (the dough is quite soft, but if it doesn't seal, very lightly moisten the edge and press again). Along the flat side of the half-moon, use your thumb to push the dough and filling in as you bring the two corners together and pinch them closed to form the dumpling. Put the dumplings on the sheet pan as you complete them, and cover them so they don't dry out. Continue with the remaining dough and filling.

Bring a large pot of water to a boil.

➡ recipe and ingredients continue

Pine Nut Chile Oil

2 tablespoons	pine nuts
2 tablespoons	extra-virgin olive oil
⅛ teaspoon	fine sea salt (1 gram)
½ teaspoon	peperoncini (dried Calabrian chile) or red chile flakes (1 gram)

Yogurt Sauce

8	labne balls (about 6 ounces), homemade (*page 251*) or store-bought, drained (or substitute ¾ cup labne)
4 tablespoons	(½ stick) unsalted butter
1 teaspoon	fine sea salt (5 grams)
½ teaspoon	ground turmeric (2 grams)
2 tablespoons	roughly chopped fresh cilantro, for garnish

Make the pine nut chile oil: In a small heavy-bottomed pan, combine the pine nuts, oil, and salt. Put the pan over low heat and cook until the pine nuts are golden, swirling the pan occasionally to keep the nuts toasting evenly, about 10 minutes. Remove from the heat, mix in the peperoncini, and set the pan aside. (This step can be done up to 1 week in advance and stored in the refrigerator or even made in large batches.)

To the pot of rapidly boiling water, add all the dumplings and adjust the heat so the water gently simmers when the pot is full. Scoop out 1 cup of the poaching liquid and set aside. Poach until the dumplings are cooked through, about 6 minutes. (The dumplings may float before the meat is cooked through so check at least one before removing them all from the water.)

After dropping in the dumplings, immediately make the yogurt sauce: Put the labne balls and reserved 1 cup water (or ¾ cup water if using labne) into a blender and blend until smooth. In a large heavy-bottomed skillet, combine the labne mixture, butter, salt, and turmeric over low heat, whisking constantly, until all the ingredients are well combined and the sauce is smooth and just barely warmed through, about 5 minutes. Taste and adjust the seasoning, and make sure the sauce is ready before the dumplings have finished cooking.

When the dumplings are cooked, use a spider to remove them from the pot, shake off any water, and add them to the pan with the yogurt sauce.

Gently fold the dumplings in the sauce to coat them. Remove from the heat and transfer to a serving dish or divide evenly among individual plates. Drizzle on the pine nut chile oil and garnish with chopped cilantro. Serve hot.

recipe Mansaf ◆▶ *page 262*

Mansaf

Famous for being Jordan's national dish, mansaf is a complete meal with meat, rice, and bread. The rehydrated dried yogurt (jameen) in the stew tenderizes the meat and adds intense tangy flavor to the rice. The chewy flatbreads make everything fun to eat and are traditionally used in place of utensils: Use torn pieces to make yourself a little "taco" with all three components in every bite. To save time, you can make the bread while the stew cooks, but don't cook too far ahead, as this is one stew that is best eaten on the day it's made.

Serves 8

Lamb Stew

1 pound	jameen (any size balls or powder)
2 pounds	lamb stew meat, cubed
1 cup	labne
1	medium yellow onion, cut into ½-inch cubes
3	cardamom pods
2	bay leaves
1	cinnamon stick
	Salt and freshly ground black pepper

Rice

2 cups	basmati rice
2 tablespoons	unsalted butter
1 teaspoon	ground allspice (2 grams)
1 teaspoon	ground cinnamon (2 grams)
1 teaspoon	fine sea salt (2 grams)
1 teaspoon	freshly ground black pepper (2 grams)
½ teaspoon	ground turmeric (2 grams)
⅛ teaspoon	saffron threads (n/a)

Make the lamb stew: Choose a container that will hold the jameen completely submerged in water (size will depend on what type of jameen you are using). Cover the jameen with 6 cups water, plus more as needed. Soak overnight. Reserve 6 cups of the soaking liquid for blending the jameen and adding to the stew.

Crumble the soaked jameen into a blender and blend until smooth, adding the reserved soaking liquid as needed to help the machine run. Set a fine-mesh sieve over a bowl and pour the blended liquid through it. Return any solids in the sieve to the blender and repeat, using more of the soaking liquid, until no pieces of jameen remain and the mixture is completely smooth (you may need quite a bit of the liquid to accomplish this).

In a large pot, combine the blended jameen mixture with any of the remaining reserved soaking liquid, the lamb, labne, onion, cardamom, bay leaves, and cinnamon. Bring the mixture to a boil, then reduce the heat so the stew simmers gently and cook, uncovered, until the lamb is completely tender, 1 to 2 hours depending on the meat. Remove 1 cup of the braising liquid and set aside. Keep the stew warm.

Make the rice: Wash the rice in a large bowl of cold water by swirling it with your hand, then pour off the water while keeping the rice in the bowl. Repeat until the water runs clear.

In a 10-inch heavy-bottomed skillet, melt the butter over medium heat. Add the drained rice, allspice, cinnamon, salt, pepper, turmeric, and saffron and stir to evenly coat the rice with the spices.

Add the reserved 1 cup lamb braising liquid and 3 cups water and stir to combine. Bring the mixture to a boil, then adjust the heat so it simmers and cook, uncovered, until the pan is dry and the rice is tender, 10 to 15 minutes. Cover the pan, remove from the heat, and let the rice steam for 10 minutes more. Keep warm.

Bread

2 cups plus 2 tablespoons	all-purpose flour (300 grams), plus more as needed
1 teaspoon	fine sea salt (5 grams)
½ cup	sliced almonds, toasted (*see page 99*), for garnish

Make the bread: In a stand mixer fitted with the dough hook, combine the flour, 1 cup water (240 grams), and the salt and knead on medium-low speed, adding flour as needed if the dough is sticky, to form a smooth dough, 8 to 10 minutes. Cover the bowl with plastic wrap and let the dough rest for 15 minutes.

Divide the dough into 8 equal portions (about 70 grams each) and roll them into balls. Keep covered to prevent the dough from drying out. Lightly dust your work surface with flour.

Heat a large nonstick skillet over medium heat. Working with 1 dough ball at a time, use a rolling pin to roll the dough into a thin 10-inch round, flouring as needed to prevent sticking. Lay the dough round on the pan. When the bread is lightly browned, flip and cook until the other side is lightly browned, 30 to 45 seconds per side (if your dough is taking longer than 45 seconds to brown, increase the heat). Remove the bread from the pan and cover with a towel to keep warm. Continue rolling and cooking the remaining dough 1 piece at a time.

Return the lamb stew to a simmer if necessary, then taste and season with salt and pepper. Put 1 piece of bread on every individual plate or arrange them all on a platter. Top with the rice, then spoon over the stewed meat, and finally drizzle with some of the braising liquid. Garnish with toasted almonds and serve hot.

Meat & Fish

لحم و سمك

et ve balık

בָּשָׂר וְדָגִים

گوشت و ماهى

κρέας και ψάρι

Միս և Ձուկ

Basturma

One of my bestselling La Boîte spice mixes mimics the taste of basturma, an air-cured beef with a garlicky, sweet-savory flavor. I named the blend Ararat, after the mountain between Turkey and Armenia—two countries with a tradition of making basturma.

ORIGIN AND HISTORY

Basturma, pastirma, pastourma, and basterma are all names for this flavorful cured beef similar in texture to bresaola. The name is thought to come either from *bastırma,* the Turkish word for "compression," or from an old Turkish salt-curing technique called pastron. It's possible that when the Ottomans settled in Istanbul and adopted many of the existing dishes, they began calling pastron "pastirma." The technique for making the cured beef was spread across the region by the Ottomans during their reign (when it was adapted by Romanians and became pastrami), then much later by Armenian refugees in the early twentieth century. It's popular in Turkey, Armenia, Egypt, Lebanon, Syria, and Iraq.

Basturma was originally made with goat, camel, lamb, water buffalo, and beef—now it is mostly made from beef. Whatever meat is used, it's coated in a thick spice mix called chemen, made from paprika, fenugreek, and fresh garlic and sometimes additional spices such as cumin, allspice, and black pepper.

PRODUCTION

Usually a lean and tender cut of beef like eye of round or tenderloin is used. The meat is covered in salt to draw out excess moisture and may be pressed at this stage. Once much of the liquid has seeped out, the salt is rinsed off. The meat is

What I love most about Middle Eastern cuisines is the creative use of simple ingredients like legumes, grains, and produce. That said, meat and fish are also key parts of the diet, and preserved proteins even more so. Traditionally, because of the climate (and until recently, the lack of refrigeration), any parts of an animal that weren't going to be eaten immediately had to be preserved to prevent waste.

I've chosen two of my favorite versatile preserved meats to highlight: basturma, which is a type of cured beef, and sujuk, a fermented and spiced dried sausage. The techniques are simple, but I think it's the creative use of spices that makes them stand out. Dried and salted fish is a commonly made and used product in the region, but I would venture to say that none of it is exported. Salt cod, however, *is* a product you can find easily and is used in many parts of the Middle East. So I've included it here.

then strung up to dry until firm, anywhere from three days to two weeks depending on temperature—drying in a cold environment takes much longer—and the size of the cut. After the meat is dried, it's rubbed all over with chemen and then left to dry again. When the spice blend is dry to the touch, the basturma is ready.

APPEARANCE AND FLAVOR

It's a bit smoky, sweet-savory from the fenugreek, and pungent from the ample garlic. Since it's not fully dried, the texture is somewhat tender and similar to Italian bresaola. It's very lean, and you'll most often find it made with beef or lamb. It should have a dark brown or reddish crust and deep red interior.

SOURCING AND STORING

Find basturma in Middle Eastern stores, particularly Turkish or Armenian grocers, and online. It's usually sold thinly sliced, and while you can buy a whole basturma and slice it yourself, I buy it presliced for easier prep. As always, look for the shortest ingredient list possible with few additives. A uniform color and nice, thin slices are also desirable.

Store basturma in the refrigerator. Wrap whole or sliced basturma tightly in plastic, because it can be spoiled by humidity, and keep in the refrigerator for up to 3 months.

TRADITIONAL USES

Eggs with basturma (breakfast dish) — *throughout the region* (see Basturma Eggs, *page 272*)
Savory pastry filling — *Turkey, Armenia, and more*

Recipe Ideas

1. Tear up slices of basturma and fry in a little oil before adding other ingredients to infuse the flavors into any savory dish.

2. Add basturma slices to a pan of vegetables or chicken before roasting.

3. Sauté diced basturma, then mix it into a rice or grain stuffing for dolma or vegetables.

4. Drape over flatbread as you might with prosciutto on pizza.

5. Treat it like any cured meat and add it to a cheese or charcuterie platter.

Basturma Spice Blend

This amount of spice blend is more than you need for making DIY Basturma (*page 271*)— use the extra to make a bigger batch of basturma (up to three total) or to generously season red meat bound for the grill or high-heat roasting.

Makes about 1 cup (90 grams)

½ cup	dried fenugreek leaves (6 grams), ground
½ cup	sweet paprika (58 grams)
1 tablespoon	ground allspice (6 grams)
1 tablespoon	freshly ground black pepper (7 grams)
2 teaspoons	garlic powder (6 grams)
1 teaspoon	cayenne pepper (2 grams)
1 teaspoon	fine sea salt (5 grams)

In a small bowl, mix the fenugreek leaves, paprika, allspice, black pepper, garlic powder, cayenne, and salt until thoroughly combined. The spice blend will keep in an airtight container in a cool, dark place for several months.

Sujuk

Sujuk is not well known outside of Turkey—yet. Think of it as Turkish chorizo and use as you would any other dried sausage.

ORIGIN AND HISTORY

Sujuk (also known as sucuk, sudzhuk, or soudjouk), a fermented and spiced dried Turkish sausage, is believed to have been one of the earliest sausages. Some historians believe that Phoenician sailors (from what is now Syria, Lebanon, and Israel) either came up with the concept of spicy dried sausage or brought it back to the region. The method would, of course, work for anyone who had meat to preserve, not just sailors, and thus spread far beyond the Mediterranean coastline and into the Turkish heartland. The Ottomans also did their part a few thousand years later, bringing sujuk to much of their empire. It's very popular with modern-day Armenian, Lebanese, Egyptian, Syrian, Iraqi, Israeli, and Palestinian cooks.

PRODUCTION

Beef, frequently mixed with lamb, is most often used to make sujuk. The meat is coarsely ground and seasoned with spices that vary from recipe to recipe, but fresh garlic, salt, black pepper, fenugreek, cumin, allspice, cinnamon, sumac, and ground chiles are all common. Some fat may also be added to the mix, depending on what cuts of meat are used. The mixture is kneaded, then stuffed into casings. The traditional drying and fermenting process lasts three to four weeks in a cool, dark spot. Sujuk can also be dried for only four or five days to make a softer, only lightly fermented version.

APPEARANCE AND FLAVOR

Most often formed into a 2-inch-thick cylinder, sujuk can also be sold in bricks. Not quite as dry as a salami or Spanish chorizo, the sausage has a smooth exterior and ranges from a brick red to a dark wine color depending on the spices. The flavor is slightly gamy if there's lamb in the mix, and it will have a pungent flavor from both the cumin and the fermentation. It has a nice amount of salt, and depending on how many chiles were used, some versions can be quite spicy. Because the interior of the sausage is chunky instead of smooth, there's some texture, and you'll get wonderful hits of flavor and fat as you chew.

SOURCING AND STORING

If basturma is hard for you to source where you live, sujuk will probably be harder, but it can of course be found online. Look for the most comprehensive but shortest ingredient list when shopping for sujuk—meaning a label that lists the cuts of meat used to make the sausage and as spare an ingredient list as possible (allowing for the unavoidable nitrates necessary for preservation). The sujuk should be whole, with a uniform size and smooth shape. Once you cut into it, you're looking for a somewhat coarse texture, a good amount of fat, and full flavor.

It will keep unopened in the refrigerator for months, but once you've sliced into it, you should aim to use it up within about one week.

TRADITIONAL USES

Sandwich filling — *throughout the region*
Savory pastry filling — *throughout the region*

Recipe Ideas

1. Slice or crumble over flatbreads before baking, as in Sujuk Pide (*page 275*).

2. Pan-fry to crisp and render some of the fat, then serve with eggs.

3. Cut into thick slices and char on a grill or sear in a pan.

4. Crumble over vegetables or meat before roasting, so the fat flavors the other ingredients.

5. Make Sujuk Manti (*page 278*).

Salt Cod

This is an ingredient that takes some planning—you can't decide to eat salt cod on a whim, as it takes one to three days to soak and desalt it and it still needs to be cooked. But with just a little forethought, it's a delicious fish that can be used in dozens of ways.

ORIGIN AND HISTORY

Salt cod is made from Atlantic cod and is an imported product in the Middle East. There is, however, a long-standing practice of salting and drying fish in the region. Long ago, in order to transport fish from the coast to the hot inland areas, it had to be preserved. Salting fish to extract moisture and drying it was the best way to preserve a large number of fish for transporting over long durations, and salt improved both the fish's taste and shelf life. With the advent of refrigeration and air transport, dried fish continued to be eaten because people liked the taste.

Most of the dried fish products from the Middle East never leave the region. Salt cod's omnipresence on the international trading scene starting around the seventeenth century, however, meant it was adopted throughout the Mediterranean. It's especially popular in Cyprus and the countries of the Arabian Peninsula.

PRODUCTION

Fresh cod are scaled, gutted, and cleaned and then salted with 17 to 20 percent salt by weight and stacked to press out the water. Traditionally the fish was air-dried by the sun and wind until the final water content was around 40 percent, but now the drying process mostly happens in ovens. After drying, the fish is ready for storage.

APPEARANCE AND FLAVOR

The dried fillets are white or off-white, usually with a layer of salt covering the surface, and very stiff. After rehydrating, the texture is wonderfully flaky and a little chewier than fresh cod. It has an ocean-rich, iodine flavor from curing and a more robust fish (but not fishy) flavor.

SOURCING AND STORING

Salt cod is sold at specialty food stores and by fishmongers who can talk to you about sourcing (a fishmonger can also cut the fillets into more manageable pieces for you). The ingredients should be just fish and salt. Look for a uniform white color, with no dark coloration anywhere. If you're buying pieces, look for ones that include some of the thick center cuts and not just the thin ends.

Refrigerate dried salt cod, and if not in a vacuum-sealed package, wrap it tightly in plastic to protect it from humidity. Dried salt cod will keep in the refrigerator for up to one year. After soaking, it should be cooked right away.

TRADITIONAL USES

Madrouba malleh (rice porridge) — *Oman*
Biryani — *UAE*

Recipe Ideas

1. Braise with tomatoes, lemon, and herbs.

2. Poach with aromatic vegetables such as onion, fennel, and the like.

3. Make Salt Cod and Green Olive Stew (*page 280*).

DIY Basturma

I invite you to make this at least once. It does require a number of weeks to cure, but thankfully there's no special equipment or ingredients beyond pink curing salt (which can be found online or at some butcher shops and may be called Prague Powder or Insta Cure).

Makes 1 basturma

3 tablespoons	fine sea salt (48 grams)
½ teaspoon	pink curing salt (3 grams)
3 tablespoons	Basturma Spice Blend (*page 267*; 21 grams)
1½ pounds	beef eye round, 1 inch thick

In a small bowl, combine the sea salt, pink curing salt, and 1 tablespoon (7 grams) of the basturma spice blend.

Coat the beef with half of the spiced curing mix (29 grams) and seal in a plastic bag, then press the air out of the bag. Refrigerate for 1 week, turning the bag over daily. Save the remaining spiced curing mix for the following week.

After the first week, remove the beef from the bag, pat it dry, then coat with the reserved spiced curing mix (29 grams). Seal the meat in a fresh plastic bag and press out the air. Refrigerate for 1 more week, turning the bag over daily.

After the second week, rinse the meat and pat dry. Make a 12-inch square of doubled-up cheesecloth and put the meat onto it. Coat the meat with the remaining 2 tablespoons (14 grams) basturma spice blend, pressing firmly. Working carefully so the spices do not fall off, wrap the beef with the cheesecloth and tie the ends tightly with string.

The basturma will need to hang in the refrigerator, ideally toward the back so it's out of your way but with air moving all around it. If you can tie the basturma to a shelf and hang it so it touches nothing, use that. Otherwise, lay a wooden spoon across two tall stacks of containers and tie the basturma to the spoon so it hangs with air all around. Put a plate underneath to catch any spices. Leave for 2 weeks, turning after 1 week so the side facing the back of the refrigerator now faces out, to make sure the front and back are both getting good airflow.

After 2 weeks, unwrap the cheesecloth and check the meat. The texture should be firming up (similar to bresaola or prosciutto). Make sure there is no mold, and if there is, trim the mold from the surface, change the cheesecloth, and make sure there is ventilation all around the hanging meat. Hang again.

Check every week until the meat has absorbed the spices, tastes pleasantly salty, and may have even started to form crystals like you find in prosciutto. If you think your basturma is ready, slice a small piece from the end. The meat will be dark and oxidized but should be a consistent color and texture throughout. This can take 4 to 7 weeks of hanging (for a total curing time of 6 to 9 weeks).

Use a very sharp knife to slice the basturma as thinly as you can manage right before serving.

Storage Directions
Store the basturma tightly wrapped in plastic and inside a sealed bag in the refrigerator for up to 1 month.

Basturma Eggs

Warmly spiced basturma and fresh parsley add dimension to rich and silky scrambled eggs for a perfect brunch dish. If you can't wait for your homemade basturma (*page 271*) to cure before you try these eggs, it's easy enough to find at a Turkish or Armenian grocer. You can even source it from small producers online, on sites like eBay.

Serves 2

5	large eggs
1 tablespoon	extra-virgin olive oil
6	thin slices basturma, cut into short matchsticks
2 teaspoons	roughly chopped fresh flat-leaf parsley
	Salt and freshly ground black pepper

In a small bowl, whisk the eggs with 2 tablespoons water until no streaks of yolk or white remain.

In a small nonstick skillet, heat the oil over medium heat. When the oil is warm, add the beaten eggs. Using a silicone spatula, gently move and fold the eggs to slowly form moist ribbons of scrambled eggs that are softly cooked and still creamy, about 3 minutes.

Remove from the heat and fold in the basturma and parsley. Season with salt and pepper to taste. Serve immediately.

Sujuk Pide

Somewhere between a pizza and a calzone and not unlike khachapuri, pide is a famous filled Turkish bread. My version is stuffed with spiced sujuk and plenty of Turkish kaşar (also called kasseri), a young cow's or mixed-milk cheese that melts wonderfully. The bread is topped with a runny egg while still in the oven and then as many toppings after baking as you like, including fresh and dried herbs, sesame seeds, and a salty, pungent Turkish goat cheese called tulum. I highly recommend using a rectangular baking stone (at least 18 inches diagonally), because it cooks the bottom of the pide quickly. If you don't have one, use an inverted sheet pan. As you shape the pide, dust a pizza peel or upside-down sheet pan with a little coarse semolina flour to help make the transfer to the baking stone easier (the long, narrow shape is, admittedly, a little hard to handle); if all-purpose or fine semolina flour is all you have, use that.

Makes 2 large breads

Dough

¾ cup	lukewarm water (180 grams)
1 teaspoon	instant yeast (3 grams)
½ teaspoon	sugar (3 grams)
2 cups	all-purpose flour (280 grams), plus more for dusting
2 teaspoons	extra-virgin olive oil (10 grams), plus more as needed
1 teaspoon	fine sea salt (5 grams)

Filling and Assembly

4 ounces	sujuk, peeled and roughly chopped
½ teaspoon	coarse semolina flour (optional)
5 ounces	Turkish kaşar cheese or mozzarella, grated
2	large eggs

Make the dough: In a small bowl, mix the lukewarm water, yeast, and sugar and let sit until the yeast is foamy, about 10 minutes.

In a stand mixer fitted with the dough hook, mix the flour, oil, salt, and yeast mixture on medium speed until they come together to form a rough dough. Continue to knead on medium until the dough is smooth and elastic, adding more flour if the dough is sticky to the touch and stopping and pulling it off the hook if it sticks, 8 to 10 minutes.

Oil a large bowl. Lightly flour your work surface and turn the dough out onto it. Use your hands to shape the dough into a ball and place the dough ball inside the prepared bowl. Cover the bowl with plastic wrap and proof until the dough has doubled in size, 1 to 1½ hours.

Remove the dough from the bowl and set it on the lightly floured work surface. Divide the dough into 2 equal portions and shape each into a smooth ball. Cover the balls with a clean kitchen towel and leave to proof again until doubled in size, about 1 hour.

Meanwhile, prepare the filling: In a food processor, pulse the sujuk until the sausage is crumbly. Refrigerate until ready to use.

Position a rack in the center of the oven and put a baking stone large enough to fit an 18-inch bread diagonally across it on the rack. If you don't have a baking stone, use an overturned sheet pan. Preheat the oven to as high as it will go—at least 475°F.

Fill a small bowl with water and put it by your work surface. Lightly flour the work surface again and use a rolling pin to roll each dough ball into an 18-inch-long oval shape with a 6-inch-wide center and narrow, pointed ends.

◆→ recipe and ingredients continue

Suggested Garnishes

¼ cup crumbled Turkish tulum cheese or feta

Dried oregano

Sesame seeds, toasted (*see page* 128)

Ground sumac

Fresh cilantro

Extra-virgin olive oil

Prepare two sheet pans (or a pizza peel): Turn the sheet pans upside down and sprinkle each with ¼ teaspoon of the semolina flour (if using) or all-purpose flour, to ensure the bread slides off easily. Place one of the rolled-out doughs onto the semolina and make sure it's not sticking. Repeat with the second dough.

Evenly sprinkle one piece of dough with half of the cheese, leaving a 1-inch border on both sides but going all the way to the pointed ends so the ends aren't plain once baked, then repeat with half of the sujuk. Brush the ends lightly with water and pinch the last 2 inches or so of each side over the fillings and together to seal, so the ends are now closed over the filling and more pointed. Fold each of the long sides of the dough toward the center so their edges just touch. The pide should now be about 18 inches long and 3 inches wide in the center, with none of the filling exposed. Brush the outside of the dough lightly with oil.

Slide the filled pide from the sheet pan (or pizza peel) onto the preheated baking stone (or overturned sheet pan), laying one end of the pide on the farthest corner of the baking stone and slowly removing the upside-down sheet pan or pizza peel while laying the pide down diagonally across the stone to maintain its very long, thin shape. Bake for 8 minutes, rotating the pide on top of the stone if it's browning unevenly.

Crack 1 of the eggs into a small bowl, then carefully add it to the center of the pide. Continue baking until the dough is golden brown and cooked through and the egg white is set and the yolk runny, another 4 to 8 minutes. Remove from the oven. Repeat with the other dough and remaining filling ingredients.

Sprinkle the pide with any of the suggested garnishes. Cut crosswise into 2-inch-wide pieces and serve.

recipe Sujuk Manti ↔ *page 278*

Sujuk Manti

Manti are small dumplings that can be boiled, but in Turkey they are perhaps more often baked in intricate patterns in huge batches. I prefer the light and crispy outcome of this somewhat nontraditional version with its extra-thin, delicate dough stuffed with a flavorful, rich sujuk filling. The hot mantis are complemented by a cold garlicky yogurt sauce. Yes, they are quite a production, but in Turkey it's said the smaller the manti, the more a cook cares. To get the thinnest, crispest dough, I use a pasta machine, though the manti can also be made without one. Note that if the dough is rolled by hand and isn't quite paper thin, you may need to make another batch of dough to use all the filling (there is enough filling here for about 70 manti).

Serves 8 to 10 as an appetizer

Dough

1 cup	all-purpose flour (140 grams), plus more as needed
1	large egg
⅛ teaspoon	fine sea salt (1 gram)

Filling

8 ounces	sujuk, peeled and roughly chopped
1	small onion, cut into 1-inch chunks
½ cup	chopped flat-leaf parsley
2 teaspoons	sweet Turkish pepper paste
1	garlic clove, peeled
	Butter, for the pan

Make the dough: In a stand mixer fitted with the dough hook, mix the flour, egg, salt, and ¼ cup (60 grams) room-temperature water on medium speed to form a rough dough. Continue kneading until smooth, dusting with flour if the dough is sticky, about 5 minutes. Cover the bowl and let rest for 2 hours.

Make the filling: In a food processor, pulse the sujuk until it starts to break down, then add the onion, parsley, pepper paste, and garlic. Pulse until the filling is finely chopped and well combined. Test the mixture by gently pressing a handful—you want it to hold together. Refrigerate until ready to use.

If using a pasta machine to roll out the dough: Set up the machine and lightly flour your work surface. Divide the dough into 2 equal portions and cover one while rolling the other.

Put the machine on the widest setting. Shape one piece of dough into a rectangle about the width of the rollers and lightly flour. Gently feed it through the machine while cranking or with the motor running. Fold the dough into thirds like a letter, then rotate 90 degrees and feed it through the machine again (this helps get the edges straight). Repeat this rolling and folding step, flouring as needed.

Adjust your machine so the rollers are one setting closer, then feed the dough through again. Continue, moving the rollers two settings closer each pass, flouring as necessary so the dough doesn't stick to itself, and cutting the sheet in half if it becomes too long to manage, until you reach the thinnest setting. Run the dough through twice on the thinnest setting. Flour the dough so it won't stick to itself, cover with a clean kitchen towel, and repeat with the other half.

If rolling by hand: Divide the dough into two equal portions and cover one while rolling the other. Dust your work surface and rolling pin lightly with flour. Roll one of the dough portions into a rectangle that is 4 inches wide and paper thin (the length is not important), dusting with flour as necessary to keep the dough from sticking. Cover the dough with a towel and repeat with the other half.

Yogurt Sauce

1 cup	labne
3 tablespoons	extra-virgin olive oil
2 tablespoons	roughly chopped fresh flat-leaf parsley, plus more for garnish
2 tablespoons	freshly squeezed lemon juice
1	garlic clove, grated on a Microplane
½ teaspoon	fine sea salt (3 grams)

For both methods: Trim the edges and cut the dough into 2-inch squares. Keep them covered so they don't dry out. Fill a small bowl with water and keep it by your work surface. Flour a sheet pan to store the finished manti or line the pan with parchment paper if you plan to freeze them.

Put 1 teaspoon of the filling onto the center of one square of dough. Very lightly moisten the left and right sides of the square. Bring the dough edge closest to you up over the filling and press the corners and sides together so they are joined, the dumpling is now a rectangle, and the filling is exposed at the opening along the edge facing away from you.

Set the manti onto your work surface with the opening facing up and press the sides together, pushing out any air while at the same time pinching the dough with both hands and pushing the dumpling down to make a flat bottom. The final dumpling should have the filling peeking out a little from the top and the sides closed around the meat, and it should be able to stand up on its own. Transfer to the prepared sheet pan and keep covered so it doesn't dry out as you make more manti.

Continue with the remaining dough and filling. (If freezing, make sure they are not touching on the pan, and when finished, transfer the pan to the freezer. Once solid, transfer to a bag and freeze for a few weeks. They do not need to be thawed before baking.)

Preheat the oven to 350°F. Butter a 10-inch round baking dish. (You can also cook the manti on a buttered sheet pan or cook a partial batch in a smaller round baking dish.)

Starting from the sides of the pan and working inward, make rings of closely packed manti until the baking dish is full.

Bake for 15 minutes, then rotate the pan. Continue baking until the dough is cooked and the edges are crispy and golden brown, about 15 more minutes (add up to another 10 minutes if baking from frozen).

Meanwhile, make the yogurt sauce: In a medium bowl, mix the labne, oil, parsley, lemon juice, garlic, and salt until thoroughly incorporated.

Serve the warm manti garnished with parsley and with the yogurt sauce for dipping, or spoon some of the sauce onto individual serving plates, top with 7 or 8 manti, and garnish with more parsley (do not put the sauce on top of the manti or they will get soggy).

Salt Cod and Green Olive Stew

Even after soaking for a few days, dried salt cod retains some salinity and has a beautiful flaky texture. Stewing it allows for a gentle cooking that keeps that texture, and the fish pairs wonderfully with the olives, herbs, and spices in the sauce. Be sure to serve it as part of a spread with lots of accompanying dishes like steamed rice, a salad—such as Sumac Onion Salad (*page 39*)—and a vegetable, like the Spiced Silan Carrots (*page 167*), as the cod and olives together pack a (delicious) punch that needs a grain and a few salads alongside.

Serves 4 to 6

1½ pounds	salt cod
2 teaspoons	Urfa chile (4 grams)
1 teaspoon	ground cumin (2 grams)
1 teaspoon	sweet paprika (2 grams)
2 tablespoons	extra-virgin olive oil, plus more for serving
2 tablespoons	pine nuts
1	large yellow onion, cut into ¼-inch dice
	Salt
1	large garlic clove, finely chopped
1 cup	pitted green olives
1	lemon, halved crosswise and seeds removed, 1 half finely diced
1 teaspoon	ground turmeric (3 grams)
1 cup	fresh cilantro leaves

First, to desalt the salt cod, place it in a container large enough to fit it. Cover with water and transfer to the refrigerator. Soak for 3 days, changing the water once a day.

In a small bowl, mix together 1 teaspoon (2 grams) of the Urfa chile, the cumin, and paprika. Drain the salt cod and pat dry with a paper towel. Cut the salt cod into 3-inch cubes and season all over with all of the spice blend. Set aside.

In a large skillet, heat the oil over medium-low heat until hot. Add the pine nuts and toast, stirring often, until lightly golden, 3 to 5 minutes. Remove the pine nuts with a slotted spoon, leaving the oil in the pan, and set aside.

Add the onion to the pan and season with salt. Increase the heat to medium-high and cook, stirring occasionally, until the onion is slightly softened and browned, 5 to 8 minutes. Reduce the heat to medium-low, add the garlic, and cook for 1 minute, until fragrant. Add the olives, diced lemon, remaining 1 teaspoon (2 grams) Urfa chile, and the turmeric and cook until warmed through, 1 to 2 minutes. Pour in 1 cup water and bring to a simmer. Cover the pan, adjust the heat so the mixture continues to simmer gently, and cook for 10 minutes.

Remove the lid and nestle the cod pieces in the stew. Return to a simmer, cover, reduce the heat to low, and cook for 10 minutes to heat the fish through.

Remove the pan from the heat and garnish with the cilantro and fried pine nuts. Squeeze the reserved lemon half over the stew and drizzle with oil. Serve hot.

CONTRIBUTORS

EMILY STEPHENSON

has worked on all aspects of numerous cookbooks from writing to editing to recipe testing to cooking on photoshoot sets. She is the author of *The Friendsgiving Handbook* and *Pantry to Plate* and coauthor of more. She cooked every recipe in this book in her Los Angeles kitchen.

DAN PEREZ

is one of Israel's top food photographers. His work appears regularly in local and international culinary magazines, advertising campaigns, books, and other publications. He has created a distinctive style of food photography that uses chiefly natural daylight, and it has become a trademark of his work. In the past few years he has collaborated with local and international chefs on more than twenty bestselling cookbooks. He is constantly documenting food culture and Middle Eastern food artisans, exploring culinary history and food travel in Israel and elsewhere.

CHRISTINE FISCHER

is a German art director based in Zurich, Switzerland. Her passion and sensibility for typography has led her to take part in many books and editorial designs for German, Austrian, Swiss, and American publishers. Christine divides her time between designing and exploring the most beautiful places in Switzerland.

RESOURCES

To shop for the products used in this book, see a complete list of sources consulted, and find more resources, use your phone to scan the QR code (right) or visit www.laboiteny.com.

ACKNOWLEDGMENTS

This book, like all of my culinary adventures and journeys, is not a dinner for one. A tribute to my beloved region, its people, places, and incredible flavors, *A Middle Eastern Pantry* would not have come to life without many people, most of whom I've known for more than thirty years.

Thank you to my parents, Moshe and Ayala, my sisters, Shelly and Iris, my wife, Lisa, and our sons, Luca and Lennon.

Many thanks go to Raquel Pelzel, Aaron Wehner, and Francis Lam at Clarkson Potter; Emily Stephenson, for her magical writing and enthusiasm; Dan Perez and Nurit Kariv, for the stunning photographs and food styling; Helen Park, for creating this book with me and testing all the recipes; Myriam Eberhardt, for the dessert recipe development; Christine Fischer, for the amazing design work; Dor Vanger, Oriel Sheinman, and the whole La Boîte team; Thomas Schauer, for his ongoing support and mentorship; and to all those I've forgotten to mention.

Finally, to all the farmers, growers, artisans, and beautiful people of the Middle East. Yalla!

Row 1, l to r: Roni Bitan; Zohar Rudolph; Yonit Crystal
Row 2, l to r: Moshe Lev Sercarz; Ziad Fandi; Abu Hamdan Allama
Row 3, l to r: Hassan Fauzi; Bshaer Barhum; Ahmad Zedan Assle

INDEX

Library of Congress Cataloging-in-Publication Data
is available upon request.

ISBN 978-0-593-23563-8
Ebook ISBN 978-0-593-23564-5

Printed in China

Photographer: Dan Perez
Photography Assistants: Boris Korotkov and
Sharona Cantor
Recipe Developers: Helen Park and
Myriam Eberhardt
Food and Prop Stylist: Nurit Kariv
Stylist Assistant: Chai Talbi
Editor: Raquel Pelzel
Editorial Assistant: Bianca Cruz
Book and Cover Designer: Christine Fischer
Production Editor: Terry Deal
Production Manager: Kim Tyner
Compositor: Merri Ann Morrell and Nick Patton
Copy Editor: Kate Slate
Proofreaders: Kathy Brock and Rachel Markowitz
Indexer: Eldes Tran
Marketer: Andrea Portanova
Publicist: Natalie Yera

10 9 8 7 6 5 4 3 2 1

First Edition

Spices

Olives

Legumes

Dairy

Meat &

Fish

Condiments